To LORD CARNARVON and HOWARD CARTER
who restored life to King Tutankhamen and gave back to man a
page of his history

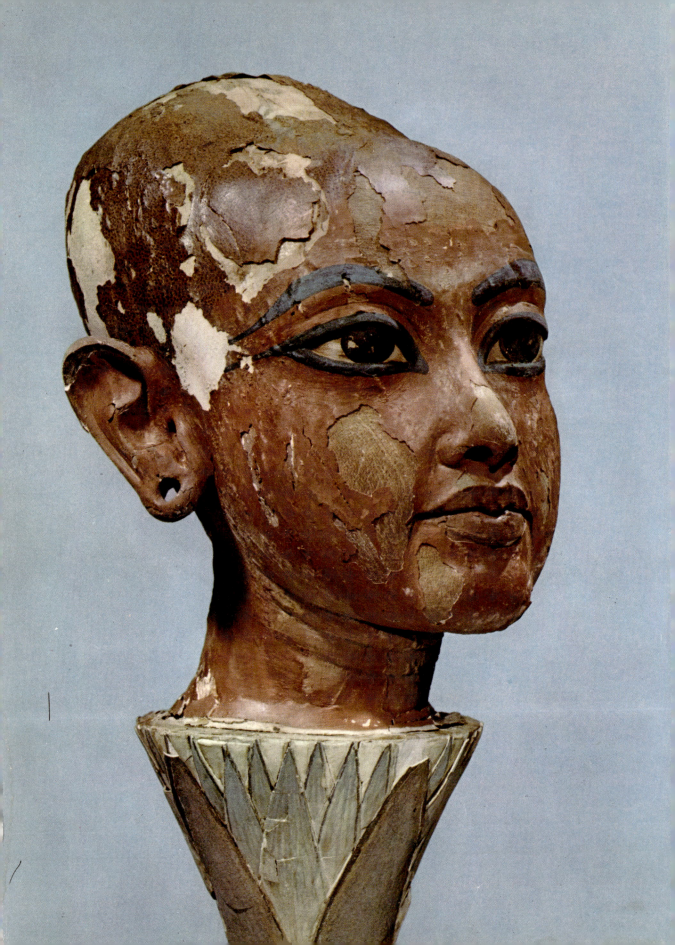

Life and death of a pharaoh

Tutankhamen

CHRISTIANE DESROCHES-NOBLECOURT

With 75 colour photographs by F. L. Kenett

Preface by His Excellency Sarwat Okasha,
Member of the Executive Council of UNESCO

Notes on the colour plates by Dr A. Shoukry,
Director General of the Antiquities Service of the UAR

THE CONNOISSEUR

and MICHAEL JOSEPH

Translated from the French by Claude

© George Rainbird Limited 1963

First published October 1963
Second impression October 1963
Third impression January 1964
Fourth impression May 1964
Fifth impression February 1965
Sixth impression March 1967
Seventh impression December 1969
Eighth impression June 1971
Ninth impression May 1972

Published in Great Britain by The Connoisseur and Michael Joseph Ltd, London

This book was devised and produced by
George Rainbird Limited, Marble Arch House, 44 Edgware Road,
London W2

Designed by George Adams

Composition by Filmset Ltd, Crawley;
colour reproduction by Amilcare Pizzi S.p.A., Milan,
printing by Westerham Press Limited, Westerham, Kent, and
binding by Webb Son & Co. Ltd, Southgate, London

SBN 7181 0765 9

PRINTED IN UNITED KINGDOM

Preface

THIS VOLUME WILL occupy a place of honour in the future amongst the revelatory moments which history vouchsafes from time to time when it lifts for a moment the mysterious curtain which has hidden from our eyes a representative individual or a significant episode in man's experience.

Could anything be more stirring to the imagination than the burial treasure of the romantic young king Tutankhamen who died prematurely after a short but sumptuous reign?

The amazing discovery of this treasure by the Englishmen Carter and Carnarvon constitutes a landmark in the history of Egyptology, as exciting—if not as important —as the decipherment of hieroglyphics by Champollion, whose genius restored to us several millennia of our history and gave meaning to the evidence they left behind. If Champollion allowed us to penetrate the writings and ideas of pharaonic times, the discovery of the two Englishmen has enabled us to see in tangible form and in brilliant colour the material and semi-divine existence of this young god-king.

After forty years of study and patient scientific conservation the doors open again and these relics are revealed once more to the world. Henceforth we shall be able to form an exact idea of the composition of a royal funerary ensemble from the only one which has survived to this day almost intact after more than 3,000 years.

I had the satisfaction, as Minister of Culture and National Guidance of the United Arab Republic, of being able to second this exceptional work. I am very pleased that I could do so, for a study of Tutankhamen's treasure could not have been confided to a scholar more highly qualified in the world of art and archaeology than Madame Christiane Desroches-Noblecourt. She is an Egyptologist of the first rank: her writings, her masterly work at the Louvre Museum and School, her practical work in the field carried out on sites explored on behalf of France in Upper Egypt, the performance of her official duties as a special consultant of UNESCO to my government—all single her out as a worthy heir of the great traditions of Egyptology and of her illustrious predecessors.

I gave her what assistance I could, not only as a tribute to her abilities and to her determination to continue the work of Mariette Pasha, but also in appreciation of her sincere and cordial feelings of friendship towards Egypt at all periods of its history.

Saroit Okacha

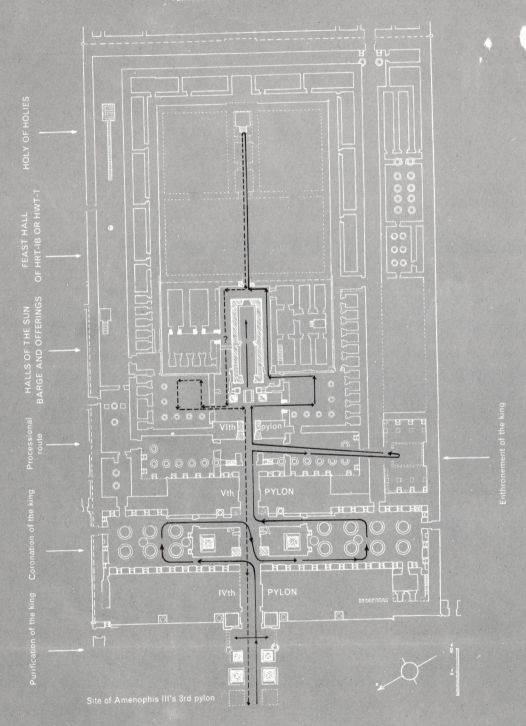

Tuthmosis III's Hall of the SED feast

HOLY OF HOLIES

FEAST HALL OF HRT-IB OR HWT-T

HALLS OF THE SUN BARGE AND OFFERINGS

Processional route

Coronation of the king

Purification of the king

Enthronement of the king

VIth pylon

Vth PYLON

IVth PYLON

Site of Amenophis III's 3rd pylon

Diagram of the temple of Karnak, known as Ipet-sut during the XVIIIth Dynasty (after P. Barguet). The arrows show the route followed by Tutankhamen on his coronation day. The roman figures by the pylons refer to their present-day numbering. (See Chapter 6)

Contents

Throughout the text the roman numerals refer to colour plates, the arabic numerals to monochrome illustrations

Acknowledgments

I have pleasure in acknowledging my debt of gratitude to Dr Sarwat Okasha who, when he was Minister of Culture and National Guidance of the UAR, allowed the objects to be removed from their cases and photographed in colour for the first time since the treasure of Tutankhamen has been on show in the Cairo Museum.

I would like to thank Dr Anwar Shoukry, Director General of the Antiquities Service of the UAR, who allowed us to set up a special photographic studio in the galleries of the museum; Mr Mohammed Abd-ur-Rahman, Curator of the Tutankhamen treasure in the Cairo Museum, for his unfailing help; Mr Zaky Iskander, Chief of the museum laboratories, who gave unsparingly of his time to ensure that the objects were not harmed while they were being moved; Mr Shehata Adam, Director of the Nubian Office and the Ministry of Culture, who eased many administrative problems; and Mr Abdul Hamid Zayed for his courtesy and help.

I must warmly thank the staff of the Ashmolean Museum and the Griffith Institute for allowing me to consult the archives of the discovery and to draw upon the records and notebooks of Howard Carter. I would like to thank in particular Mr R. W. Hamilton, Keeper of the Ashmolean Museum, Dr Rosalind Moss, Mrs Burney, and Miss Helen Murray; and above all Sir Alan Gardiner who gave me the warmest encouragement at all stages of my work.

I am also grateful to Lord Carnarvon for his forthright information and for his reminiscences of his father, which add an element of first-hand experience to a work of objective scholarship.

Finally I would like to thank my former students, now my colleagues at the Louvre, who checked my references, found many of the black and white illustrations and took important burdens off my shoulders. I would single out Mademoiselle Janine Monnet, Madame Diane Harlé, and in particular Mademoiselle Monique Kanawaty and Madame Ruth Antelme. The last named gave me invaluable assistance in correcting the proofs of the French edition and by drawing up the index and the critical appendices.

I owe also a debt of gratitude to Mrs Joy Law of George Rainbird Limited, who, in the course of preparing this book for press, shared with the author the many responsibilities which an archaeologist assumes in the pursuit of accuracy and which she has discharged with unfailing patience and understanding.

Last but not least I must thank Mr George Rainbird; without him I would not yet have written what I know and feel about this most attractive period which has been the subject of my teaching for so long. It was his pulsating enthusiasm and his determination to produce the book with Mr Kenett's colour photographs that forced me to find time—I know not how—during the years I was occupied with the preservation of the Nubian monuments to devote myself to Tutankhamen.

C.D.-N.

The author and the publishers express their gratitude to Eve and Delves Molesworth for their help in getting the book started; to Cyril Aldred for advice about the transliteration of the proper names for this edition; to Madame R. Antelme for assuming responsibility for the correctness of the archaeological details in the translation; and to the following who have supplied monochrome photographs, drawings and maps: Griffith Institute, Ashmolean Museum, Oxford; Lt-Col. the Rt Hon. the Earl of Carnarvon; Cairo Museum; Louvre Museum, Paris; Giraudon, Paris; The Times, London; Antiquities Service of the UAR, Cairo; Radio Times Hulton Picture Library, London; Clive Tunnicliffe of George Rainbird Limited, London; Librairie Hachette, Paris; Hassia; Professor I. E. S. Edwards; Trustees of the British Museum, London; Abdel Badia; Ehemals Staatliche Museen, Berlin; F. L. Kenett; Mrs N. de Garis Davies; Mme Henri Maspero; Staatliche Museen, Berlin; Metropolitan Museum of Art, New York; Museum of Fine Arts, Boston; The University Museum of the University of Pennsylvania, Philadelphia; Pierre Tetrel; Museo Egizio, Turin; Egypt Exploration Society, London; Centre de Documentation sur l'Egypte Ancienne, Cairo; Rijksmuseum van Oudheden, Leyden; Oriental Institute of the University of Chicago; Maurice Chuzeville, Bollingen Foundation, New York; Damascus Museum; Professor Claude Schaeffer, Paris; Professor Fairman, Liverpool.

Nowhere is the temptation to write a romance instead of an historical study more compelling than here and it is for that reason that the greatest care has to be taken in the use of all these documents.

WALTHER WOLF

Zwei Beiträge zur Geschichte der achtzehnten Dynastie

My mind is not so timid that I deny the existence of mysteries. But I am wary of those who profess to live by them, who with their finger to their lips, proclaim themselves God's elect and keep the uninitiated in ignorance.

JACQUES DE BOURBON BUSSET

Moi, César

1 Return to the past

EXACTLY ONE CENTURY elapsed between the founding of Egyptology and the extraordinary discovery of Tutankhamen's tomb.

In Paris, on 22 September 1822, Jean-François Champollion the younger wrote his famous *Lettre à Monsieur Dacier, secrétaire perpétuel de l'Académie royale des inscriptions et belles-lettres, relative à l'alphabet des hiéroglyphes phonétiques*. On that day he opened the great book of Ancient Egypt, sealed for some two thousand years and now at last decipherable.

West of Thebes, on 25 November 1922, the first stone was removed from the wall closing the entrance of Tutankhamen's tomb, allowing Lord Carnarvon, his daughter, Lady Evelyn Herbert, and Howard Carter a glimpse of the most incredible burial treasure in existence today (1).

From its very beginning, Egyptology had inspired genuine scientific vocations. Fragments of four thousand years of human experience on the banks of the Nile were gradually pieced together; customs as old as the world itself, humble details of daily life, philosophical enquiries of scribes and wise men, elaborate theologies, social and religious reforms, military campaigns; all contributed to the historical reconstruction of this vanished civilization.

What have been the sources of our knowledge? Immense archaeological discoveries on sites which since the foundation of the Egyptian Antiquities Service have been scientifically controlled; the study of temples and tombs dedicated to the eternal life and power of the gods, kings and peoples of the Nile valley; the remains of cities, long-buried under sand and rubble, rich in moving evidence of the past; and finally the objects and monuments in the first Egyptian collections assembled at the time of Bonaparte's expedition and the admirable *Description de l'Egypte* published between 1809 and 1816 in which the scholars who accompanied him recorded their work (2).

Among the wealth of dynasties, kings, monuments and colossi, Tutankhamen was an inconspicuous, shadowy figure: few objects bore his name, among which two important monuments seem to suggest that, willingly or under compulsion, he had restored the official cult of the dynastic god Amun, abandoned by the king of Tell el Amarna, Amenophis IV-Akhenaten, at whose court

1. The archaeologists' first sight of the treasure

2. Scholars who accompanied Bonaparte's expedition to Egypt measuring the hand of an enormous statue near Memphis (Description de l'Egypte)

Tutankhamen had spent his childhood during one of the most attractive periods of Egyptian history—the epoch of the Solar Globe, Aten. These two monuments point to the implacable hatred with which the king had been pursued. We learn from the stele of the restoration of the Theban cult and temples (3) that, in order to strengthen the official position of the court, Tutankhamen was prevailed upon to have the temporarily abandoned shrines immediately reopened and restored, starting with those of Amun. But the stele no longer bears the sovereign's names for they were replaced by those of King Horemheb.

The other piece of evidence is the magnificent black granite group (4), a true memorial of the reconciliation with Theban Amun, added to the Louvre collection shortly before the discovery of the king's tomb. In this, he is shown standing before the seated figure of the imperial god. The god's broken hands, the king's shattered head, limbs and obliterated names are so many proofs of the ruthlessness of his enemies. This splendid group, though disfigured, nevertheless provides an idealized, but recognizable, portrait of the king in that of Amun, for Egyptian gods depicted anthropomorphically had always closely to resemble their "dear son" or earthly incarnation. In this group the face is very like those portraits of Tutankhamen familiar to us from statues at Karnak and certain bas-reliefs at Luxor; all, however, appropriated by Horemheb.

In fact, practically nothing was known of Tutankhamen, when Howard Carter, the archaeologist, encouraged by his findings in the Valley of the Kings, undertook, with Lord Carnarvon's moral and material support, to find his grave.

No royal sepulchre had ever been found *intact* in the burial grounds, and Biban el Moluk, the Valley of the Kings, seemed fated to disappoint the exca-

3. *Tutankhamen making offerings to the god Amun and the goddess Mut. The top part of the stele of the "restoration of the Theban temples" (Cairo Museum)*

4. *Amun protecting Tutankhamen (Louvre)*

5. *The reaction of the world press at the time of the discovery of the tomb and after the death of Lord Carnarvon*

vators. But they still clung to hopes of surpassing the discoveries of their predecessors, Sir Gaston Maspero, Loret, Naville, and Theodore Davis. These hopes were realised when Howard Carter's experience and perseverance and Lord Carnarvon's farsighted generosity breached the barrier which had protected Tutankhamen's final resting place from living intruders for 3,265 years.

The "shattering" discovery at once became world news (5). The announcement of the riches held by those few tiny rooms, scarcely designed for receiving such a treasure, caused as much surprise as wonder. Like Ali Baba's cave, the new tomb in the Valley of the Kings began, as fast as the clearing and the painstaking scientific recording allowed, to yield riches of unimaginable variety. The closer the searchers came to the sarcophagus, the more precise, tangible, and fantastic grew their conception of the treasure.

As might be expected after so sensational an event, many problems arose. New organization was required for the excavations, and a foolproof guard system had to be installed. Additional funds were urgently needed for removing the tomb's contents under proper conditions, yet the wealthy patron died shortly after the discovery. Other troubles arose: difficulties with the administration, Carter's legitimate insistence on autonomous working conditions, and, of course, the inevitable consequences of fame. Journalists demanded information on the spot; swarms of visitors from the four corners of the earth threatened to paralyse the archaeologists' work; and the countless mundane tasks which the diggers could not avoid slowed down the work. Only if one has lived in an archaeologists' camp under such climatic conditions can one appreciate the merit of Carter's team and also make allowances for attitudes of his which may sometimes have seemed exaggerated.

Carter and his men were worn out by having, in addition to their proper duties, to act as guides to celebrities of the day or to determined travellers who streamed to the tomb as to a fashionable show. Each visitor wanted to see

18

everything; and was deeply offended if his welcome was not of the warmest or if
he was not shown, already restored, the very latest object to be dug up (6).
Everyone wanted to go down and look at the wall bearing the royal names.
Everyone wanted the unique sensation of entering a tomb where so many
thousands of years, locked between hastily white-washed walls, must surely
communicate some occult message.

Demands, pleas, protests, interference, molestation by the press—the scholars were spared nothing. But when all the tumult had died down, it was the
universal fame of Tutankhamen that remained. This little-known ruler evoked
all by himself the mystery of the pharaohs, the idea of legendary—yet real—
treasure, and, for many, the myth of vengeance associated with the story of the

6. *Visitors at the entrance of the tomb at the time of the discovery*

discovery, with the young king himself, and with the formidable magicians and wise men of ancient Egypt.

The excavations and work within the tomb were completed by 1928; it took almost six full years to empty the sepulchre and to restore, on the spot, every piece of the most complete set of burial objects known to this day. The Cairo Museum's permanent exhibition of this treasure was prepared during the same period. It was actually ten years before proper study of the antiquities permitted completion of the first general publication: *The Tomb of Tut·Ankh·Amen* (Vol. 1 by Howard Carter and A. C. Mace [1923]; Vols. 2 and 3 [1927, 1933] by Howard Carter alone).

Obviously, such an incomparable collection could not be divided up, and Pierre Lacau, Director General of the Antiquities Service, decided wisely, though in the face of much opposition, to keep everything together in Egypt. In return, the Egyptian Government indemnified Lord Carnarvon's widow for all expenses incurred since work started in the Valley of the Kings.

Neither the excitement of the search nor the almost miraculous quality of the discovery made so short a time before the digging concession expired, nor even the vastness of the wealth exhumed could, however, make anyone forget Lord Carnarvon's fatal illness contracted a few months after the opening of the tomb. The Egyptian climate had helped it to develop rapidly. Unlike the young lord in Théophile Gautier's *Roman de la Momie*, in the hour of his triumph Lord Carnarvon could not look upon the remains of the prince with whom his name will always be linked. To the sensation-loving public, fate, in denying him this rare satisfaction, seemed to have acted unfairly, even provocatively. So some cause had to be found for the tragedy, an invisible avenger invented, responsible for every misfortune. Why not the pharaoh himself? Egypt, land of the mysterious sphinx, had already inspired many fantastic legends in which the magic of the ancients was continually invoked. People now recalled inscriptions dating back to earliest times, threatening the worst to "the living who come to violate the tombs." Clearly Lord Carnarvon had broken the powerful law which forbade the disturbance of the kingdom of the dead. The angry shade had struck and Lord Carnarvon was condemned.

Then, after leaving the tomb, Georges Bénédite, head of the Department of Egyptian Antiquities at the Louvre, died of a stroke brought on by the stifling heat of the Valley of the Kings. His death was followed by that of another member of the team, Arthur C. Mace, Assistant Keeper of the Department of Egyptian Antiquities at the Metropolitan Museum of Art in New York. The legend of a curse became firmly established. Nevertheless, others who took part in the work or studied the history of the discovery were in no way affected. Howard Carter, in particular, does not seem to have met with swift retribution; he died on 2 March 1939. Those who lived on until the Second World War and after were: A. Lucas, Director of the Chemical Laboratory of the Egyptian Government's Antiquities Service, who treated almost all the objects; Harry

7. Luncheon in a tomb in the Valley of the Kings: J. H. Breasted, Harry Burton, A. Lucas, A. R. Callender, Arthur Mace, Howard Carter and Alan Gardiner

Burton, the photographer to whom we owe the innumerable beautiful pictures of the discovery; R. Engelbach, Chief Inspector of Antiquities and later head of the Cairo Museum; Dr Derry of Cairo University, who analyzed the king's mummy; Jean Capart, who had the honour of showing the treasure to Queen Elizabeth of Belgium shortly after the discovery; and Gustave Lefèbvre, a member of the Institut de France (then Chief Curator of the Cairo Museum, responsible for laying out the permanent exhibition of the treasure as we see it in Cairo today), who died in 1957. Nor should we forget that the digging team also included A. R. Callender, Carter's assistant and his two draughtsmen, Hall and Hauser. Finally, Charles Kuentz, Pierre Lacau, Bernard Bruyère, and Sir Alan Gardiner were all present at the opening of the tomb or were actively engaged in subsequent work: evaluating the importance of certain objects, deciphering inscriptions, and so forth; although the last three are now well over eighty, they are still extremely active in the field of Egyptology.

From time to time the revenge of Tutankhamen shares the front page of the popular press with the Loch Ness monster. The ghost of a long-dead pharaoh torments some sensitive collector or appears to him in a terrifying form. How to escape from the pharaoh's curse? For of course the object responsible for these hallucinations could never have belonged to anyone less than a king, and is itself too much feared to be destroyed: the solution, then, has been to donate it to a museum. How often, in the world's great public collections, has some un-solicited gift been put aside for study; a harmless stone with hieroglyphics or a fragment of a wooden sarcophagus from a humble grave—the flotsam of a superstition as lively as ever in the twentieth century. Indeed, as often as not, the supposedly malefic object is an obvious fake.

However, if one cannot take seriously the many "mysterious" stories concocted after the discovery of the treasure, one must acknowledge two curious incidents, the only ones of their kind, which were related to me by Lord Carnarvon's son, the sixth earl, in London in July 1961 and then at his family seat, Highclere. To place them in context, we must recall the circumstances which led Lord Carnarvon to undertake archaeological research in the Valley of the Kings, and to place Howard Carter in charge of the work.

Carter had begun his career in Egypt as a draughtsman and in this capacity accompanied Percy Newberry to Beni Hasan and to El Bersha in 1892. He then worked with the American, Theodore Davis, in the region of Thebes, and collaborated on the drawings for the publication in which Sir Gaston Maspero and P. E. Newberry described the tomb of Amenophis III's parents-in-law, Thuya and Yuya. Carter was appointed inspector of Lower and Middle Egypt in 1903, and in 1907 Maspero introduced him to Lord Carnarvon who the previous year had applied for permission to dig at Thebes West in Upper Egypt.

Lord Carnarvon was not an Egyptologist; his decision to visit Egypt in 1902 was taken upon medical advice, as the climate was considered beneficial to delicate constitutions. A great sportsman and a keen traveller before suffering a serious motor accident, as well as a man of taste, he was the epitome of the *grand seigneur*. He was an extremely rich man, but was averse to spending his money without getting a return for it. On Lord Cromer's advice, he decided to subsidize archaeological research, and, with Maspero's help, obtained a permit to dig from the Egyptian Antiquities Service. It was understood that scientific responsibility for the work would be entrusted to an expert, and Carter was that man. From 1908 to 1912 Carnarvon and Carter explored the western region of Thebes on the left bank of the river. *Five Years' Exploration at Thebes* (Oxford, 1912) is the account of their first findings, which were encouraging. These included the famous wooden tablet (since known as the Carnarvon tablet) which bore written in ink the first account of the wars of Kamose, one of Egypt's liberators after the invasion of the Hyksos. (In 1954 a historic stele was discovered at Karnak, in which thirty-eight lines set forth the sequel to the events mentioned in the Carnarvon tablet.)

Then Carter decided to dig in the delta, and attempted to make Sais, at Sakha, his new site. But water from the Nile soaked the region and made it impossible to begin work before April; the temperature rose sharply, and the diggers were literally chased from the site by an invasion of cobras. So perhaps it is because of these sacred serpents that we find Carnarvon and Carter resuming work near Thebes shortly before the First World War.

IIIa. *Tiny statuette of Amenophis III found in*
a small mummiform coffin. Solid gold
b. *An earring. In the centre of the clip is the*
little king flanked by two sacred serpents

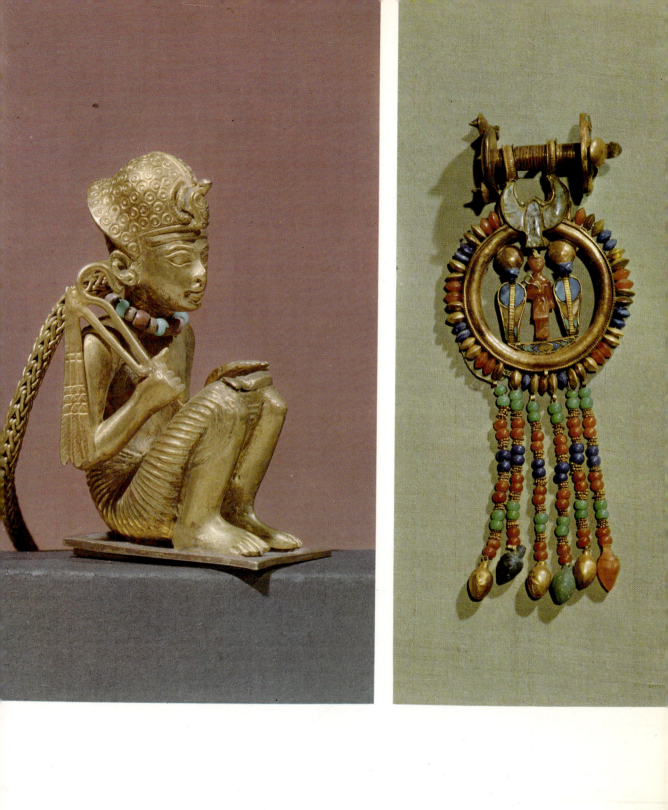

8. *The Theban peak towering above the Valley of the Kings. The entrance to the tombs of Tutankhamen and Ramesses VI is on the right*

The war itself greatly slowed their work. Carnarvon was unable to return to Egypt, but Carter was conscripted locally. During this period he discovered the tomb of Amenophis I, which had unfortunately been pillaged, and the one prepared for the princess Hatshepsut before her accession to the throne. It was a good omen. Thus, from 1919 to 1921 Carter systematically and steadily prospected the whole sector of the Valley of the Kings between the tombs of Merenptah, Ramesses III, and Ramesses VI (8).

When the concession had only a few more weeks to run, Carter became discouraged: in England, Lord Carnarvon began to wonder if there was any hope of making an important discovery. But on the morning of 4 November 1922, when the last rubble-covered corner under Ramesses VI's tomb had been cleared down to the rock and after the remains of the XXth Dynasty workmen's

IV*a. A footstool used by the boy-king at the beginning of his reign*
   b. A scribe's palette in ivory and a case for writing-reeds made of wood plated with gold and inlaid with glass-paste

dwellings below the entrance to the syrinx had been thoroughly removed, Carter saw what looked like the beginning of a step hewn in the rock. It was followed by others which led to a screen of stones, plastered over and bearing the seals of the royal necropolis. He then made preparations for the ceremonial opening of the tomb. With his devoted assistant Callender, he cleared the last four steps and reached another wall of stone blocks, again roughly plastered and bearing the imprint of the royal seals. After sixteen steps, which seemed to acquire almost magical importance, they saw, upon the last barrier between the living and the

9. Highclere Castle, the home of Lord Carnarvon

dead, the name of Nebkheprure-Tutankhamen. On 6 November Carter informed his patron, at Highclere: Lord Carnarvon and his daughter landed at Alexandria on the 20th and were able to reach Luxor on the 23rd. On 25 November, the day Carter called "the day of days, the most wonderful that I have ever lived through, and certainly one whose like I can never hope to see again," the first stone was removed from the tomb's wall. Through the small opening, after Carter's first quick glance, Carnarvon, peering into the gloom, saw strange animals, statues, and gold.

I have visited the great park of the Carnarvon estate (9), strolled on its cedar-dotted lawns and by the lake with its white marble belvedere. I was shown the stud farm and pastures, the neo-Gothic hall, the priceless library, the old masters, the collection of valuable furniture, including Napoleon's desk from Elba and his chair, its arms scratched by irritable imperial fingernails. Nothing at Highclere hints at the Egyptian adventure of its late master: the fabulous collection he began in 1907 was disposed of far from the British Museum, in the United States, by Lady Carnarvon's wish. Not a single object or photograph is left to evoke the land of the pharaohs.

As we stood before a portrait of the fifth earl, his son told me the epilogue to the extraordinary discovery and described his father's death. Lord Carnarvon had spent Christmas in England, and returning to Upper Egypt early in 1923, he visited the Valley of the Kings daily. In March he was bitten by a mosquito; the bite turned septic, and as the infection spread rapidly, he decided that he would return to Cairo, where his family hoped to have him looked after more satisfactorily. The infection yielded to treatment, but towards the end of March he contracted pneumonia, and his son, Lord Porchester, who was serving with the army in India, was summoned urgently. Since the discovery of Tutankhamen's tomb everything connected with Lord Carnarvon had become of public interest, and news of his grave illness travelled fast. Everything was done to hasten the young Lord Porchester's voyage from India to Egypt, and throughout the crossing Moslem pilgrims prayed for the stricken earl.

Lord Porchester reached the Continental Hotel in Cairo just a few hours before his father died there at five minutes to two on the morning of 5 April 1923, without having recognized his son. At this precise moment the two incidents referred to earlier occurred. In Cairo, all the lights in the hotel went out and remained out for some time. Next day, the new earl, on a formal visit to the High Commissioner, Field Marshal Lord Allenby, learned that every single light in the city had gone out also. Lord Allenby asked the English engineer in charge of the electricity service the cause of this strange power failure but received no satisfactory technical explanation. The other incident concerns the dog which Lord Porchester had left in his father's care when he sailed for India, and which had grown so fond of its new master that it had pined in his absence. At the exact moment of Lord Carnarvon's death in Egypt, the animal left in England howled inconsolably and died.

These, then are the only authentic events connected with Lord Carnarvon's death. According to his wishes, he is buried on his estate, on top of Beacon Hill, on the spot where he had once previously engaged in archaeological research, and his grave faces the house. His destiny was shaped at the time of his decision to support archaeology; whether he lived a few years more or less mattered little, since his partner in glory had been awaiting him in the shadows for more than three thousand years. From the day the royal tomb was opened, three names were to become jointly famous: those of Tutankhamen, Carter and Carnarvon.

Tutankhamen, the unknown, became world famous overnight, yet his burial treasure, testifying to a refined culture, to funerary rituals and practices which had to be pieced together and understood, revealed little or nothing of his own life and personality. The king who seemed to have been taken out of his historical and personal context was now rescued from oblivion; yet he himself remained shrouded in mystery. "To speak the name of the dead is to make them live again," say the funerary inscriptions, it restores "the breath of life to him who has vanished." Innumerable prayers exhort the pilgrim to perform this rite when passing near a tomb. The harshest punishment for delinquents was to change their names, and thus remove their real identity. The names of enemies and invaders were never to be spoken, for they had no citizens' rights among the men of Egypt. Criminals disappeared from this world and from the orb of the eternal world even before their deaths, since their names had been effaced and destroyed. Thus they became nothing, and fell back into the void.

Carter and Carnarvon were certainly the greatest benefactors of a king whom they rescued from this fate, making his name "live again," as adjured by the priests of the necropolis.

It is clear from the outset of this study that in spite of Tutankhamen's youth and the brevity of his reign, he was the victim after death of a systematic attempt to erase him utterly from history. Ruthless hatred disfigured those of his monuments which his tomb could not protect.

Vengeance, if vengeance there was, came not from him but from Amun, or rather from the supporters of Amun who tried to remove Tutankhamen's name from the stone so that he might die a second death and vanish forever (10). Only by identifying the author and assessing the motives of these criminal attempts can one hope to reconstruct the life of the young king.

10. *The back of the statue of Amun protecting Tutankhamen showing the obliterated inscription* (Louvre)

V. *Painted ivory plaque from the lid of a coffer showing Tutankhamen and Ankhesenamun in a garden. The lower frieze shows young women plucking mandrakes*

2 The world of the dead and life west of Thebes

*Tales of mummies,
kings and brigands*

THE AREA AROUND Thebes (11) is the main setting for this story. Although we will follow the river to Tell el-Amarna in order to reconstruct Tutankhamen's early years, we must always return to that supreme city of high antiquity and its environs. When we examine its bricks and stones, we go back in time to the fourteenth century B.C., to the heart of a civilization throbbing with life.

Today the temple at Luxor sprouts like a garden of magnificent sturdy plants on the bank of the Nile. Approaching it, one senses the power of the gods and priests of Egypt, who were the principal beneficiaries of Pharaoh's prodigality. Luxor, however, was created primarily as the great god Amun's harmonious Opet of the south, the centre of his family and personal life, where he went during the eleven days of his divine emergence for the great feast of Opet. Throughout the whole of his journey he appeared to his faithful worshippers in his magnificent ceremonial barge sparkling with gold.

Karnak is a world of temples, a maze of sanctuaries and pylons, its doors and walls covered with figures of kings and gods (12). The great gods of the Egyptian empire were all honoured in chapels and sanctuaries. Chief among them was Amun, whose name means the Hidden One, but who is represented everywhere bestowing strength and eternal life on the king. Two tall plumes rising from his head-dress symbolize his celestial origin. He is thus at once an invisible demiurge in the firmament and a god on earth, served by his priests, who exacted from the pharaoh all the moral and material support Amun could wish for.

Among the many evocations of the Theban kings an eloquent image adorns the seventh pylon of the great temple: that of Tuthmosis III, seventeen times conqueror of the Asians. He is consecrating before the charming little goddess-Thebes (under the aegis of Amun) a huge human cluster of enemies kneeling to implore mercy. Elsewhere, a gigantic panel depicts heaps of gold, rare jewels, and exotic produce brought back by the king from victorious campaigns and nearly all presented to the deity of the sanctuary as a thank-offering.

Every Egyptian monument evokes with intensity an event, an instant in the life of its vanished people. With so much evidence available about the history of

VI. *The back of the gold-plated throne: the queen Ankhesenamun
is putting the finishing touches to the king's toilet*

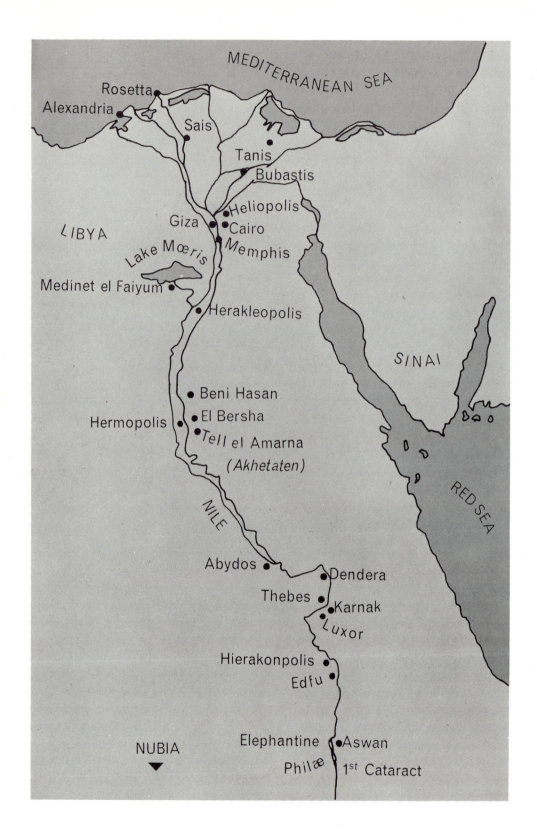

11. Sketch map of Egypt

12. Karnak: view of some of the sanctuaries taken from the top of the first pylon facing south

Tuthmosis III, the great conqueror, it eventually became possible to establish the link between a detail on the surface of an obelisk, confirming the inscription at its base, an image on a Theban chapel wall, and a cylinder (now in the Louvre) with cuneiform inscriptions in the name of Ashurbanipal. This cylinder tells us that when the Assyrian king sacked Thebes, during the reign of Tanoutamun, he sent back to his palace two columns, or obelisks, which had stood at the temple gate. Made of electrum, an alloy of 75 per cent gold, 22 per cent silver, and 3 per cent copper, their combined weight was 2,500 talents, or 166,650 pounds.

It is easy to guess the hold of the priests of Karnak over the crown. Queen Hatshepsut affirms it on the base of her obelisks at Karnak:

"... I sat in my palace and thought of him who created me [Amun] ... My heart bade me make for him two obelisks of electrum ... Then my soul stirred, wondering what men would say who saw this monument after many years and spoke of what I had done. ..."

But the queen found she had not enough of the precious alloy. She therefore

33

continues her story on the obelisk base:

> "Concerning the two great obelisks which my majesty has had *covered* with electrum for
> my father Amun, that my name may live forever in this temple, throughout the centuries:
> they are hewn from a single stone which is of hard granite, with no joints ... I have shown
> my devotion to Amun, as a king does to all the gods. It was my wish to have them cast in
> electrum, [as this was not possible] I have at least placed a surface [of electrum] upon them."

In other words, the queen had to be content with gold-plating the two obelisks. They are still at Karnak, and one can discern near the corners the grooves in which Hatshepsut's goldsmiths set the sheets of electrum.

Tuthmosis III's overseer decorated the interior of his own funerary chapel at Thebes with a complete pictorial account of the works carried out under his supervision in the workshops of the temple of Amun at Karnak. One illustration shows two obelisks, and a fragmentary inscription suggests that these were indeed entirely of gold alloy. What had been beyond the resources of the world's first great queen was achieved by her successor, who employed the same overseer. Tuthmosis III's Asian campaigns drained the treasuries of Egypt's new vassal states and the victorious monarch was able to offer to the god and his priests two solid images of the vital ray in gold alloy in appreciation of Amun's help. These are probably the two obelisks, mentioned in the Louvre cylinder as weighing 1250 talents (83,325 lbs) each, which stood in the sanctuary at Karnak, and which the Theban clergy surrendered to Ashurbanipal to avert the sack of the city. Only under Tuthmosis III could such wealth have been brought into Egypt.

There is no doubt that this king owed everything to the priests of Amun. With their help he had deposed his aunt, Queen Hatshepsut, under whom he had endured a long period of tutelage. However, the time came when the great conqueror was forced to shake off the yoke of the insatiable priests. In Karnak itself he reminded them of the limits they so often seemed to have overstepped, countering with a tangible symbol, the presence of another god, the most powerful of all, the Sun. In earliest pharaonic times tall pillars of matched stones were dedicated to this god; they looked like one huge dressed stone, and at the top was a point in the form of a small pyramid. Such a *tekhen* was the only object of worship in the sun temples of the Vth Dynasty (about 2,500 B.C.). Later they became more slender, like needles made from a single stone, and appeared in pairs flanking the temple entrances. When the civilization of the pharaohs had begun to decline, Greek mercenaries, making fun of these strange sacred shapes which they did not understand, dubbed them *obelisks*, or "spits".

Towards the end of his reign Tuthmosis III planned to erect within the precincts of Karnak—in a temple dedicated to the rising sun, to the east of the great temple of Amun—a *single* obelisk. It was not to be consecrated to the overpowerful lord of the empire, Amun, but to the Sun. The immense stone needle was not set up in Tuthmosis's lifetime, and its inscriptions tell us that it lay by the sacred lake at Karnak after his death. His successor, Amenophis II, added monuments and statues to Karnak's glories, but ignored the obelisk. However,

13. The sphinx of Giza still buried in sand

the next king, Tuthmosis IV, completed the work begun by his grandfather, and installed within Amun's very sanctuary, in the centre of a courtyard in the east temple, the *single* obelisk, the revolutionary symbol of Re Harakhti, the rising sun (now in the piazza of St John Lateran in Rome).

The new king's freedom of action was hampered by the formidable Theban clergy. They could make or unmake kings, and appeared to have played an active if cold-blooded part in the probably fratricidal feuds of the Tuthmosides. However, they must have reached some kind of compromise with the scholar-priests of Heliopolis, who worshipped the sun—for how otherwise could a new Tuthmosis prince have become the fourth pharaoh of that name? At least, that is the implication of a monumental stele at the breast of the great sphinx at Giza (13), discovered when the sands which had accumulated since Roman times were cleared away. For here Tuthmosis IV openly declared that he owed his throne to the god Harmakhis.

According to this stele the future pharaoh was not originally in the line of succession. One day, while hunting in the Memphis necropolis, he fell asleep at noon in the shadow of the "guardian of the necropolis," and Harmakhis (Horus-in-the-Horizon) appeared to him in a dream. The god was suffocating beneath the heavy weight of sand, and told him that in exchange for deliverance from the intolerable burden he would ensure that his benefactor wore the double crown of the reigning monarch. Awaking with a start, the hunter drove his chariot swiftly home and at once ordered that the god be freed from the weighty shroud of desert sand. Shortly afterwards Amenophis II died, and during a procession in the great pillared hall of the temple at Karnak the statue of the god, borne

35

14. The Dream Stele at Giza at the time of its discovery

by the priests, forced them to turn aside from their appointed path and approach the silent and devout Tuthmosis in a dark corner of a transverse aisle. The god had imposed his choice as heir to the throne.

Thus Amun continued to crown his kings, but Tuthmosis IV preferred to ascribe the outcome to the intervention of Re, the sun god, relieved of his burdens and represented in his aspect of repose as the sphinx reclining on the horizon, ready to take wing like Pharaoh at the dawn of his accession. The inscriptions did not lie; at the beginning of this century excavations uncovered an earth-brick wall built by Tuthmosis IV to keep the desert sands from the sphinx: the bricks all bore his royal stamp (14).

Karnak and its temples, the sanctuaries of Egypt, despite the thousands of years that have elapsed since they were built, evoke so vividly those stirring times that it is fairly easy to relive them: the monarchy, the solemn occasions of pharaonic life, and the dazzling New Empire, particularly during the XVIIIth Dynasty, the outburst of one of history's greatest religious reformations, one

36

15. The pylon from the temple of Luxor after the clearing away of the rubble

which actually succeeded in checking the power of Amun. Within the sacred precincts a mystical, headstrong pharaoh confronted prelates who clung blindly to an authoritarian dogma out of touch with a rapidly evolving society.

Amun's temporary disgrace in the city of temples sacred to official theology and to the divine person of the pharaohs resulted in the gradual desertion of the shrines and eventually in persecution. Fire even ravaged the great wooden portals studded with bronze and cracked the stone lintels. Ironically, it seems, after those titanic deadly struggles, fate was to crown a mere child, Tutankhamen, who, guided by a shrewd mentor, was to drive the intruders from the abandoned temples.

But it is not in the religious and royal centres of Karnak and Luxor that one should look for clues to the colourful daily life of those times. These can only be found on the left bank of the river, west of Thebes—the bank of the dead—where an Egyptologist's life is an extraordinary adventure compounded of past and present. On the right bank, where in ancient Thebes palaces and hovels were scattered indiscriminately between colossal temples, modern buildings now cover the ruined dwellings and conceal what is left of the richest capital of antiquity. True, for some years past the Antiquities Service have been cleaning the temple at Luxor; its pylon is now clear and no longer obscured by the accumulated rubbish which had raised the level of the terrace in front of the tall trapezoid towers. The colossi by the walls are now visible in their entirety and so is the base of the eastern obelisk, the twin of the one presented to France by the Egyptian government as a tribute to Champollion. A very fine *dromos* or sacred way adorned by a human-headed sphinx has now been exposed (15); the road to Karnak used by the last of the native dynasties has re-appeared; but the earth-brick city is still buried under the present-day township of Luxor.

Let us therefore leave Thebes of the Hundred Gates, whose great stone portals still stand, and cross the river westward. I have often done this, in every season and at all hours of the day, and it has never been quite the same on any two occasions. Yet the Theban mountain, with its pyramidal peak, its colours shifting from pink or blue at dawn, through the pale gold of daylight to scarlet at the brief moment of dusk, is always there, beckoning. Those who have spent some time there know the delight of crossing the river in an ageless *felucca*, with its patched triangular sail and flat white seat cushions. Sometimes a boy takes the helm and a pair of rowers sing as they raise and lower the crude oars, but more often the wind swells the skilfully set sheet, for these men have always been great sailors. When the level of the Nile drops after February, sand shoals (the famous *tchessou* of the ancient texts) emerge and impede river traffic, and the people at once plant tomatoes and marrows on them. Sometimes one passes a boat laden with peasants singing to the beat of a *darabukka*, possibly a wedding party; or sometimes a great rough *felucca*, bulging with goods, timber, live-stock, and passengers—the ferry for the west bank villages of Qurna, Qurnet Murai and El Khokha (16).

On the west bank there are donkeys waiting for the traveller reluctant to use the local taxi, but not everyone can emulate the villagers and ride them bare-back. Here you will seldom see the roadside markets common on the other bank, with their displays of food, clothing, and porous earthenware jars which keep the water cool and fresh, nor are you likely to encounter palm-decked carts full of crouching black-veiled women or brilliantly clad girls chattering like birds (17). The west bank is calmly confident of its stately heritage: you feel you are in the presence of the pharaohs' subjects and are treading the sacred soil where their forebears were buried. It is also magical, treasure-bearing soil. A police station stands near the landing-stage, and those who do not actually live on the west bank must leave it by sundown.

A raised dyke leads away from the river through fields of sugar cane, cotton, wheat, and *berseem* (a variety of clover). Like everything in the poetic Egyptian landscape, mud-brick villages which could be ancient or modern cluster about

VII. *The gilt shrine which originally contained the statuettes of the royal couple*

On the two following pages: VIII. *Details of the exterior of the gilt shrine:*
  a. *The queen brings unguents and flowers to the king*
  b. *The queen fastens a necklace round the king's neck*

IXa. *The king pours a perfumed liquid into the queen's hand*
  b. *The queen helps the king in a ritual hunting scene*

38

the heart of an oasis of palms and sycamores where donkeys, *zamouses* (water buffaloes), and dromedaries live. The riverside *shadoofs*, which the peasant still uses to irrigate his fields after the floods have subsided, soon give way to *sakiehs*. Patient buffaloes work these water wheels, encouraged by a small boy armed with a whip, chanting nasally yet raucously in time to their steady creaking.

The first village to be reached presents a sharp contrast with the landscape. It is new and still uninhabited, built of elegant houses in the Saidi, or southern, style—often reminiscent of Nubian dwellings, which have retained their archaic character. In 1948–9 the Service of Antiquities started to build this model village to rehouse the inhabitants of Qurna, in an attempt to clear these inveterate grave-robbers out of the chapels and sepulchres of the Theban nobles. Here we are entering a strange world on the fringe of the necropolis, and even within it, for these villagers—if one may so call them—reluctant to waste a single foot of cultivable land, have settled in the very heart of temple and tomb (18).

Beyond the green valley, past the site of Amenophis III's funerary temple of which only the famous colossi of Memnon remain—huge, dramatic witnesses of a vanished world—lies the desert. Without any transition, the fertile humus gives way to arid sand and rock; all vegetation abruptly disappears. The relative coolness of the river ends and it is as though one were suddenly struck in the face by the atmosphere of a blast furnace. This is the real left bank, the realm of the Theban dead, of family vaults and priests, mummifiers, coffin-makers, grave-diggers and cemetery guardians, a region where life pulsated in the shadow of the treasures and monuments raised by the kings of the New Empire: Deir el Bahri, the Ramesseum, Medinet Habu. . . .

These names evoke the shrines of dead kings whose graves in fact no longer adjoin their chapels. During the XVIIIth Dynasty the whole underground section of the royal burial complex was separated from the temple and installed at the back of the imposing cliff of Deir el Bahri and its outcroppings, in the parched *wadis* known as the Valley of the Kings and the Valley of the Queens. Emulating their royal masters, the Theban nobility built their eternal homes along the front of the cliff. The finest *mastabas* (bench-like tombs) of the Ancient Empire, built of limestone blocks, had their inner chapel walls decorated with friezes depicting in coloured relief scenes of daily life. When Thebes became the capital of the kingdom and the sovereigns elected to crown all their syrinxes with a copy of the natural pyramid capping the Theban mountain, courtiers and senior officials were granted royal funerary concessions on the slopes of the hill. The finest of these tombs are at the lower level, where the stone is magnificent. The carved friezes within were made by the most skilful artists of the day

X. *The gilt throne. The back is decorated with a scene which is perhaps ritual but evokes the private life of the royal couple. The other parts of the throne are decorated with official and religious motives*

16. *The villagers from the west bank waiting for the boat to take them across the Nile to Luxor*

18. *Women returning to the village of Qurna having drawn water from the Nile*

17. *Peasant girls travelling in a cart on the right bank of Thebes*

and examples from the reign of Amenophis III can be seen in the famous chapels of Khaemhet, Kheruef and Ramose. Higher up, the stone is of inferior quality and is not always suitable for carving and sculpture. Here the chapel walls were often smoothly rendered and directly painted upon, in strips whose colours remain fresh and vivid to this day.

Every aspect of Theban life is dealt with on these walls, and at every social level: noble guests at royal celebrations, magistrates on the bench, even the king's vizier attending to his duties. In the painted gardens, trees and multi-coloured flowers surround a rectangular fishpond with birds and lotus flowers. We see the gardener's *shadoof*, unchanged by the centuries, and craftsmen setting the final touches to a statue or piece of furniture. Workers are making clay bricks and building a wall; a shepherd, beautiful as a young god, leads his flock homeward. A girl pauses in her gleaning; a labourer asks his friend to remove a thorn from his foot. A peasant sleeps under a tree from which hangs his waterskin, and the barber plies his trade in the fields (19). Every craft is represented in the painted reliefs or the flat paintings; for example, the goldsmith

19. A barber working in the fields. Scene in the Theban chapel of Woserhet

20. Singing and dancing: a scene from the walls of a Theban chapel (British Museum)

putting the finishing touches to sumptuous jewels beside the gold-founder smelting his precious metal. Lavish banquets bring together the elegant citizenry of Thebes, waited upon by pretty girls and entertained by musicians and dancers (20).

In every tomb there are endless variations on the same themes. Two of these, traceable to earliest times, are those of hunting and fishing. With the XVIIIth Dynasty they reached their apogee of stylized elegance. On either side of a great thicket of papyrus the owner of the tomb is shown in a coracle, accompanied by his wife, sometimes by his children. In one picture he is throwing boomerangs at waterfowl. In the other he is spearing two great fish. This traditional design, usually very prominent in the chapels, was long believed to illustrate the pastimes which the dead man hoped to enjoy in after-life.

The world of the dead, especially in the Theban funerary chapels, offers the most comprehensive record of life in pharaonic Egypt. A well-shaft ending near the chapel led below ground to the burial chamber which was private and might not be visited after burial. Here the mummy, enclosed in its coffins and surrounded by its effects, slept out eternity.

It is not hard to reconstruct the atmosphere peculiar to these parts of the necropolis nearly four thousand years ago, for so much remains, preserved, though often damaged, beneath the sands or the layers of a nitrogenous deposit called *sebakh*. But to do so, one must leave Qurna and Qurnet Murai, and follow a dry *wadi* between the Valley of the Kings and the Valley of the Queens, leaving behind on one's left the funerary temple of Ramesses III, which rises from the romantic ruins of Djeme, the ancient Coptic city. On the road to the Valley of the Queens there is a cavern, surrounded by votive inscriptions to the goddess of the district, "she who loves silence," the snake goddess who also reigns on the peak of the mountain. During the New Empire, at least, pairs of cobras were probably worshipped there, as today some reptiles are respectfully tolerated in certain households in Qurnet Murai.

The path leads on to the *wadi* of Deir el Medineh. There the Cairo *Institut français d'archéologie orientale* spent forty years clearing *sebakh* from the ancient remains of a large walled village which, for several generations during the New Empire, had housed the workmen of the necropolis. In addition to its homes the village contained a main street and a public square where one could fetch water. A police station at each gate protected and probably kept an eye on the villagers. Nearby was the *gebel*, or desert mountain, the haunt of wolves, hyenas, and brigands.

One by one the ruined dwellings came to light, their door-posts and the bases of the columns supporting their roof-trees marked with their owners' names, and it became possible to establish the connection between locally-found papyruses, tombs in the nearby necropolis (21), and the newly-discovered dwelling. The many fragments, especially *ostraca*, found in the earth-brick walls, the houses, the rubble, or in a cache in the well-hole of the North Temple, were highly informative about the daily life of the village. (An *ostracon* is a sliver of calcareous stone or pottery, then used by the Egyptians for correspondence in hieratic—or simplified cursive hieroglyphics—to save costly state-monopolized papyrus.) They outlined local working methods and described the hilltop path the gangs followed down to the neck of the valley at the foot of the Theban peak. These gangs, divided according to whether they lived on the right or left of the village street, would then set up camp on either side of the path to the Valley of the Kings. This would be their base during the ten-day working week to follow. At the end of this period they would return to their village, Set Maat, the Place of Truth.

These workmen were not, as has so often been stated, prisoners of war or slaves subjected to cruel forced labour and put to death when the royal tomb was finished. Papyri referring to them and thousands of *ostraca* contain fascinat-

21. Reconstruction of the ancient necropolis of the workmen of Deir el Medineh

ing proof of this: for instance, the excuses for non-attendance proffered by the lazier workers: one has had to take a sick donkey to the vet, and another has buried the same aunt for the third time! A workman applies for promotion while another indents for replacement of tools; and we learn of work held up when a gang encountered "the stone," a vein of silex which genuinely slowed them up. One foreman's accounts show the number of wicks issued to his team for their oil lamps used for work underground.

The whole of village life is recorded—schoolchildren's homework corrected in the teacher's red ink, artists' sketches, and illustrations of popular fables. . . . Here is a study of a royal profile to be reproduced in a tomb, there a hyena hunt with ravening dogs, and, just as Aesop and La Fontaine described them, the wolf and the kid together, playing the flute! A worried mother complains to a neighbour about an unruly son pelting schcolgirls with stones from behind a wall. Thanks to the *ostraca*, one can follow, step by step, the route of the god's statue, called in as an oracle to settle a dispute. One can retrace its trip from the village gates to the very spot where the god identified the guilty party. No detail is lacking, down to the small bundles of papyrus slips, each with a different inscription, used for drawing lots. The official records of the Theban necropolis even tell us the ingredients and the amount of the day's rations, and that at one time these had to be fetched from near the temple of Medinet Habu. On one occasion the men complained: "We are weak and starving because we have not been given the rations which Pharaoh ordained," and they went on strike.

Sometimes we encounter accusations, as in the case of Hai, a foreman of works, who was said to have spoken offensively of the pharaoh. The private necropolis tribunal was convened, and the account of the trial shows what exceptional privileges these specialized artisans enjoyed. Hai was judged by the *kenbet*, a court of his peers, four "right" and four "left" men of Deir el Medineh, presided over by a fellow worker of his own standing. The accused was given every chance to state his case, and justice took its course.

An *ostracon* often provides the missing link between scraps of information already obtained perhaps from a fragment of papyrus, as a jigsaw puzzle is pieced together. An observant Egyptologist, watching a workman clear a column, notices the name of the owner of the house upon it, Paneb. He knows that Paneb was foreman of works at Set Maat, at the heart of which was situated Deir el Medineh, and he immediately thinks of Paneb's tomb in the hillside whose western slope overhangs the workers' village. Archaeologists have suspected that Paneb was responsible for the murder of the headman Neferhotep. Would his house now confirm his infamy? A fragment of wood covered in gold leaf had once been found in Pawah's cellar and had provided irrefutable proof of his thefts from the tomb of Ramesses III which the law had failed to discover in the twelfth century B.C. But Paneb was prudent and left no new evidence of his guilt. His contemporaries, however, watched him carefully, and if one collates the information in the Salt papyrus No. 124 and the Cairo *ostracon* No. 25,521, one is forced to the conclusion that Paneb's bad reputation was not undeserved.

Paneb lived at the time of Siptah II, between the reigns of Sethos II and Ramesses III, at the beginning of the XXth Dynasty. He took advantage of his official position as deputy chief of works in the necropolis to feather his own nest, setting his artisans to work for him personally without payment and using state goods and labour as his own. From one he exacted that he paint his coffin, from another, that he plaster the inner walls of his tomb, jobs which were clearly outside the normal range of duties of the pharaoh's specialized workman. He even compelled another man, Nebnofer, son of Ouadjmes, to feed his ox for a whole month at government expense, and yet another necropolis worker, Raouben, was forced to make the reed mats for his house. It was scandalous, but apparently Paneb made no distinction between his interests and those of the state. His immediate superior, Neferhotep, chief of the workmen, denounced him, and lodged a formal complaint with the vizier; but the righteous without protection need all their courage to expose an embarrassing truth. Not only was Paneb dishonest, but probably a murderer, too, since apparently Neferhotep died suddenly from unknown causes, and was promptly succeeded by Paneb. Completely unscrupulous, he seemed unafraid of divine retribution, unlike some of the pious sinners of his time such as Neferabou, a worker at this same necropolis, whose sins were punished by blindness. Conscience-stricken, he made a public confession that he had caused injury to his neighbour and his sight was restored at once by the merciful goddess of the peak, Meresger.

Paneb was not the only Theban of the XXth Dynasty unaffected by moral considerations, as several papyri conclusively prove. Of these the most famous are the Abbott papyrus (British Museum), the Amherst (New York), and the Leopold II (Brussels). The two latter are complementary; the lower portion of the four sheets is the Amherst (known since 1874), and the upper portion was found by the Belgian Egyptologist Jean Capart in the wooden base of a statuette. The documents thus reassembled were published in 1939. Other papyri now in Liverpool, at the British Museum, and in Turin enlarge upon the vital information these contained, and make it seem unlikely that a royal sepulchre would ever be found intact.

Graffiti on the rocks of the royal necropolis show that inspectors regularly checked the condition of the tombs, but it was not suspected that robber bands systematically pillaged them for gold and precious oils. However, this might have been foreseen, as the royal burial treasures were common knowledge from the time of their making. Moreover, they were displayed in the funeral processions from the right bank to the left and cannot have failed to arouse in many onlookers feelings of greed and cupidity rather than respect for the dead and fear of the supernatural. A case of grave robbery was discovered under Ramesses IX, and the ensuing trial shattered the equanimity of high officials. Certainly it was a case for jurisdiction higher than that of the *kenbet*, although most of the accused were apparently humble folk. The trial was held, it seems, in a temple of the right bank, in the great hall of the goddess Maet, patroness of justice and truth, and judged by the high court of the city, composed of the vizier, the high priest of Amun, and other high-ranking notables. According to the necropolis records, the accused were imprisoned in the temple of Mut, at Thebes, where they were interrogated "with strokes of the cane on their hands and feet." This was no trifling matter; times were harsh and violent, and the country's political decline was thrown into stark relief by a succesion of bad harvests and widespread starvation.

Gold was scarce and some people did not mind where they got it from. The scandal came to light when Pesiur, mayor of Thebes, discovered that royal and noble tombs were being raided. His zeal was probably activated by desire to expose the complicity or incompetence of Pawer, the mayor of western Thebes. He promptly informed Khaemweset, the vizier, and enquiries, arrests, and interrogations followed. There were even reconstructions, *in situ*, of the crimes, which included the desecration of several noble graves, among others those of Queen Isis, the great royal spouse of Ramesses III, and of King Sekhemre-Shedtawy, Sobekemsaf and his wife Nubkhas. Of course, Pawer had no alternative but to denounce the culprits, in spite of the powerful protection which they enjoyed. But the vizier managed to take advantage of indiscretions on Pesiur's part to save them, for Pesiur, infuriated by Pawer's double dealing and the cynicism and venality of the police, had not been able to keep his righteous indignation to himself. Incautious statements of his were carried back to the vizier, who promptly quashed the enquiry, acquitting and releasing the accused.

Pawer was "put in the wrong," and as a sop to administrative bureaucracy, a report was placed on record in the vizier's official archives. There is reason to believe that some of the robbers of Sebekemsaf's tomb were in fact executed, but others escaped thanks to the protection of Pawer, and no doubt of Khaemweset himself who probably took a share of the spoils.

Such indulgence—indeed, such complicity—could only encourage the robbers who turned their attention to the great tombs of the Valley of the Kings. Once again they were apprehended and tried, this time more scrupulously. For instance, the desecrators of the tomb of Queen Tiye, wife of Sethos I and mother of Ramesses II, were suitably punished. The tombs of these two kings were also violated, and until the XXIst Dynasty the fabulous necropolises of western Thebes suffered frequent thieving incursions. Even the priesthood was involved, and a papyrus in the British Museum states that the Ramesseum—the funerary temple of Ramesses II—was pillaged by its own priests. It is an index of the state of penury and confusion to which the country had been reduced by incessant Libyan invasions that the priests should violate the sanctuaries which they were supposed to guard.

At last recognizing the virtual impossibility of guarding their ancestors' tombs, the kings of the XXIst Dynasty removed the royal mummies to communal hiding places. The most important seems to have been that situated to the north-west of the *cirque* of Deir el Bahri, where a twenty-seven foot-long underground chamber hewn in the rock sheltered thirty rough sarcophagi, including those of the greatest pharaohs: Amenophis I, Tuthmosis II, Tuthmosis III, Ramesses I, Sethos I, Ramesses II and Ramesses III. Sequenenre, liberator of the valley of the Nile, lay also with these masters of antiquity, his face pierced by a Hyksos arrow. And this pathetic "crypt," improvised by the last kings of Thebes and their faithful scribes and necropolis inspectors (such as Butehamun), brings us back full circle to the modern inhabitants of the Theban necropolis.

Their territory stretches from the hillside dwellings to the depths of the surrounding *wadis* (22). From childhood their playground is the *gebel*, whose most inaccessible corners they know by heart, and where they have often located caches which they draw upon regularly like a money-box. In 1874 Maspero noticed the appearance on the antique market of figures bearing royal names of the XXIst Dynasty, of a wooden tablet inscribed in ink purchased by a collector (the Rogers Tablet, now in the Louvre), of a papyrus belonging to Queen Nedjmet, and so on. He sent inspectors to investigate, as detectives rather than

XI. *Details from the ceremonial footstool of the king:*
  a. *The adversaries of the north: a Syrian and a Libyan*
  b. *The adversaries of the south: a Nubian and a Sudanese*
  c. *The enemies of Egypt conquered and placed beneath the yoke of the pharaoh (a variation of the scene of "Union of Two Countries")*

officials, but it took some time to collect the evidence. At last, in 1881, the organizers of the thefts were found to be the Abdelrassoul brothers of Qurna and Mustapha Agha Ayat, consular agent in Luxor for Britain, Belgium and Russia! With the permission of Daoud Pasha, *moudir* (governor) of Qéneh, Maspero had Ahmed Abdelrassoul taken into custody and interrogated, but to no avail. When appealed to, the mayor and notables of Qurna testified on oath that Ahmed was the most honest and disinterested man in the land, that he had never "dug" and never would, and that he could never have misappropriated an antique, let alone have desecrated a royal grave. An ironic echo of the Theban high court's exoneration of Pawer and his thieving necropolis workers three milennia earlier! Abdelrassoul was released under surveillance. Shortly afterward denunciations reached the administration: quarrels had sprung up between the Abdelrassoul brothers; the one who had been to jail, feeling that he could no longer rely upon the protection of Agha Ayat, demanded compensation from his partners in crime, insisting upon a half-share in the profits from the treasure instead of the fifth with which he had been content ever since it had been found in 1871. On 25 June 1891, Mohammed, the elder Abdelrassoul brother, turned informer to the *moudir* of Qéneh, Daoud Pasha, and on 6 July, at Deir el Bahri, the Antiquities officials followed him into the last Theban resting place of Egypt's greatest pharaohs. Their trappings had long since disappeared, their elaborate golden sarcophagi plundered and melted down by the robbers of antiquity. Their mummies, re-wrapped by priests of the XXIst Dynasty, lay, beside those of commoners, in plain wooden sarcophagi, sometimes bearing only an indication of their names.

Thus a *fellah* with an eye for treasures gave back to Egypt more than thirty of her greatest ancestors. They could not, however, be left a day longer in their insecure cache, for the men of Qurna, lured by village gossip, came rushing to find the alleged hoards of gold inside the tomb and were even prepared to attack the small team of archaeologists. Forty-eight hours of incessant work was needed to remove the sarcophagi and what was left of the burial furnishings (24) from the mountainside, for everything had to be man-handled to the river; a heavy sarcophagus sometimes took sixteen men and an eight-hour journey. On the evening of 11 July everything had reached Luxor, and three days later, on 14 July, the steamboat *Menshieh* left for Cairo with its royal cargo. It narrowly escaped attack from a village near Karnak, and its progress along the Nile was signalled by the usual mysterious grapevine, so that men and women left their fields and houses to line the banks ululating shrill mourning choruses and putting ashes on their heads as did the mourners of the pharaohs (23). Thus to a chorus of lamentation the great kings reached Cairo during the summer of 1881.

When Victor Loret discovered Amenophis II's grave in the Valley of the Kings in 1898, he also came upon another royal cache where priests of the

XII. *Pharaoh's ecclesiastical throne. Remains of the openwork decoration between the feet refer to the "Union of Two Countries"*

22. *The ancient workmen's village from the Theban necropolis at Deir el Medineh*

23. *Female mourners at the tomb of Woserhet (Thebes west)*

54

24. *The discovery of the first royal cache at Thebes west: preparations for the removal of the mummies*

XXIst Dynasty had concealed thirteen mummies, including those of Amenophis II, Sethos II, and Siptah. But this find had nothing to do with brigands— he had long been seeking the missing tombs among the forty in the royal necropolis visited by the Greek geographer Strabo during his tour of Thebes.

What the ancient thieves left behind them was manna to the latter-day Qurnis. When they "struck it rich," the Theban antique market blossomed with precious objects, often with revelatory inscriptions. They used the ancient burial chapels as common rooms, and in time of danger, such as when the police was after one of them they followed the well shafts through the burial chambers into the network of connecting tombs, for the entire hillside is like an immense anthill where one can travel freely without ever having to emerge above ground.

Sometime in September 1916 it became obvious that an old Qurni, Mohammed Hamad, had suddenly become wealthy, since he decided to take a second wife, a very young girl. His circle of friends increased, and their overheard conversations often centred upon gold coins. Thus the police were alerted to his discovery of treasure. One day at dawn the police and the *mamour* (prefect) arrived on horseback, and Mohammed and his young bride were awakened by the agitation of the villagers; the gold had to be removed from the village unseen at all costs. The pretty girl filled a basket with coins, covered them with flour, and placing it on her head, strolled down the hill, gaily exchanging jests with the guards she met on the way. As she turned the corner at the bottom, however, the final *shaweesh* playfully struck her basket with his baton and the basket fell to the ground, scattering gold pieces everywhere. Police and Qurnis joined in the ensuing scramble, and Mohammed Hamad and his cronies were taken to Luxor, although only the former actually went to jail.

Then the story was pieced together. In July 1916 some Qurnis visiting the "Monkeys' cemetery" in the southern valley had been caught by an exceptionally heavy cloudburst. After the downpour they saw a continuous stream of water flowing from the cliffside, suggesting a crack in the rock. The nimbler among them roped themselves together and descended from the mountainside, to find themselves in a virtually inaccessible, and, so they said, inviolate, tomb. Its contents were immediately sold to receivers, who gradually disposed of them abroad—no less than the burial treasure of three Syrian princesses, all secondary wives (and not concubines) of the great Tuthmosis III.

Some years later Winlock was digging in the district and employed Mohammed Hamad as a labourer. Thus the American Egyptologist was able to study on the spot the remains of the treasure—much of which was acquired by the Metropolitan Museum. The jewels in the tomb were exceptional, among them a bandeau decorated with two gazelle heads and a golden head-dress inlaid with blue and red paste—the monumental wig-cover of one of the princesses. Will there ever be an answer to the question of this triple burial? Did the three princesses die at the same time of some epidemic? Or were they involved in one of the famous conspiracies so often hatched in royal Egyptian harems? At any rate, their tomb was not apparently robbed in ancient times, for the necropolis inspectors had passed and recorded the dates of their visits upon the rock: "Year 22, first month of the season of Akhet, twentieth day [of the reign of Pinedjem, 1047 B.C.]—the royal scribe Butehi came." On the other side of the *wadi* a second rock inscription tells us that the "Scribe of the Place of Truth of the Horizon [the necropolis] Butehamun," came too, accompanied by "the Royal Scribe in the house of Eternity," Tuthmosis (his own father), and followed by Ankhefamun, his son. Perhaps these were the men who helped their king to bury the pharaohs' mummies in their last hiding place. At that time nothing struck them as suspicious, and there was no apparent need to remove the bodies of the three princesses to the communal tomb.

Thus can one evoke kings and brigands. Sometimes the necropolis was well guarded; at others, its workmen and inhabitants regarded the old kings and their treasures as their own rightful heritage. Many attempts were made to evict

56

the *fellaheen* from their lairs in Qurna, even to trying unsuccessfully to smoke them out in 1763. Nothing worked. The Qurnis even received Bonaparte's commission of scholars with volleys of stones. Even thirty years ago some parts of the village were still a sort of *maquis*—a penultimate halting place of outlaws bound for the *gebel* behind Deir el Medineh.

Such, then, was the setting, the atmosphere, in which the Egyptologists camping upon the west bank of Thebes lived and worked. Howard Carter was to stir up perennial stories of brigands and police enquiries in searching through the Valley of the Kings for a lost tomb.

25. A villager of Qurna and his village built on the necropolis of the Theban nobles

(*See page 184*)

Prelude to the discovery

During the winter of 1906 Theodore Davis, who was excavating in the Valley of the Kings, discovered in a cache near Carter's future working site a blue-varnished pitcher with the name of Tutankhamen upon it. The following year he entered a subterranean chamber, more than seven yards below ground, also in the Valley of the Kings and situated to the north of Horemheb's tomb. Torrential floods had filled this room with mud which had since dried up and from it the diggers extracted a broken wooden casket containing several leaves of embossed gold upon which, among others, were the silhouettes of Tutankhamen, his wife Ankhesenamun and the "Divine Father" Ay. Some days later these two discoveries were complemented by finding a number of pieces of pottery in a well-shaft some hundred yards to the south of the tomb; among them was a very elegant long-necked wine bottle, now in the Metropolitan Museum. Some of the pots were still stoppered with lids bearing the seal of the necropolis (Anubis, the dog, watching over nine prisoners) and the name of Tutankhamen, "beloved" of various gods, including Ptah and Khnum. One container was wrapped in a piece of cloth dated year 6 of Tutankhamen. Small bags—the contents of which had turned to dust—were found next to a heap of linen which had probably been used for embalming and wrapping the mummy. Remarkable among these were three semicircular handkerchiefs or wig covers of sorts, and fifty mummification bandages, not cut from a large piece of material, but especially woven with selvedges for the purpose.

Davis and his colleagues were then convinced that they had found all that remained of Tutankhamen's tomb. It seemed to them that it must have been pillaged like so many others such as Horemheb's which Davis was to find the following year, 1908. Shortly after he abandoned the search during which between 1903 and 1909 he had unearthed seven tombs with inscriptions, and nine others without, in the Valley of the Kings. The preface of the book describing his last excavations ends with this phrase: "I fear that the Valley of the Kings is now exhausted."

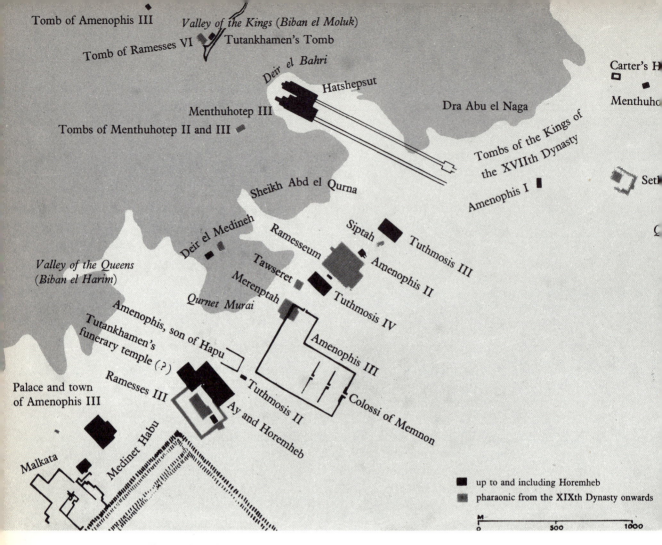

Tomb of Amenophis III   Valley of the Kings (Biban el Moluk)

Tomb of Ramesses VI   Tutankhamen's Tomb

Deir el Bahri   Hatshepsut   Carter's H

Menthuhotep III   Dra Abu el Naga   Menthuho

Tombs of Menthuhotep II and III   Tombs of the Kings of the XVIIth Dynasty

Sheikh Abd el Qurna   Amenophis I   Set

Deir el Medineh   Ramesseum   Siptah   Tuthmosis III

Valley of the Queens (Biban el Harim)   Tawseret   Amenophis II

Merenptah   Tuthmosis IV

Qurnet Murai   Amenophis, son of Hapu   Amenophis III

Tutankhamen's funerary temple (?)   Colossi of Memnon

Palace and town of Amenophis III   Ramesses III   Tuthmosis II

Malkata   Medinet Habu   Ay and Horemheb

■ up to and including Horemheb

■ pharaonic from the XIXth Dynasty onwards

M
0   500   1000

26. The region of the funerary temples and the necropolises to the west of Thebes

Maspero was less convinced; he thought that Tutankhamen's tomb must originally have been in the western branch of the Valley of the Kings, not far from the syrinx of Amenophis III. Sacked by King Horemheb at the time of his first attacks upon the memory of his predecessors, its scattered elements must have been collected by the faithful and buried in the hiding places discovered by the American archaeologist. Indeed, the objects Davis found did resemble the type of equipment used for the special rites of Tutankhamen's burial and for the banquet served in or near his tomb. Everything connected with the corpse and all the utensils and linen used during this banquet had been carefully concealed there. Davis even found three great floral necklaces of cornflowers and blue lotuses interlaced upon a ground of olive leaves and mingled with blue varnished beads, which had been worn by the guests during the funeral meal.

Theodore Davis's investigations seemed to confirm that that area of the Valley of the Kings contained caches or graves dating from the end of the XVIIIth Dynasty and belonging to those who had taken part in the religious revolution at

60

27. The entry to the funeral chamber of Ramesses VI in the Valley of the Kings

Tell el Amarna. In 1907, in that same region, he had also found fragments of a canopy in the name of Queen Tiye, mother of Amenophis IV and wife of Amenophis III—as well as canopic urns, a sarcophagus containing the mummy (as he thought) of the heretical king Amenophis IV-Akhenaten—all assembled without order in a hiding-place rather than a tomb (Tomb No. 55).

4 November 1922 at the entrance to the tomb

All these clues incited Carter to search the area between the tombs of Ramesses IX and Ramesses VI. When he arrived at the site on the morning of 4 November 1922, the whole atmosphere of the dig was totally different from that of the preceding days. He was awaited in an impressive silence, and understood that his workmen had reached the goal of the search. A step carved in the rock below the tomb of Ramesses VI (27), and until then entirely covered by rubble,

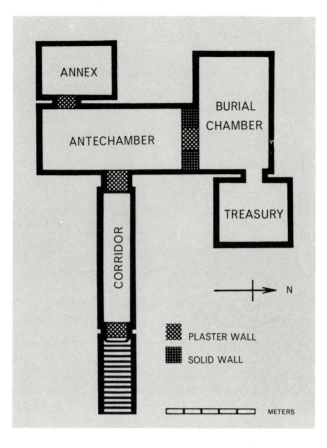

28. *Plan of the tomb and identification of the rooms at the time of the discovery*

had been cleared. After this fifteen more were exposed, forming a stairway 5 ft 3 in. wide by 13 ft 2 in. long leading to a door, a rectangular opening with a heavy timber lintel and entirely blocked up with stones which had been plastered over (3 ft $\frac{1}{2}$ in. thick and 5 ft wide). The side facing the archaeologists bore traces of seals. On the upper part of the wall they were all seals of the royal necropolis: a scroll framing Anubis the dog dominating nine crouching figures with their hands tied behind their backs—the nine imprisoned enemies of Egypt. On the lower part of the wall were other seals containing the coronation name of Tutankhamen: Nebkheprure. It was clear, too, that the tomb had been pillaged, for there were visible traces of two successive openings which had been replastered. The archaeologist's apprehensions were thus confirmed, for when the rubble was being cleared from the stairway, he had noticed that a tunnel large enough for a medium-sized man had been dug and later refilled with stone chips and rubble darker in colour than the surrounding material.

On 25 November the door was completely pulled down; behind it, beyond the sixteenth step, was a passage twenty-five feet long hewn in the rock and also filled with rubble. Here, too, debris of blackish stone indicated clandestine penetration. The passage led to a second door—that of the antechamber of the tomb—of the same type as the first; it also had been opened, reblocked, and resealed.

When this second door was opened on 29 November it revealed the most unimaginable accumulation of extraordinary and unexpected objects, and the diggers at first believed that they had stumbled upon an apparently almost inviolate storehouse of the royal funeral cult. The most hopeless disorder reigned in the chamber. A striking feature of the unique display was the mixture of objects apparently of both daily and religious usage: boxes of preserved food for funeral purposes (pieces of beef, mummified ducks, etc. . . .), bunches of flowers, a golden throne inlaid with coloured glass-paste, great beds in fantastic animal shapes, dismembered gold-plated chariots, an armless dummy of a young man wearing a royal head-dress, and alabaster vases of unfamiliar design.

The antechamber or south room

This first room was some twenty-six feet long by twelve feet wide, with bare whitewashed walls. Looking like a typical storeroom, it resembled the cache where Theodore Davis had found the canopy with Queen Tiye's name and the mummy-shaped sarcophagus in which he thought he recognized the body of Amenophis IV. The tomb itself was oriented on a south–north axis perpendicular to the eastward-opening corridor.

It is not possible here to describe in detail everything that was found in the tomb. Several authors have already done so, especially Carter, who published three volumes, the fruit of ten years' work, on the young king's treasure. Moreover, to provide exhaustive information on each object would require as many monographs as there are items. However, one would wish to convey to the reader some idea of the atmosphere in which twentieth-century men were first privileged to see a royal burial ensemble almost completely as it was left in the dark ages at the end of the XVIIIth Dynasty, in the fourteenth century B.C. We shall return to the main elements of the treasure when we study the king's life and especially the ceremonies surrounding his death.

The floor of the antechamber was strewn with rubble, fragments, pottery shards and vegetable matter from the bouquets and scattered baskets. The thieves who had apparently twice broken into the tomb had displaced a number of pieces, burst open chests and coffers, and removed the precious oils from the vases; stoppers of unbaked clay wrapped in fine linen littered the ground. But nearly everything was still there, and it was an unbelievable sight. Carter's working diary informs us that this first room alone contained one hundred and seventy-one different objects and pieces of furniture, but among these one must include chests and coffers which in turn contained many other items. Far from being a jumbled mass of unconnected objects, as seemed likely from remains found in the rubble in the corridor, the *tessons*,—certain fragments of containers with the names of Amenophis III, Smenkhkare, Tutankhamen, and Amenophis

IV-Akhenaten, and even a scarab of Tuthmosis III—suggested at one point that this might be a storehouse.

Most of the objects in the antechamber were marked with Tutankhamen's name, and many of them had obviously been displaced by the grave-robbers. It is impossible, for instance, to determine the original position of the lotus-shaped alabaster cup (XXIII) with its lateral bouquets crowned with crouching spirits. From the threshold it seemed to greet the diggers, for upon its rim, after the formal titles of Tutankhamen, was the wish:

> "May thy *Ka* live! Mayest thou spend millions of years, O thou who lovest Thebes, seated with thy face turned to the north wind and thine eyes contemplating felicity!"

Nor does one know where the head of the young king mounted on a plastered and painted wooden lotus flower (II) was placed at the time of his burial. On the west side of the antechamber coffers and seats had hastily been pushed back against the wall: stools, a chair with the spirit of eternity upon its fretted back (XIV), and the dazzling gold, silver and glass-paste throne decorated with poetic evocations of Tutankhamen and his wife (X). Various trunks containing clothes and jewellery seemed almost untouched. Opposite these was a pile of four dismantled chariots (29), and reeds, walking sticks, weapons, and decayed baskets together with pottery and alabaster vases.

Nearly all the boxes and coffers were rectangular, some with flat lids, some with a triangular front flap, some domed. A few were made of reeds, but many were of wood or had panels of painted ivory. Sometimes their contents were listed in hieratic script in black ink, like the box which bore an inscription stating that it contained seventeen blue lapis-lazuli objects. In fact, sixteen blue libation vases were found in it—the seventeenth, removed by the robbers, lay in another room of the tomb.

In front of a great statue of blackened wood was a remarkable painted timber chest, the panels of which depicted for the first time masterly battle and hunting scenes, the forerunners of those sculpted upon temple walls during the XIXth and XXth Dynasties (XVI). Its hieratic inscription said: "Sandals of His Majesty. Life, Health, Strength!" and in it were indeed several pairs of pharaoh's sandals. Another was stated to contain "the golden rings of the king's funeral procession"; on yet another were listed the elements of "His Majesty's wardrobe when a child". But the contents had been stolen or mixed with those of other chests. For instance, the beautiful painted box with the hunting and battle scenes said to contain the royal sandals also held among other things a gilt-wood headrest, royal robes and a garment of material decorated with gold sequins, probably imitating pelt-markings as the wooden head attached to it resembled that of a cheetah (31).

Alabaster, ebony, gold, lapis-lazuli, turquoise and ivory were the materials used for most of these funerary objects. There were also fly-whisks trimmed with ostrich feathers, reed dressing cases, jewels scattered on the floor or still

64

29. *Dismantled gilt chariots found in the south-east corner of the antechamber*

30. *Candlesticks under one of the funerary couches in the antechamber*

31. *Sandals, jewellery and ritual clothing in one of the coffers in the Treasury*

within their caskets, calcite vases, torch-holders of wood and bronze shaped like a "sign of life" with arms holding a wick of twisted flax resting in a cup containing oil (30). Sceptres, walking sticks, even trumpets—nothing was missing, not even four examples of the famous unit of length, the cubit (1 ft 7½ in.). Beside the thrones and seats, there were lots of stools decorated with images of Egypt's enemies (folding stools with legs carved into wild-ducks' heads). Further boxes contained rolls of linen and cases in which rings and other jewels were packed, together with the king's clothing, such as riding gloves with which he could grasp his horse's reins more comfortably.

In one long chest was a bronze trumpet with the images of Ptah, Amun and Harakhti, three great gods of Egypt and patrons of three army corps; some walking sticks with granular decoration, and a riding crop belonging to the king who, says the inscription, "appeared upon his horse like Re when he shone". Close by were the famous batons whose curved handles were shaped like the body of a Negro or an Asian, or both together (XVIII). The most disparate objects were assembled in heaps; for instance, a delicate ivory casket containing an aragonite wine strainer and a pectoral, adorning a corselet of pharaoh, showing the king with a black face like that of Osiris at the time of his rebirth. Elsewhere lay very rudimentary gilt wooden sistrums; another dome-lidded chest held linens, scarves, wooden headrests, and a royal robe. And of course there were the magnificent wooden *ushabti*, or royal funeral statues, and the dummy mentioned earlier in this chapter.

Next to the four dismantled chariots were the remains of a fairly light canopy. Its base was a sort of horizontal tray with columns over which a light veil must have been draped. Finally, close to the door communicating with the annex, the open doors of a small naos, or shrine, of gilt wood (1 ft 9¾ in. high) showed that it had been pillaged. What had been taken? At least one solid gold statue, judging from the remaining ebony base and dorsal pillar (4¾ in. high, 2⅛ in. wide) which bore the name of Tutankhamen. Shallow relief decorations on the side panels and doors depict the king and his young wife Ankhesenamun. The dimensions of the naos (10¼ in. wide by 8⅝ in. deep) are such that this little shrine may well have contained not merely one but two solid gold statuettes which were subsequently stolen. It rested upon a wooden sledge covered in silver leaf (VII, VIII, IX).

A third walled door with numerous seals of the necropolis and the royal cartouche took up almost the whole north wall of the antechamber. Two black varnished wooden statues of the king, with batons, sceptres, jewels, loincloths and gilt sandals stood one on either side (LVI). Carefully arranged bunches of olive and persea had been offered to both statues; one bunch had fallen but the other still leaned against the wall. These life-size statues, probably of the king's own height, between 5 ft 6 in. and 5 ft 7 in. are most impressive likenesses, and differ from each other only slightly in the type of headgear and the shape of the loincloth. They were in the name of "the royal *Ka* of Harakhti, the Osiris-Tutankhamen".

32. *The two life-size statues flanking the sealed door which led to the burial chamber*

33. *Oars and ritual objects placed against the north wall of the burial chamber*

34. *The outside of the gilt shrine: the linen veil studded with gilded bronze daisies and the polychrome wall paintings in the burial chamber*

When Carter and Carnarvon held a flickering light through the opening into the antechamber, they saw first the great animal-shaped funeral beds (XXVII, XXIX, XXX), especially the middle one. On it were piled chests and seats, and beneath it were stacked forty-eight white oblong boxes containing animal offerings. Next, on the right, they saw the two great black varnished statues pointing the way to the rest of the tomb. But for the time being the archaeologists proceeded no further. For the next two years, after installing a photographic workshop in Queen Tiye's storehouse and a laboratory in the tomb of Sethos II, they concentrated all their efforts on removing the treasures from the antechamber. To avoid any damage in transit they carefully strengthened each of the objects *in situ* before covering them with paraffin and binding them on to special trays built for the purpose. Then, in the improvised laboratory, they were repaired so that they could be handled safely.

The burial chamber or west room

On 17 February 1923, they at last pulled down the wall, or door, between the antechamber and the burial chamber guarded by the two great statues (32). Traces of plastered-over openings showed that the thieves had passed there, too, but the immense shrine of gilded wood (10 ft 10 in. by 16 ft 5 in. by 9 ft) which the archaeologists found did not seem to have been pillaged. It filled the burial chamber (13 ft 2 in. by 21 ft) almost entirely. The room was oriented on an east-west axis and the level of the floor was below that of the antechamber. In fact, it contained not one gold shrine but four, one within the other, and corresponded to the "golden room" of the royal tombs. The first and outer shrine was of gilt wood inlaid with blue lapis-lazuli glass-paste. Its two doors were no longer held together by the customary seal of stamped clay, complementary to the ebony latches, showing that they had been opened after the original closure of the tomb.

The paintings on the four plastered walls of the room showed the pharaoh ritually "reanimated" by his successor and then surrounded by infernal deities after he had entered his tomb in the form of a mummy sheltered by the catafalque and drawn upon a sledge (34).

There was hardly room—only 2 ft 5½ in.—to pass between the sides of the golden shrine and the walls of the chamber. In these interstices there were also other objects; some, such as the necklaces by the door to the antechamber, were probably where the thieves had dropped them. But in the south-west and north-west corners of the room—at the end of the small western wall—were two emblems of Anubis. In the form of animal skins, wound around a staff stuck into a "mortar", they had clearly been set there ritually. In addition to specifically funerary objects, such as two double boxes, one shaped like a naos

XIII. *Unguent box (?) in the shape of a double cartouche, probably used for ritual purposes*

68

and one like a pylon, blackened with varnish and containing burial equipment, the floor of the northern corridor was littered with eleven wooden steering paddles (33), a bouquet of persea, and wine jars dated year 5 and year 9 of Aten's domain, the western river. In front of the partly opened door of the shrine, facing east, there were also baskets and the statue of Amun's sacred goose, covered in black varnish and wrapped in linen; a silver trumpet with the images of the gods Re, Atum, and Ptah; and finally, two lamps of milky alabaster with an over-elaborate floral design. On the inside of one of these was a painted scene visible on the outside only when the lamp was lit.

Opening the doors of the first shrine all the way, a second shrine was revealed (36); it was covered with a yellowed veil sprinkled with tiny daisies of gilded bronze. A wooden frame kept the veil in place above the second shrine. The doors, fitted with ebony latches, had not been opened since the burial, and the strings tying their bronze rings together were still intact and sealed with clay. Instead of a frieze of *djeds* (the amulet of Osiris) and knots of Isis, which the first shrine bore, this one was decorated in incised relief, and like the remaining two shrines, it featured representations of infernal deities and spirits surrounded by hieroglyphic texts. Outside the first shrine was a magnificent staff embellished with lotus flowers inlaid with gold, silver and glass-paste, and several others were found in front of the second shrine. The two most beautiful, one of silver and one of gold, had pommels portraying the king when very young.

Among the weapons and canes outside the closed doors of the second shrine were two alabaster containers of exceptional shape: the one closest to the shrine displayed a traditional royal scene, "the Union of the Two Lands" (35). Two standing spirits evoking the god Nile and wearing plants on their heads entwined the vase with the emblems of the North and South—the papyrus and the lily— thus linking the two regions of the king's domain. These were also symbolized by two serpents, one wearing the red crown of the North, and the other, the white crown of the South. On the rounded flank of the vase were the names of Tutankhamen and his wife, Ankhesenamum. On the ground nearby was another unguent jar, a sort of cylindrical box covered with hunting scenes. Heads of Africans and Asians formed the four feet, and on the top a peacefully recumbent lion wrinkled its brow and stuck out its red tongue (XLIII). There was also a double box, shaped like a royal cartouche, of gold inlaid with multicoloured glass-paste (XIII).

Within the second shrine was a third, its seals also unbroken. Around it were more weapons, ceremonial bows and arrows, and a fly whisk originally trimmed with ostrich feathers and decorated on both sides with scenes of an ostrich hunt and the triumphant return with the game (XX).

Then came the fourth and last shrine, also of gilded wood. Its shape differed from the two preceding shrines and its cornice and roof were of a single piece.

XIV. *Back of a chair decorated with royal names and with
the spirit of "millions of years"*

35. Unguent jars and canes heaped up between the two outer golden shrines and the linen veil studded with gilded bronze daisies

This fourth shrine contained a magnificent red sandstone sarcophagus inscribed with the names and titles (style) of the king, each corner decorated with a beautiful high-relief of a goddess protectively spreading her winged arms. The lid, found smashed in two, was of rough granite painted to match (38).

Four golden burial shrines, a linen canopy with golden daisies and a quartzite sarcophagus were still not adequate shelter for the mummy of an Egyptian king. The searchers were about to uncover even greater marvels: within the sarcophagus were three mummiform coffins, one within the other (37). The first, wrapped in linen, was in the form of the god of the dead, Osiris. His hands, folded on his breast, held the emblems of royalty inlaid with blue and red glass-paste; the vulture and serpent on the brow were similarly inlaid. The coffin was of gilded wood, the face and hands being of slightly duller gold leaf. The lid had silver handles. Several anomalies came to light as the diggers reached the depths of the tomb: the doors of one of the catafalques had been wrongly hung and the sarcophagus and its lid though for the same king were of different materials. It now became apparent that to allow for the positioning and closing of the lid, the extremities of the feet of the mummiform outer coffin which was wrapped in shrouds and lay immediately within the sarcophagus, must have been planed. The whole had been lavishly anointed with unguents.

36. The excavators opening the doors of one of the gilt shrines

72

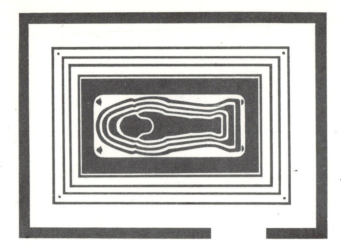

37. *Diagram showing the four golden shrines, the linen veil, the stone sarcophagus and the three mummiform coffins*

Within the first coffin was another, fitting so exactly that a little finger could not be inserted between them. It, too, was of wood covered with gold leaf, but this time inlaid all over with multicoloured glass-paste. A small wreath of flowers had lain on the first coffin; on the breast of the second, however, was a great necklace of olive and willow leaves and blue lotus flowers (39, 40).

The opening of the first coffin on 10 October 1925, marked the beginning of a most exciting period for the archaeologists and their guests. A third mummiform sheath, wrapped in a red linen shroud, was revealed where the priest had left it, with only the face exposed to the darkness of the tomb. A necklace of flowers on a backing of papyrus plants still lay on the breast and the side-pieces of the wig. The coffin, of solid gold, was incised with a religious pattern of touching purity: the interlaced wings of the goddesses Isis and Nephthys, and then, in gold cloisonné and shallow relief upon the king's arms, the great goddesses of Upper and Lower Egypt, Nekhabet, the vulture, and Wadjet, the serpent. This golden coffin combined the ornamental elements of the two others, the first of which was clasped in the feathered arms of Isis and Nephthys, and the second embraced by the outstretched wings of Nekhabet and Wadjet. This last coffin which disposed all four goddesses about the body of the dead king was opened on the morning of 28 October 1925. It revealed the extraordinary gold death mask—a most striking portrait of the king (XXVI)—placed upon a mummy almost burned away by excessive use of unguents.

More than a hundred and forty-three gold jewels were distributed in a hundred and one different spots over the swaddled body.

A very low lion-shaped bed of gilt wood bore the entire weight of the three coffins, including the solid gold one containing the bejewelled mummy. (This adds up to a weight of some 3,030 lb.—the solid gold one alone $\frac{1}{10}$ in. to $\frac{1}{8}$ in. thick, accounting by itself for 2,448$\frac{1}{8}$ lb. of pure gold.)

38. *The sarcophagus and the first gilt wooden coffin*

39. *The second gilt wooden coffin wrapped in its shroud and decorated with garlands of flowers*

40. *The face of the second coffin with garland of natural flowers*

75

41. The four spirits in the niches where they were hidden in the walls of the funeral chamber
    a. The pillar djed   b. Anubis the dog

Following the footsteps of the discoverers, one has the impression of penetrating successive spheres, from the first shrine to the moment when, having removed layer upon layer of bandages, piece after piece of jewellery and amulets, they reached the naked mummy with its golden mask, the final sign laid on the head. In fact we have gone back in time and followed, albeit backwards, the path which will help us, later, to reconstruct the king's death and his funeral ritual and to accompany him to his final resting place. The mummy, in a very bad state of deterioration, was treated—and that is indeed the right word—by Dr Derry, and after its restoration was found to be approximately 5 ft 5½ in. long. From Dr Derry's calculations the king must have been about 5 ft 6 in. tall at the time of his death.

Once the burial chamber had been completely emptied, the shrines taken down and the coffins removed, leaving only the stone sarcophagus, it remained to be confirmed that the traditional protective statuettes had indeed been concealed in the walls. One was *djed*, the pillar (southern niche, facing east); the second, Anubis, the dog (western niche, facing north); the third, a funerary spirit with a human head (northern niche, facing west); and the fourth was a statuette of the god of the dead, Osiris (eastern niche, facing south) (41).

This was the only decorated room in the tomb, and once it was empty, the designs on its walls could be properly observed (34). On a rather dark ochre background, under a black band representing the sky of Egypt, tall human figures painted in bright colours—predominantly yellow, red, white, and black —occupied the full height of three of the walls. The fourth and western wall was divided horizontally into four strips: the bottom three showed baboon spirits of the first hour of the night, in the funerary realm through which the

c. A funerary spirit   *d. A statuette of Osiris*

dead king had to pass. Above these was the funeral procession, showing the sledge upon which the bier containing the mummy rested; it was drawn by high officials of the court and the two viziers.

On the north wall Ay, the king's successor, was shown accomplishing the funeral ritual, after which the king would be enabled to enter the domain of the funerary deities. Accompanied by his *Ka*, or double, he embraced the god Osiris, as if to become one with him.

The southern wall of the burial chamber had not been hewn from the rock, and at the point where it communicated with the antechamber it was made of mud-brick plastered over and painted with pictures of gods, among whom were the goddess of the west and Anubis, with Tutankhamen between them. This wall was partly demolished when the Egyptologists broke down the door, and among the images, that of the goddess Isis is missing.

The so-called Treasury to the north

A low opening in the north-east corner of the burial chamber led into a small room 13 ft 2 in. long by about 11 ft 2 in. wide, and the passage did not seem to have been blocked by masonry at any time. Clearly it had been entered by the thieves, for certain coffers had been partially emptied of their jewels. Its wall and ceiling were bare. Carter dubbed it the Treasury, and, indeed, it contained the most precious objects to have served in the funeral rites. Others believe it to be the "canopic recess", since the most important object found in it was a monumental chest shaped like a sacred pavilion. Under multiple wrappings it sheltered the king's viscera in canopic urns (XXXII, 42).

Only a small clay brick with a magical inscription upon it and a reed torch affixed to it guarded the entrance. From the threshold one could see a great chest of gilded wood, pylon-shaped, with its carrying poles. On it reclined a majestic black-painted statue of Anubis, the dog, wrapped in linen with a fringed border, and showing only the slim-muzzled head; the eyes were inlaid with gold and the ears edged with the same metal. Under the cloth (dated year 7 of the reign of Akhenaten) was a linen scarf, covered with a floral necklace of lotus and cornflowers. Between the silver-clawed forepaws lay a tiny ivory palette which had belonged to one of the daughters of Amenophis IV, Merita-ten, Tutankhamen's sister-in-law. Within the compartments of the chest itself some religious objects and jewels remained: a pectoral, scarabs, amulets, and simulacra. Behind it was a magnificent gold-covered wooden cow's head with lyre-shaped copper horns (XLVIII). This animal, its neck wrapped in linen, evoked the goddess Hathor, known as "Re's Eye". Beyond, three vases supported by stands still contained remains left over from the funeral rites.

Certainly the most important object in the room was the magnificent canopic ensemble, a sort of wooden shrine entirely covered in gold leaf, resting upon a sledge against the western wall of the Treasury. The four corner posts supported a cornice with a pattern of serpents crowned by the solar disc; this

42. Diagram showing the position of the coffers, the canopic urns and the small canopic sarcophagi

XV. *Votive shield showing the king slaying two lions*

On the two following pages: XVI. *The famous painted box which shows Tutankhamen in his chariot*

XVII. *Details of the painted box:*
    a. *Destruction of the black Africans*
    b. *Destruction of the Asians*

78

formed a protective canopy for the central chest, itself topped by a cornice and another frieze of serpents. The whole was covered with hieroglyphic texts and religious images. On the outside of this shrine were the familiar four protecting goddesses—Isis, Nephthys, Neith, and Serket—their faces turned sideways to underline their vigilant attitudes and touchingly concerned expressions, their winged arms spread around the receptacle in a gesture of protection (XXXI).

Sheltered by this gilded shrine was an alabaster chest set upon a sledge; the same guardian goddesses are shown in shallow relief at its four corners in similar attitudes. It had been covered with linen, and its lid was still held in place by sealed ties. Inside were to be seen the tops of four alabaster stoppers, each covering a vase-shaped compartment hollowed out of the solid alabaster, and each portraying Tutankhamen's head wearing the *nemset*, with the sacred vulture and cobra on the brow (XXXIII). When the human-headed stoppers were lifted, there lay beneath, in each compartment, a miniature coffin of cloisonné gold (XXXIV), containing the mummified viscera of the king. Each stopper of the canopic urns was dedicated to a male deity, and the belly of each, to a female one, a combination which had faithfully been observed since the use of canopic urns had begun. Carter noticed, however, that the ritual siting and compass orientation of certain goddesses had not been followed. This great shrine, nearly six feet high, had been deposited against the west wall of the Treasury.

Along the southern wall lay small containers each in the shape of a naos made of blackened wood. All were shut and sealed except one, the open door of which revealed a magnificent and strange glittering gilt wooden statuette of the king placed on a walking cheetah. This group was wrapped in linen like the other statuettes found in the sealed boxes. The other small black naoses contained only statues of the king or of gods; they were made of wood, and either gold-plated or blackened with resin. There were seven statuettes of the king and twenty-nine of gods and spirits, their eyes inlaid with alabaster, obsidian, bronze, and even glass-paste. Most of them were wrapped in linen, like a mummy, and wore round their necks garlands of leaves, including those of the olive tree.

Upon these tall boxes rested a fleet of boats, prows to the west, in every form —from the papyrus cockle used for hunting hippopotamuses to the funeral barge or the vessel which conveyed the dead through the other world with the sun-god (XXV). All these boats had rudders, chapels, or small pavilions. There were two more in the north-eastern corner of the room, and a last one, much larger and more elaborate than the others but also painted in bright colours, had a central cabin and a tall mast from which two yards still hung. Small deck cabins fore and aft completed the vessel, which rested on the model of a primitive granary. Perhaps it was a model of the barge in which Tutankhamen sailed the Nile.

XVIII. *The lower ends of ceremonial canes showing the two*
        adversaries of Egypt: the black African and the Asian

In the south-west corner of the room, beneath several of the black chests, was a long narrow box containing a frame outlining the mummiform silhouette of the god Osiris. It contained alluvial Nile mud sown with corn. The grains had germinated in the darkness of the tomb, and had thus recreated a sprouting and new-born outline of Osiris, symbol of resurrection. Of human size, it had been wrapped in linen like a mummy. In a wooden chest a hand mill for grinding the grain was discovered, and immediately beside this were two strainers on a stuccoed wooden box, with central discs of pierced copper designed to serve as beer filters.

Opposite the gloomy chests (along the south wall) with their black and gold statuettes of the king and the spirits, on the north side of the room and to the left of Anubis on his naos, were six chests of different shapes. They were aligned side by side, but their disordered condition was evidence of thieving, and their lids were no longer closed by ties bearing the seal of the necropolis. The chest nearest to the entrance had a domed lid and was superbly worked in ivory and ebony marquetry, of which Carter counted up to forty-five thousand inlaid pieces.

Among the objects in this chest spared by the robbers was a sumptuous pectoral, on which was a boat with a scarab in its centre, pushing a solar disc. The wide ribbon of worked gold, like a baldric, upon which it hung was decorated with similar scenes; but here the boat was replaced by a basket. The combination of scarab-basket-sun signified the king's "first name" or coronation name: Nebkheprure. All this was of gold, semi-precious stones and marquetry.

The second box, of reddish wood with three horizontal bands of blue hieroglyphs on its panels, was shaped like a royal cartouche, the elongated ring within which were inscribed the royal names (44). On the gold-plated and ebony-bordered lid, inlaid in ivory and ebony, were the hieroglyphs making up the name of Tutankhamen, the birth name by which he was known before his coronation. Everywhere else Nebkheprure, his coronation name, is used, but on this chest at least was the name by which the young king is now known to the whole world.

The contents, in great disorder, were almost exclusively jewels (45). First there was a box containing several pairs of earrings, some of a reddish-gold. Nearly all the other jewels were decorated with scarabs, the essential element of the king's coronation name. Gold, lapis-lazuli (for the scarab), inlays of glass-paste and amethyst were the principal materials, as well as turquoise, cornelian, and red jasper. The bracelets were golden circles widening out into medallions for the scarab or else ribbons of coloured beads and amulets fastened by a large ornamental clasp. Next came a mirror box in the shape of the *ankh*, or sign of life, gold plated and entirely edged with silver; the mirror, probably also of silver, was missing and presumably stolen. Beside this were pendants, including a very handsome pectoral representing an elegant boat bearing the rising sun.

43. Anubis at the entrance to the room called by Carter "the Treasury"

84

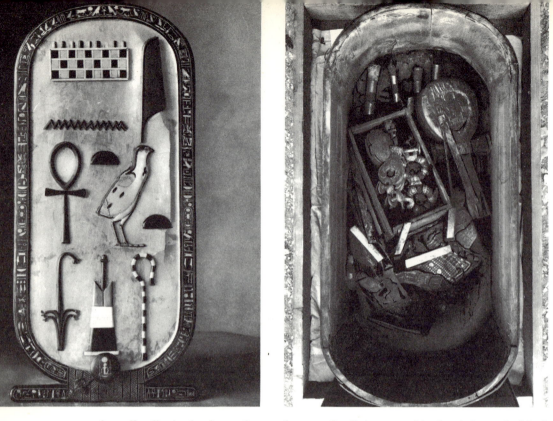

44. *A small coffer in the shape of a royal cartouche. It is unusual in that it bears the king's birth-name, changed after the return to Thebes*

45. *The inside of the same coffer containing precious objects and earrings worn by the king as a child*

Just below were two pairs of "Osirian" sceptres, the crook and flail of gold and dark-blue glass-paste imitating lapis-lazuli, mingled with obsidian; the smaller pair bore the name of Tutankh*aten*, the larger, that of Tutankh*amen*. There was also a sort of ceremonial scarf composed of seven rows of tubular blue glazed terracotta beads grouped between rows of gold ones. At the ends, four "signs of life" hung from a cartouche containing the king's name.

Then came a very rough chest with a white-painted domed lid, which had been almost entirely emptied by the thieves. Only a pair of leather sandals and some anklets of stone were left. Like other similar coffers it must have contained garments, some of which had probably been replaced in other boxes.

The fourth chest, also on four small feet, was square, of cedar and ivory inlaid with black pigments and plated with silver and gold. The fretted decoration, consisting mainly of friezes of magical signs of divine life (the hieroglyphs *ankh* and *ouas* resting on baskets), stood out on a dark background. The sixteen regular compartments within must have held gold and silver flasks for perfumes and cosmetics (46), but other things had been tossed into them: an entirely gold-plated mirror-box, for instance, with a spirit representing eternity crouching on it. The gold mirror it had probably contained was missing, like its silver counterpart from the other box. There was also a small flat box made of reeds with a portrayal of the king surrounded by gods on the lid. It contained a

86

46. *Inside of the large coffer with sixteen compartments*

scribe's complete equipment: a small, very shallow ivory bowl, an ivory palette bearing Tutankhamen's name, two cakes of ink (red and black), and the calamus, or reed pen, and another palette covered with gold leaf. Next to this was a calamus case shaped like a palmiform column (IVb) and an ivory papyrus-smoother in the form of a small mallet; on its handle was the (futuristic) outline of an ionic column (87).

Immediately beside this a fifth chest, white like the third and with a domed lid, bore an inscription in black ink similar to that on the first chest . . . "procession of the funerary chamber". Its contents seemed to reduce thousands of years to a moment: a fan made of thirty ostrich feathers, alternately white and brown, and still almost quivering with life, joined to a semicircular piece of ivory. The curved ivory handle, decorated with sculptured papyrus plants, was completed by a violet glass button on a gold base. And three persea fruits were still also in the box.

The sixth chest was behind this row; its four compartments were quite empty, and the lid bore a hieratic inscription in ink, again alluding to the "procession of the funerary chamber". The thieves had removed this lid and placed it on a nearby cartouche-shaped box. After careful study of the boxes and their contents Carter and his assistants came to the conclusion that about sixty per cent of the jewels and treasures had been stolen. Judging by what remained, the richness of what was used at the funeral procession must have been unbelievable.

Furniture had also been piled up along the north wall of this room, with the boat mentioned earlier at the top (47). In the north-west corner was a long triangular chest designed to hold the king's bow. It was inlaid with marquetry, with areas of gold depicting the king as a sphinx; in the centre was a desert hunting scene, and at each end a finely sculpted cheetah's head. This case still bore the copper ring by which it was attached to the sovereign's chariot. Indeed, against the same wall were the dismounted pieces of two separate light hunting chariots. Among the objects Carter found one which might prove of the greatest importance: though merely a whip, it bore a problematical inscription: "the son of the king, captain of the troops, Dhutmose". Who was this prince?

The last corner of the room remained to be cleared—the north-east corner, its walls half covered by a heap of boxes and chests and ten wooden kiosks painted black: once more strictly funerary material. All these kiosks on small sledges contained burial statuettes called *ushabti*, supposedly images of servants who would perform the tasks demanded of the king in the other world. But these servants bore a marked resemblance to their sovereign: they were not identical, and the head-dresses varied, yet the attitude was the same—that of the king in a mummy-shaped sheath, gazing at eternity and holding the emblems of "Osirian" royalty or tools for tasks he might be called upon to perform.

These statuettes were of the most varied types and materials: some were masterpieces, strikingly lifelike portraits of the king; others, mere varnished terracotta figurines executed in the most rudimentary style. There were altogether one hundred and thirteen *ushabti* with funerary inscriptions. Their tools were also shown, individually marked, and eighteen hundred and sixty-six were found. Some of these were made of iron, a metal very rarely used; of the tomb's treasures only a miniature headrest, *Wedjet*-eye, and dagger—all of them found on the mummy—were made of this material. Six of the most handsome statuettes had been presented by two of the king's high officials; five of them had been dedicated by the commander-in-chief, Nakhtmin, and the sixth, by the superintendent of the treasury, Maya.

Maya had also offered another rather different gift: within a small wooden sarcophagus lay the mummiform image of the king upon a bed with lion's heads and low legs, attended by two birds—one, human-headed, near his heart and the other, a falcon, on his right side (LIV). The inscription which ran the length of the bed stated that the precious model had been made by a servant of His Majesty, superintendent of works in "the place of eternity", royal scribe, superintendent of the treasury, Maya.

Only in this room was anything found alluding to the king's courtiers, and after these came a most unexpected reference to his family: upon the pile of kiosks was a small wooden coffin tied with linen string and secured with the necropolis seal. It was about 2 ft 6 in. long and blackened with resin like the boxes containing the funerary materials; it bore a gift inscription and contained a second small gilded coffin in the image and name of King Tutankhamen. Inside was found a small statuette of Amenophis III in solid gold (III) with a little chain attached. It was wrapped in a piece of linen for mummification and then placed against the legs of a third sarcophagus, much smaller and made of

88

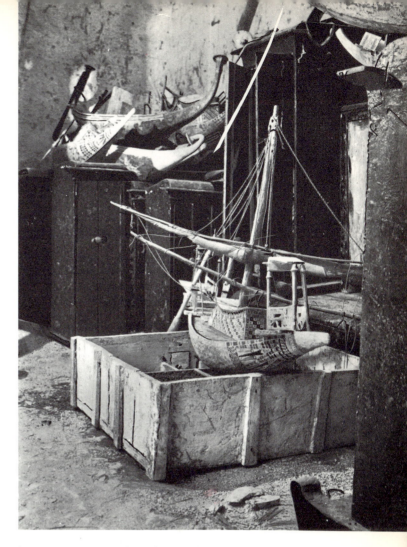

47. *Objects stacked up in the Treasury, consisting of boats, coffers, statuettes and a miniature granary*

plain wood. And within this one there was yet another tiny anthropoid sarcophagus, about 5 in. long. The latter had been heavily anointed with unguents and bore the titles of Queen Tiye; within, carefully wrapped in linen, was a curl of her auburn hair.

An even greater surprise was to be found in another box of blackened wood upon the pile of objects to the north-east of this wall, by the great canopic chest. This box contained two small anthropoid coffins placed side by side, head to foot. The inscriptions on the outside referred to an Osiris with no other name. Each of these coffins contained another smaller one, of gold, and in each of these was the mummy of a foetus preserved like an adult body. Their sizes differed slightly, and analysis showed that one was probably a six- and the other a seven-month foetus. On the smaller was a burial mask far too big for it; the larger had none. The diggers' first assumption was that these were still-born children of Tutankhamen and his wife Ankhesenamun. But were they correct? At any rate, the discovery of the tiny bodies temporarily overshadowed the magnificence and riches of the burial furnishings, which never revealed anything of the king's own life. Now that the still-born corpses had been found, would they add to the meagre information about the sovereigns themselves, or simply increase what was known of the funeral rites? A reconstruction of these may perhaps provide the answer.

The Annex—oriented eastward

We must now return through the burial chamber to the antechamber. As soon as they had cleared this room and removed all the objects heaped against the funerary beds, the diggers had noticed a door in the south-west corner; at some time it had been broken open and was still gaping, exactly below the great bed in the shape of the hippopotamus goddess, Tueris. This door led to a chamber 13 ft 2 in. long by 9 ft 10 in. wide. The diggers called it the annex, and according to Carter this description exactly fitted its purpose.

If the other three rooms had apparently been partly set to rights by the necropolis inspectors after being pillaged, this one was in the wildest disorder. Everything was scattered around or piled up indiscriminately by the grave-robbers, and the inspectors had just left it there; they had not even bothered to brick the door up again. At first it seemed that the objects in this annex, whether stored there originally or subsequently moved there by the thieves, had simply been dumped without any plan or pattern. The diggers concluded that objects intended either for the burial chamber or for the Treasury had carelessly been added to the original contents of the annex. Because of the heterogeneous nature of its contents, of the four rooms in the tomb this one is perhaps the most difficult to analyze.

However, some traces of seals still remained at the top of the blocked door, and they provide a clue. These practically illegible texts were deciphered on the spot by Professor Breasted and Dr (now Sir) Alan Gardiner, although it took these two great philologists a full seven days to make out the characters. The inscriptions were quite different from those on the other doors and they were of four different types. The first read: "The King of Upper and Lower Egypt, Nebkheprure, spent his life making images of the gods so that they daily give him incense, libations and offerings". The second: "Nebkheprure, who made images of Osiris and built his house as at the beginning". The third: "Nebkhe-prure-Anubis triumphing over the nine bows". And the fourth and last: "Their Lord Anubis triumphing over the four captive peoples".

The precarious balance of the tall piles in this annex, which seemed ready to collapse at the merest puff of air, set the diggers a trying task: to consolidate the wobbling heaps so that each piece might be removed separately. The objects had been stacked haphazardly, broken; chests had been opened and

XIX. *Detail from the inside of one of the state chariots*
  a. *The king as a sphinx trampling the enemies of Egypt underfoot*
  b. *The enemies of Egypt vanquished and enslaved*

overturned, and boxes disembowelled; one bow-container showed footprints, probably those of the thieves. There were even greasy fingerprints on certain jars from which the precious oils had been stolen.

Five years after the archaeologists had entered the tomb, on the last day of November 1927, they were ready to start work in the annex.

After examining this conglomeration of apparently unconnected objects, Carter was convinced that no method had informed the selection of the room's contents. He realized however that they fell into two distinct categories: firstly the articles found in the annex but belonging elsewhere and secondly—and these were far fewer in number—the articles originally intended for it. This interpretation was probably too rigid and may not quite correspond with the facts which will emerge when we try to reconstruct the funeral.

On top of the pile was a bed with a wooden frame, short feline legs, and a mattress of plaited straw. In fact, there were four of these beds, each with a single end-board, not at the head but at the foot. Two were of ebony, of which one bed, heavily gold-plated, possessed considerable sculptural beauty; the other, gilded, was a pendant of the first, but less fine; both were decorated with the heraldic plants and the scene of "the Union of the Two Lands". Another was collapsible and lay against the south wall of the room.

In the south-east corner, majestic and oddly out of place in this chaotic ensemble, was an ebony throne inlaid with ivory. The seat was concave and rested on crossed legs shaped like ducks' heads and necks; but the back, which had been added to it, bore stylized geometrical designs and divine symbols, as well as hieroglyphic inscriptions bearing the names of Aten and Amun. The marquetry work on the seat suggested a leopard-skin pattern. Parts of the throne were gold-plated, others inlaid with glass-paste and precious stones (XII). Its rigid severity of line seemed to indicate a liturgical purpose. Not far away was a stool of the same materials, decorated with scenes of Egypt's traditional enemies crushed beneath pharaoh's heel. Beside it, a straw chair, regarded by the diggers as a "garden chair", was against another white-painted one; the space between the legs of the latter was decorated with the two heraldic plants of Egypt. This motif was repeated on a stool on which the decorative plants were gold-plated. But most original of them all was a white-painted three-legged wooden stool with legs shaped like a dog and a fretted design, again of the heraldic plants. Its semi-circular seat consisted entirely of delicate fretwork lions with tied paws confronting each other, and it had a round beaded cushion.

In the annex there were also two precious cabinets of dark-red cedarwood and ebony. Each resting on four tall legs, they were reminiscent of the *barbières* in Europe during the nineteenth century. One of them was framed with bands of inlaid inscriptions (L), but at the base of both was a frieze of amulets; pillars of Osiris and knots of Isis upon the first, *ankh* signs of life alternating with *ouas*

XX. *The king's fly-whisk:*
  a. Front: the king hunting ostriches
  b. Back: his triumphal return with the kill

(divine strength) sceptres on the second. On the first of these cabinets, which Carter found broken, a hieratic inscription stated that it was intended to hold the king's finest linen garments. In fact, it contained four headrests, two of which were wooden, with religious decorations. Forming the base of one, the god of the atmosphere supported the semi-circle for the nape of the neck. Another, shaped like a folding stool, with its crossed legs ending in ducks' heads, had heads of the god Bes carved on its sides. The last two, remarkably restrained in style, had gold-ringed legs; one was of opaque blue, and the other of darker blue, glass-paste (XLIa and b).

In a square wooden box was a sort of mushroom hat-stand for royal headgear, of which only a few scraps of linen, fine gold, lapis-lazuli, cornelian, and feldspar remained. This ancestor of our hatboxes was tucked away among wine jars at the north end of the room.

Then came three ebony boxes with hieratic inscriptions showing them to have been "his majesty's linen chests when he was a young being (anpu)". One of them should also have contained incense, gums, antimony powder, and three golden grasshoppers. All had disappeared. Seven more almost empty boxes were found, one of them of particular interest since it is the first known example of a compendium of games, with compartments, drawers, and a most ingenious automatic closing device. It contained a tiny miniature ivory gaming set called senet, some slings, and a sort of 'lighter' for making fire by rubbing a bow along the regular rounded cavities on a hardwood blade. There were also archers' gloves to protect the left wrist, several sorts of bracelets, one of them of ivory showing hunted animals, including a horse brought to bay by a dog, and other bracelets of china bearing the names of the preceding co-regents: Amenophis IV-Akhenaten and Smenkhkare.

On top of a pile by the western wall was a crude box, broken open, revealing a series of small pale blue glazed terracotta containers (in the antechamber a similar box held the dark lapis-lazuli tableware). Near the door, on a pile of baskets, was another box in which were tapestry gloves and two liturgical linen robes of rectangular shape, like a dalmatic. These garments were partly decorated with wool embroidery and partly with a woven pattern along the sides and hem in a design composed of wild animals being hunted. The woven neck-band was floral and geometrical in pattern and bore the names of Aten and Amun. We may suppose that there was a link between these obviously liturgical garments and the equally liturgical throne in the same room. To this same group of objects must be added a ceremonial sceptre of gold-plated wood (known as the Kherep, or Aba), showing on one side the animal offerings it would consecrate, and on the other, a vertical inscription stating that the face of the king, son of Amun, dazzled "like Aten when he shines".

Among the boxes was another large bow-shaped chest containing, appropriately, bows, arrows (two hundred and seventy-eight of sixteen different varieties were found in the room), and various types of boomerangs. Among the weapons in the annex were also long sticks, curved or harpee swords, and eight shields, only four of which could have been used; two of the latter were covered in cheetah-skin. The votive shields had elaborate fretted gilt-wood decorations, showing the king as a sphinx trampling his enemies underfoot or mastering a lion (xv). Amulets strewed the ground as did models of instruments and *ushabtis*, probably from the Treasury; no doubt several small-scale models of boats were also intended for that room. To the north-west, amidst debris, lay a magnificent silver vase shaped like a pomegranate.

One must also mention the many batons and staffs of various kinds. Some were trimmed with gold or silver, others, with marquetry, and yet others, simply carved out of a magnificent and precious polished wood. All possessed most original handles and ferrules, and every type was represented, including forked sticks for catching reptiles. Fans and flails which had lost their ostrich feathers are reminiscent of those borne in processions around the king; no doubt they, too, were part of the ceremonial ensemble. One of these was engraved with the names of Akhenaten and the god Aten.

Several sets of the thirty-squared game called *senet* were found still complete with their pawns, ivories and sticks (XLIX). They were of three different sizes and made of ebony, ivory—often carved—and gold. There were also a pair of sandals decorated with real marquetry, a leather corselet, and a pair of ivory castanets ending in hands and bearing the name of Queen Tiye. To this incoherent assortment should also be added part of the small portable canopy, the remainder of which had been found in the antechamber.

To end this list of unusual objects, we must first mention a sort of *pièce montée*, or what the discoverers considered as being a centrepiece. Carved in very fine alabaster and decorated with coloured paste and gold leaf, it consisted of a rectangular basin of sorts with floral designs, in the names of Tutankhamen and his wife, Ankhesenamun. In the centre of this basin, probably a flower holder, a small plinth supported a boat with an ibex's head at each end. On a central canopy supported by four floral columns was an object similar to a lidless sarcophagus-tank, decorated with plant motifs. In the prow of the bark a delightful naked young girl clasped a lotus to her breast (XXIV), and in the stern, a female dwarf held a long punt pole.

There now remained a very battered chest abandoned in the north-west corner of the room; its magnificent lid of decorated ivory edged with a frieze of alabaster and glass-paste was found in another corner of the room. The central decoration, delicate and poetic, though somewhat over-elaborate, showed the young couple, Tutankhamen and Ankhesenamun, under a flowered canopy in a dream garden (v). The queen, standing before the childlike king, held out to him two bunches of papyrus and lotus. The inscriptions confirm the identity of the figures. On the side panels were scenes in the same style, but their themes were of hunting, fishing (176) and galloping animals. It was a sort of homely counterpart to the great chest which was found near the tall black statues in the antechamber and which showed the deeds of arms and hunting exploits of a victorious king.

48. Rolls of linen which disappointed the excavators

We must now rapidly review what Carter considered to be the only objects originally intended for the annex—in fact everything containing unguents and solid and liquid provisions. In the room there were still thirty-four vases and alabaster vessels. They were empty, but all had contained oils and unguents, apparently regarded as extremely valuable, and all were without their lids or stoppers. Some of the alabaster vessels had been used before by another owner whose name had been erased. Others bore the names of Tutankhamen's predecessors, even that of Tuthmosis III. Ancient broken vases had been mended. On two vases with the cartouches of Amenophis III the hieroglyphs of Amun's name had been hammered out. One of the vases with a fretted decoration had the outer shape of a *situla* (or libation bowl with a handle). Others, with very long necks, had rings of floral decorations inlaid with coloured paste (XL*a*). The most astonishing was shaped like a lion rampant, its head, with a tall flowered headdress, forming the neck of the vessel. One forepaw was raised and the other rested upon a hieroglyph, a magic sign of protection. Of alabaster with ivory inlays and coloured pigments, it bore the names of Tutankhamen and his wife and rested on a fretted support. Another "bottle" represented a small ibex, recumbent and bleating—or at least showing its tongue (XLIV). One lid, separated from its vessel, consisted of a flat alabaster disc on to which was fixed a cup forming a nest for a tiny, open-beaked fledgling; it was spreading its small wings,

XXI*a. The king's two daggers, one with a blade of gold and the other with a blade of iron*
    b. Below, detail of the hilt of the first dagger

96

and was surrounded by four eggs (XLVIII).

In addition, there were a hundred and sixteen baskets, chiefly containing dried fruits and seeds; there were mandragora, grapes, doom-nuts, melon seeds, and so on. These baskets were all of types still in current use, and one of them, which was bottle-shaped, still held dried raisins. Traces in the antechamber show that the original stores were even more abundant.

Finally, there were three dozen wine jars, large amphorae of almost prim-ordial historical importance, owing to the hieratic inscriptions upon their "shoulders". Most were of pottery and of classical Egyptian design, tall-shouldered, with two small handles and a pointed base. Their unbaked clay stoppers, which were still intact, yielded, in their inscriptions, still more important information about the history of the Amarnan period. For instance, they revealed that the most recent year of Tutankhamen's reign was the year 9. Most of the wines came from the vineyards of the "western river", that is, the delta. Last of all were the wine jars of foreign design, and though the wine in them may have been Egyptian (the clay seals have the same marking as those on the Egyptian jars), their ovoid long-necked shape and single handle was undoubtedly Syrian. Capsules closing the holes in the heavy stoppers provided a "safety-valve" for fermenting gases.

First lesson of the tomb

Such, broadly, was the fabulous accumulation of treasure—for treasure it un-doubtedly was, by virtue of its intrinsic value as well as the sheer quantity of objects and their artistic qualities. Nearly everything was made of precious material, and gold, with its incorruptible surface, covered this whole assortment of articles so necessary to ensure eternity for the dead. Furniture and jewels, garments and vases, household goods and images of spirits—and sometimes, too, the names of the young sovereigns—established all these dumb witnesses in their proper context. But not a single inscription shed light on the history of the dead king. Religious texts on the sides of the funerary canopies were deciphered, customary prayers and the names of certain servants were found on the statuettes. Carter searched everywhere for papyri; for a brief moment he thought he had found in a humble box (numbered 43) in the antechamber the most precious receptacle in the whole tomb. It contained rolls—but they turned out to be only rolls of linen (48). He was forced to admit that the tomb would not easily yield up the king's secrets.

Nevertheless Tutankhamen's "survival", prepared for by burial ceremonies, was heralded by the objects placed in his tomb. Their presence did little more than evoke in general terms the impersonal and purely theoretical existence of a

XXIIa. *Object in red gold openwork showing the king's triumphal return with prisoners*
   b. *Drinking cup found at the entrance of the tomb*

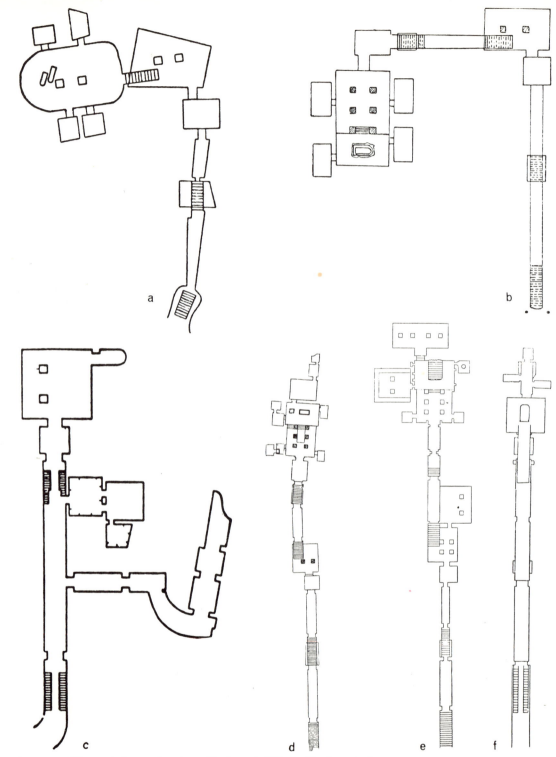

49. Plans of the tombs of: a. Tuthmosis III; b. Tuthmosis IV;
c. Amenophis IV-Akhenaten; d. Horemheb; e. Sethos I and f. Ramesses IV

king. But beyond this they had another significance and seemed to form a coherent whole with the accessories of mystical rites. Everything of a personal nature had been removed, and it was useless to expect the tomb and its contents to add many details to our knowledge of history. But at least it had yielded up for the first time an almost complete funerary ensemble which in spite of theft and depradation could tell us how the priests had used the objects in performing the burial rites. It only remained to discover why.

The observers were struck by the astonishing contrast between the abundance of magnificent pieces in the tomb, the appalling disorder in it, and the meanness and bareness of the rooms themselves. The condition in which the treasure was found suggested that it had been hastily stored in a kind of emergency depository. The chariots had had to be taken apart to get them through the doors and the narrow corridor. The gilt-wood shrines, one within the other, had been reassembled without regard for the orientation of their panels. In order to close the stone sarcophagus, it had been necessary to plane the feet of the first and largest wooden mummiform coffin and wood-shavings had carelessly been left beneath it. The dominant effect was one of casualness, even of negligence.

And yet many beautiful and sumptuous tombs were so near! There was no need even to enter the most famous of all the royal burial chambers of the Valley to find magnificent "eternal homes", since the tombs of the courtiers of the New Empire on the far side of the cliff still bore traces of their first splendour. If ministers were owners of such impressive funeral chapels, what may the tombs of the kings, sons of the gods, have been! Indeed, the most ephemeral of the pharaohs, starting with Ramesses I, were buried in elaborately decorated tombs. But it was not so for Tutankhamen: only one small room bore hurriedly executed funerary decorations.

Nevertheless, careful study of the tomb does not reveal anything in its general pattern which seems incompatible with the traditions of royal burials before the religious revolution at Tell el Amarna, during which the king was born. Throughout the heretical period the course of the sun in its direct trajectory could not be interfered with, and therefore the corridors and rooms of Akhenaten's tomb at Tell el Amarna are laid along a single axis. Before that time, as can clearly be seen in the gallery tombs of Tuthmosis III and Tuthmosis IV, the way to the burial chamber follows a pattern at right angles. This custom was followed in Tutankhamen's tomb, although on a much smaller scale (49).

It therefore seems certain that although haste may have been a determining factor in the burial, the rites had nonetheless been correctly carried out, and the tomb conformed to existing religious requirements. The most one can say is that the tomb, such as it was, had not originally been designed to receive the sovereign himself. But at least it had been prepared for him without any breach of the fundamental laws of royal funerary architecture.

Only some circumstantial evidence of the king's life and death might help to unravel these apparent contradictions. The tomb set the problem; it did not solve it.

4 The cradle of Tutankhaten

THE FAMOUS heretical king Amenophis IV-Akhenaten is one of the most attractive characters in all Egyptian history. His name immediately recalls the religious reforms of a young sovereign, so often called a mystic, who launched a genuine heresy, having possibly been prepared for it by the environment of his earliest youth. In his view, for many reasons, the time had come to react against the powerful god of Thebes, "Amun, the hidden one," whose cult served only to maintain an ambiguity more useful to the priesthood than helpful to the evolution of religious thought in the "most devout of all nations." As far as the people were concerned, Amun saw all without being seen, but his images in stone portrayed a deified pharaoh, wearing the double-plumed, mortar-shaped head-dress and flanked by the goddess Mut and the infant Khonsu.

A compromise had to be found between the remote "Unknown" and the gilded idol: a concept both lofty and simple, but accessible to all. The Solar Globe, Aten—the visible aspect of the hidden deity who manifested himself daily as the sun in the name of Re, and whose nightly avatar was Osiris—provided an appropriate symbol of the sublime power upon which the universe and the whole of life depended (51).

This heretical reform, aimed at expressing a single aspect of religion, had certainly been encouraged by those close to the young prince. At court, where his father Amenophis III reigned jointly with Queen Tiye (50), senior officials, scribes and scholars, anxious to return to the pure sources of theology, had introduced the young man to the subtle ideas of the wise men of Hermopolis.

At that time the royal family was living at Malkata on the left bank of the Nile, south-west of Thebes, in a vast rambling palace of many luxurious apartments whose walls were adorned with elaborate floral and animal friezes. Amenophis IV probably spent the first years of his reign there.

With the first official acts of the young pharaoh begins a strange and fascinating series of events which leaves us uncertain of everything, even of the tangled

50. Colossi representing Tiye and Amenophis III from the royal funerary temple to the west of Thebes (Cairo Museum)

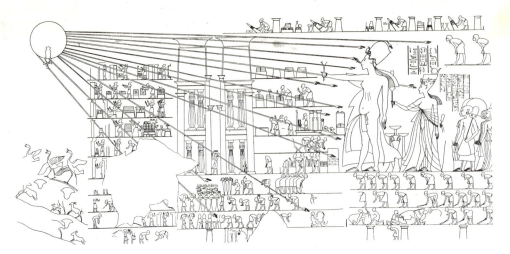

51. Worship of the rising sun in the royal tomb of Tell el Amarna

relationship between the crown and the powerful opposition party in what one might call the drama of Amarna.

There are, for instance, several contradictory and hotly-defended theories about the accession of Amenophis IV. Did he automatically succeed his father at his death or were they initially co-regents? If the latter, then, according to some scholars, the period of co-regency was for only a few years, while others extend it considerably. Lately one tendency has been to consider that it never existed at all.

Similarly, nothing is really known about the beautiful Queen Nefertiti, whose lovely sculptured face is familiar to us from the bust which has survived so many changes (52). We know nothing of her origins and any attempt to reconstruct the pattern of her life can only be conjecture.

On the other hand, the daughters of the royal couple, as they were born, appear regularly on the monuments of the Amarnan royal family. But what of the princes, if princes there were? From the time of Amenophis III, custom decreed that only princesses were to be given prominence; it is very rare to find even a mention of the prince who was to be Amenophis IV, in the XVIIth Dynasty, before his coronation. Were there other princes in the royal family?

Who was the "Divine Father" Ay, husband of Nefertiti's nurse? Were these important people related to the sovereigns?

Of what race were the parents of Queen Tiye, mother of Amenophis IV? Who, in fact, were Smenkhkare and Tutankhamen? Can we even be certain what Tutankhamen's name meant, or of the part he played which is recorded in the archives of the princes of the east, but which many modern scholars have not fully understood?

It is still too soon to attempt a final assessment of this brief but consequential moment of history. We shall, however, try to choose from current hypotheses those which seem to correspond best with the evidence.

52. Bust of Queen Nefertiti (Ehem. Staatliche Museen, Berlin)

Only on this understanding can an attempt be made to sketch the life of the young Tutankhaten (as he was called at birth), an attempt which can in no way be conclusive until the soil of Egypt one day yields up the truth which it still conceals.

Even so, a choice must be made: the first problem to be solved is that of chronology. More than fifteen authors who have studied the period, place the reign of Tutankhamen (his birth-name modified after his return to Thebes) at slightly different dates, although they all agree that it lasted nine years. For some, those years stretch from 1369 to 1360 B.C.; for others, from 1357 to 1350 or 1349. A third school of Egyptologists holds the view (which we believe to be closest to the truth) that Tutankhaten came to the throne in 1352 or 1351, and died about 1344 or 1343. He was succeeded for some four years by the "Divine Father" Ay, whereupon General Horemheb seized the throne.

This however is pure surmise, since there is still no single piece of documentary evidence to establish where Tutankhaten was born, or at whose court he grew up.

The main stumbling-block is the highly controversial question of a possible co-regency period. Although it is uncertain whether Amenophis III and Amenophis IV actually ruled jointly, co-regency of this particular type was not in itself exceptional. It is only the period itself that is exceptional. Egyptian history contains other examples of a king taking his son or his next-of-kin as his co-regent, and there are accepted instances of this in the XVIIIth Dynasty, as in the case of Amenophis IV and Smenkhkare. It is also generally accepted that Sethos I and Ramesses II ruled together at the beginning of the XIXth Dynasty.

Why then in the Amarnan story are we faced with so many limiting factors, not to mention wild surmises? We cannot establish with any certainty this sharing of royal powers, because no text has yet been found referring to a given year in the reign of Amenophis III which corresponds with a given year in the reign of his successor Amenophis IV (who later became Akhenaten) which would establish that the latter had been associated to the throne during the lifetime of his father.

It is less difficult to pinpoint the end of the reign of Amenophis IV-Akhenaten. From the dates on wine-jars in the heretical city of Tell el Amarna, it seems beyond doubt that the year 17 of Amenophis IV-Akhenaten—probably the year of his death—corresponded to the year 1 of Tutankhaten who died apparently, at the age of eighteen, and, that the last year of his reign, also mentioned on wine-jars in his tomb, was the year 9. He must therefore have been born in the eighth year of the co-regent Akhenaten.

If Amenophis III and Amenophis IV-Akhenaten did rule jointly for a time, as there is reason to suppose, the latter must have acceded to the throne between the years 27 and 30 of Amenophis III's reign.

Working from the same premises, Meritaten and Meketaten, Amenophis IV's first two daughters, must have been born before the end of the year 4 of his reign. This was at Amenophis III's court between the years 31 and 33. At the city limits of Amarna (Akhetaten), the capital where Amenophis IV-Akhenaten appears to have settled in the year 5, there was a boundary stele of the year 6, with an additional inscription of the following year, renewing the vows of dedication of the city and to which was added a portrait of the third daughter, Ankhesenpaaten. It was in the year 6 that the Amarnan king changed his name from Amenophis to Akhenaten.

Princess Baketaten, Amenophis III's last daughter, was probably born at Malkata in the year 33. And in the year 8 at Tell el Amarna (Akhetaten) the fourth little Amarnan princess was born: Neferneferuaten Tashery. Probably in

XXIIIa. *An alabaster lamp in the shape of three lotus flowers*
  b. The most precious of all the king's coffers made of ivory to contain gold rings

the same year, or at the end of the preceding one, year 36 of the old king, Tutankhaten was born at Malkata. In the year 9 of Akhenaten, or shortly before, the fifth daughter of the Amarnan couple—Neferneferure—was born. Her name did not contain the vocable *aten* which figures in the names of her four elder sisters and those of her cousins Baketaten and Tutankhaten. And in the year 9 the third jubilee of the "All-Powerful Globe reigning on the horizon at Akhetaten" was celebrated. This is an important milestone in the theology of the heresy, which indicates that the names and epithets of the tangible evidence of the deity had changed. Such jubilees must have fitted with those of the old king, which had been fairly regularly celebrated since the year 30 of his reign (the second was in 34 and the third in 37).

At the end of the year 9 of Akhenaten, the sixth daughter of the Amarnan couple appears to have been born. She was called Setepenre, and is depicted with her five sisters on a painting in the royal palace (the remains of which are at Oxford) before the names of the Globe had assumed their permanent form.

In the year 12 an impressive ceremony, which has been interpreted in several ways, took place. Whichever theory is correct, in order to establish an acceptable chronology, the presence of the six little Amarnan princesses escorting the royal couple to the canopy upon which the processions converged is of prime importance (53).

In the elder pharaoh's capital we have reached the year 39, the last date at which documents mention Amenophis III in his Malkata palace. But he cannot have died that year, because, in the tomb of his granddaughter the princess Meketaten, at Tell el Amarna, the names of the co-regents, Amenophis III and Akhenaten, enclosed in twin cartouches, appear upon the broken fragments of the great stone sarcophagus. If the evidence has been correctly interpreted, the young princess was still alive during the festivities of year 12, which took place in the second month of the second season. Perhaps she died at the end of that year, which would place the death of her grandfather, Amenophis III, some months later, probably between year 39 and year 40 at Malkata.

The year 15 of Akhenaten may correspond to year 1 of the second co-regency of the reign, when he elected to share his throne with the young Smenkhkare. He married his own third daughter Ankhesenpaaten, then about eleven or twelve, in year 16. Towards the end of year 17 the heretic and Smenkhkare died almost simultaneously, and within the same year young Tutankhaten was installed and established "upon the throne of his ancestors."

If, however, the arguments of a minority of Egyptologists, who do not accept the idea of a co-regency between Amenophis III and Amenophis IV, are to be regarded as sound, all the events of the Amarnan story and the first four years of

XXIV. *Detail of the prow of the alabaster boat : head of a Syrian ibex and a figure, thought to be that of princess Mutnedjmet*

53. *The royal couple with the six Amarnan princesses at the "Parade of foreign tribute" at Tell el Amarna*

Amenophis IV's reign at Malkata must be brought forward in time. To begin with, his coronation would then have taken place at the time of Amenophis III's death, between 39 and 40. In that case, the young Tutankhaten who in years 40–41 could have been at most five or six years old, would have been about twenty-two when, seventeen years later, he inherited the throne from Akhenaten. As he reigned for at least the acknowledged nine years, he would then have been over thirty at his death, but an analysis of his corpse, meticulously carried out by expert practitioners, showed that he cannot have been older than nineteen or twenty when he died.

There is far more evidence to support the co-regency theory than there is for the theory of a normal succession of reigns. Even so, there are still problems to be solved. One was recently stressed by Sir Alan Gardiner, concerning a letter in the famous correspondence in the Egyptian archives at Tell el Amarna, the heretical capital, consisting of baked clay tablets covered in cuneiform signs in a form of Akkadian, the diplomatic language of the whole Near East at that time. This letter, No. 27 of the Knudtzon edition, was from King Tushratta of Mitanni to Naphuria, king of Egypt (55). This most interesting missive mentions princess Tadukhipa, daughter of King Tushratta, who was sent to the harem of Amenophis III and then, after his death, to that of his son Neferkheprure-Amenophis IV, or so we believe today, assuming that Naphuria was indeed the Akkadian version of Neferkheprure (the coronation name of Amenophis IV). Until now it was thought that the hieratic superscription written on the side of the tablet when it was filed in the pharaonic archives at Malkata was dated year 12. However, the first figure of that date was reconstructed from a gap caused by a deterioration of the script, and should not be restored if there is any doubt about it. The letter therefore, may have reached Amenophis IV

110

54. *The mysterious coffin of cache No. 55 from the Valley of the Kings*

in his father's capital in the year 2, shortly after the latter's funeral, to which there seems to be an allusion in the text. It is impossible at present to settle, without further examination of the tablet itself in Berlin where it is preserved, which date (2 or 12) is correct. For the moment the problem must be left unresolved although a recent photograph seems to suggest that the old theory may after all be the right one.

Another possible objection might be raised: in spite of recent work by eminent philologists on the Akkadian and Egyptian languages, can we be quite certain that Napkhuria (or Nabhuria) and Nibphuria (or Biphuria) are the Akkadian versions of *Nefer*kheprure (Amenophis IV's coronation name) and *Neb*kheprure (Tutankhaten's)? Was there never any confusion between the two, and if so, might not the letter, if it really was received in the year 2, have been addressed to the new sovereign Tutankhaten whom foreign kings, systematically ignoring the heretic, then recognized as *sole* heir to Amenophis III?

55. *Letter No. 27 from the cuneiform correspondence found at Tell el Amarna showing the hieratic inscription dating from the year 12 (?) (Staatliche Museen, Berlin)*

(After he seized the throne Horemheb adopted the same attitude towards all the Amarnan sovereigns.) This hypothesis, however, rests on slender evidence.

From this brief outline of the more doubtful points of Amarnan chronology, let us turn to the little we know of the life of the child-king and attempt to reconstruct from the information available the background of his early years. For this purpose the co-regency theory seems least likely to mislead us.

More than at any other period, however, the leading figures and events of the late XVIIIth Dynasty stand out as separate elements with few precise connecting links. Extreme discretion veils their personal history; genealogies even of the royal family are seldom provided, and the texts are so mute concerning their intentions, identities and environment, that they seem almost like actors.

In the confusion of the period the salient feature was the revolutionary reappraisal of theological dogma whose repercussions affected the whole political situation and led to upheavals and violent reactions. Even the tombs in the necropolises were not spared: the dead were deprived of their final identity by the effacing of their names.

Thus, it has not yet been possible definitely to identify the mummy in Queen Tiye's so-called tomb (54) which would solve the riddle of Tutankhamen's family tree and that of the sovereigns who preceded him: Amenophis IV-Akhenaten, and Smenkhkare. When it was found, it was thought to be the mummy of Akhenaten, but it is now certain that the coffin, in any case, was originally made for a woman. Later it was believed to be the body of Smenkhkare; specialists who compared it with the mummy of Tutankhamen were struck by the marked similarity of the platycephalic skulls, and had no hesitation in declaring that they were those of two brothers, of nearly the same age. Smenkhkare would appear to have died at the age of about twenty-five or six.

The latest theories on the identity of the mummy, whose frontal *uraeus* bears the name of Aten, now seem to agree with the earliest. If we accept them, they would place the death of the heretic king in or about his twenty-sixth year. But, as early as the year I of his reign (as co-regent, or sole monarch if we reject the idea of joint rule) Amenophis IV had launched his religious reform; this suggests that if he was ten years old when he ordered a temple to be built and dedicated to the Solar Globe, Aten, which symbolized the very essence of the new dogma, he was either a phenomenal genius, an even more enlightened mystic than was believed, or alternatively a child deliberately brought into the foreground by a royal parent wishing his heir to reap the fruits of his own daring experiment.

In any case, it is now known for certain that his father Amenophis III greatly revered the solar gods, in particular the manifestation of the Globe (the eye of the sun) still today incorrectly called the Disc. This king's attitude was at once a reaction against the obscurantism of the priests of Amun and their paralyzing

XXVa. *A model of one of pharaoh's boats*
 b. *The bezel of a ring showing Tutankhamen's*
  veneration of the sun-god

authority, and the logical outcome of his predecessors' tentative rebellion: on a scarab of Tuthmosis IV, the old name of Aten had been restored to favour. Two of Amenophis III's architects, Suti and Hor, carved a poem for the Luxor temple which constitutes the most dazzling preface to Akhenaten's famous *Hymn to the Sun*. There is still further evidence of the king's attitude: in Nubia (Kawa) he founded a temple called Gem-Aten. His barge, too, was called *Splendour of Aten*, as was one of his regiments.

Towards year 11 of his reign, he moved away from an area where Amun's priests and followers exerted too great an influence. On some eighty-two acres on the left bank of the river (to the south of his great funerary temple, guarded by the colossi of Memnon) he built his new capital in a district which, according to certain authors, may have been the famous Djarukha ("the Search for Evening" or "The Gust of Evening"). This vast domain consisted of three principal estates: to the north that of his eldest daughter Sitamun, whom he married and made queen. In the centre was the residence with the great colonnaded courtyard which was occupied by Amenophis IV during the first four years of his co-regency with his father. There were of course numerous smaller houses and annexes for other lesser members of the family, and three large villas in a separate compound were most likely owned by Ramose—the vizier whose famous tomb fills visitors to the Theban necropolis with admiration —the royal chancellor, and the great intendant. Here, too, were the workers' village and the homes of minor officials, built, as usual, of unbaked brick, with white-plastered inner walls and painted murals. Amenophis III's own immense residence was situated to the south of this complex, beside a smaller building probably used by the "Great Royal Spouse", Queen Tiye. The king's palace was called: "The house of Nebmaetre (the king's coronation name) is Aten's Splendour", the name which was also given to his palace at Tell el Amarna. In the thirtieth year of his reign—that is at the time of his first jubilee—he renamed his palace "the House of Jubilation" a term also applied to a temple of Aten at Tell el Amarna. Today this royal compound is called Malkata, which in Arabic means "the place where things have been gathered"—an allusion to the vestiges of pharaonic times found there long before official excavating began.

Magnificent gardens naturally adorned the new city, which was connected to the Nile by a canal which broadened into a T-shape on reaching the township. This part of the canal has long been regarded as the remains of the famous Lake of Tiye, the Great Royal Spouse, to whom the king showed such marked signs of respect and love. A famous text, preserved upon several historic scarabs, mentions the foundation of an immense pool or pond, 3,700 cubits long by 700 cubits wide (148 acres) which was built for the king in fifteen days during the period when the river overflowed its banks "between the first and the sixteenth day of the third month of innundation". On the day of the "Feast of

XXVI. *Tutankhamen's funeral mask in solid gold inlaid with semi-precious stones and glass-paste*

56. *The mummy of Yuya, Tiye's father*
(*Cairo Museum*)

57. *The mummy of Thuya, Tiye's mother*
(*Cairo Museum*)

the Opening of the Pools", the sixteenth day of the third month of the floods, the tall dykes holding back the river were finished, and the king sailed on his magnificent golden barge, *Splendour of Aten*, to the ceremony, during which the irrigation basins were connected by piercing their dividing dykes. When the floods subsided leaving this immense artificial lake empty the peasants were able to cultivate it. In the year 11, a year after the arrival of the Mitannian princess in Pharaoh's harem, the Great Royal Spouse Tiye received a new token of affection: a vast estate at Djarukha which would bring her a new income and was to be administered by her own officials. The site had been well chosen, not west of Thebes as has been thought up to now, but close to Akhmim, in the district of Panoplite. It may have been the birthplace of her family.

Tiye was not a princess of the blood: her father Yuya and her mother Thuya were high ecclesiastical dignitaries in Amun's service, and also held provincial administrative appointments, probably in their own native districts. Yuya was also "Prophet of Min" and "In charge of the Oxen of Min" at Akhmim (56). Thuya was the "Superior of the Harem of Min" (57). Both had risen to the highest ranks at Pharaoh's court, and indeed Yuya bore the title of "Divine Father", which some take to mean "Pharaoh's father-in-law". He was also "Lieutenant-General of the King's Chariots" and was bound by many other privileges and duties to the king and to the domain of Theban Amun. In Thebes, Thuya enjoyed the important position of "Superior of Amun's Harem".

Queen Tiye, daughter of these two provincial nobles of Nubian origin, as seems fairly clear from their mummies discovered in the Valley of the Kings became the first lady of the empire, since Pharaoh had made her queen, thus

58. *King Amenophis III, attended by his mother Mutemweya, enthroned beneath the triple canopy of his palace*

breaking with a religious tradition, which invariably required the king to take as a great royal spouse and prospective mother of a royal heir, a daughter of Pharaoh. Amenophis III set out to inform his subjects and those beyond his frontiers of his decision to marry a commoner: on his wedding-day, in the year I of his reign, he issued a series of commemorative scarabs with the queen's name and details of her humble origins for all to know, from Naharin in the north to Karoy, in the heart of the Sudan, near Napata. It was tantamount to a declaration that all children born of the union could never be considered as bastards— manifestly flouting the priests of Amun. They would no longer be able to proclaim upon their temple walls that their god had replaced the sovereign on his wedding-day and impregnated an unquestionably royal daughter, herself descended from the god. For that is how Amun is depicted in the "Theogamy" scene on the walls of the funerary temple of Deir el Bahri, showing that Queen Hatshepsut, daughter of Ahmose, the pharaoh's daughter, had truly been begotten by Amun, the king of the gods. At Luxor, Amenophis III himself had had recorded the circumstances of his divine conception, showing his mother, Queen Mutemweya, who cannot, as has been suggested, have been of foreign stock, engaged in ecstatic amorous dialogue with a representation of Amun.

The king's marriage with a commoner's daughter amounted to a provocative attack upon the prestige of the Theban priesthood. It seems likely that during the first years of his reign, the king set out to compromise by appearing, despite his marriage, with the queen mother (58), a princess of the blood, at official ceremonies. But soon Tiye, Tiye *alone*, and always Tiye occupied the place of honour at all the feasts he attended, on all occasions, in every town he visited.

The only exception—and no doubt this was a logical consequence of their marriage—was made for the couple's eldest daughter, the princess Sitamun, whom he married and officially recognized as his wife, as if to give her a more ample share of her divine ancestry. Nevertheless this did not prevent the girl from honouring and respecting her devoted parents, the royal couple. It seems that the court tried to alter the very essence of royal genealogy and stress the importance of maternal descent: the daughters were raised above the sons and are portrayed accompanying the sovereigns on the plinths of the monumental statues in the great temples or on the walls of the sepulchres of the high dignitaries of the empire. Princes are never portrayed; yet princes there surely were, for we know that the future Amenophis IV must have been present at the Malkata court.

When the king was planning his tomb, he included two extra chambers in its depths—one for Tiye and the other for Sitamun, his eldest daughter. Amenophis IV-Akhenaten followed his example when he declared officially when he created his new city, that he would be buried there with his wife Nefertiti and his eldest daughter Meritaten.

Memorials of Sitamun were discovered in the tomb of her grandparents, Thuya and Yuya, where her portrait appears on two chairbacks. Facing Queen Tiye, she is shown offering her homage (59); or seated majestically, receiving a golden necklace. On her tall wig she wears a crown of lotuses, the prerogative of royal favourites and princesses married to their fathers. Her name was inscribed in a cartouche: a kohl-tube (now in the Metropolitan Museum) bearing the twin cartouches of Amenophis III and Sitamun provides further—and conclusive—evidence of their marriage. Finally, and most important, on the

59. *Back of one of Sitamun's chairs. The princess (the "royal favourite") is paying homage to her mother Queen Tiye*

left bank of Thebes the royal capital abounded in palaces of various princesses; many of them are still unknown to us, but none was as important as Sitamun's.

As administrator of her estates the king appointed probably the most powerful person in the country at that time: Amenophis, son of Hapu. His position in the palace hierarchy was so exalted that on his death the sovereign bestowed upon him the rare favour of building his own sanctuary near the royal funerary temples—a supreme honour to which no commoner had a right. Amenophis was born at Athribis, in the delta, probably during the reign of Tuthmosis III, and thanks to his great wisdom and sagacity, reached the advanced age—reputed to be that of the just—of 110. After his death he became an almost divine figure and his memory was revered for many centuries.

He began his career under Amenophis III as a royal scribe, and was soon in charge of the ceremonies on many official and religious occasions, as well as of military recruiting; but the position he really wanted and swiftly obtained was that of royal chief of works. It was he who at Gebel el Ahmar directed the quarrying of the magnificent sandstone, the "miracle stone", and he had huge blocks of it transported from the end of the delta to the region round Thebes. This compact red sandstone was under the protection of the god Atum and became the favourite stone of the sun-worshipping sovereigns. It is not surprising, therefore, that we find later in Tell el Amarna, the city of the Globe, the remains of an obelisk, not of granite but of sandstone. Amenophis's works can be seen all over Egypt, from Athribis to far-off Nubia, in Karnak too, and statues of himself were given a place in the temple of Amun.

Amenophis III appointed him master of ceremonies of the feast of Amun, thus conferring upon him increased importance in a field where the High Priest did not welcome a rival. Amenophis, son of Hapu, was also made a hereditary prince, with the surname of Huy, erecting within the very temple of Amun miraculous statues of himself to intercede with the god for the devout. At the base of a colossus in front of the tenth pylon of Karnak, two of his statues, showing him as a scribe, bore convincing inscriptions which showed the lengths to which the palace would go to check the power and ambitions of Amun's priesthood.

On the first statue the inscription runs:

"You, people of the South and the North, whose eyes who can see the Sun, you who have come to Thebes to pray to the lord of the Gods, all of you, come to me! I carry what you say to Amun of Karnak at the moment when you pronounce your speech of offering and pour the water [the libation]. For I am the herald, named by the king to hear your prayers and raise [to the gods] the affairs of the Two Countries."

On the other statue Amenophis says:

"You, people of Karnak, you who wish to see Amun, come to me, for I am the herald of that god. Nebmaetre [Amenophis III] named me, that I might bring [to the god] the words of the Two Countries when you pronounce the words of offering and if you invoke my name daily as is done for one of the praised."

"Herald of the God" was a title which Amenophis III had conferred upon other military personages, none of whom, however rose to the heights reached

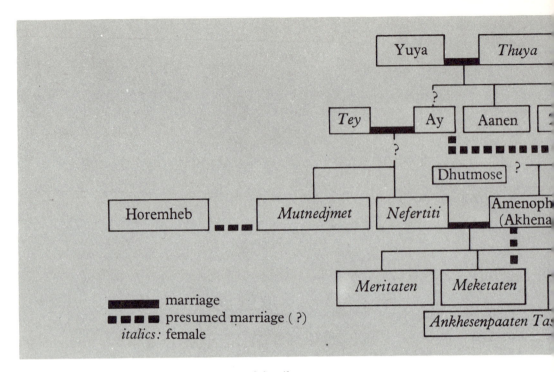

60. Genealogical tree of the Amarnan royal family

by the *éminence grise*, Amenophis, son of Hapu. He did of course belong to the officer caste, and at a time when the empire was in decline, owing to the negligence of the Theban monarchy, soldiers were more favoured than ever before. One of them, a young "Scribe of the royal recruits", may have been serving in Syria and Palestine and we shall meet him again. Preferring Memphis to Thebes, he was to become General Horemheb and to seize the throne of Egypt. At the beginning of the Amarnan heresy he must have been about twenty.

Amenophis had the freedom of the palace and knew all the "Secrets of the *Kap*". What exactly was the *Kap*? We know very little about it, but we can at least be certain that it was a military organization, probably set up within the palace precincts, at any rate during the New Empire, to educate the sons of Nubian princes brought to the metropolis after the pharaoh's punitive expeditions in the lands of Wawat and perhaps Kush, areas which correspond with modern Egyptian and Sudanese Nubia. Although under strict discipline, these "sons of rebels" were treated with great consideration, sharing the education of the pharaoh's own sons, and later, imbued with the most harmonious culture of high antiquity, allowed to place their experience at the disposal of their native country. Most of them became assistants to the viceroy of Nubia, but others chose careers in the pharaonic armies, and as childhood companions of the royal princes often remained attached to their persons at court. Many of them, indeed, spent their entire lives in the palace and tutored the children of the king whose academic and military education they had shared. Throughout their lives,

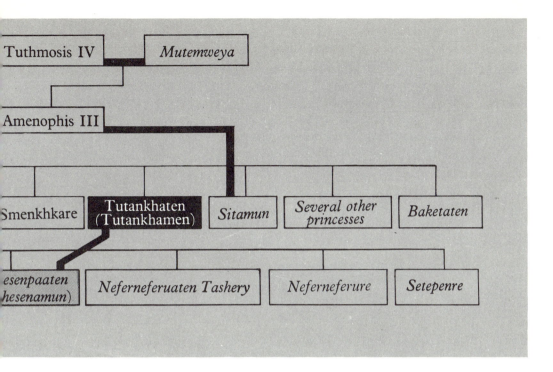

```
Tuthmosis IV —— Mutemweya

Amenophis III

Smenkhkare   Tutankhaten    Sitamun   Several other   Baketaten
             (Tutankhamen)             princesses

esenpaaten   Neferneferuaten Tashery   Neferneferure   Setepenre
hesenamun)
```

however, they retained the title "Child of the *Kap*". These chosen officials were invaluable to the rulers of the XVIIIth Dynasty, although they never abandoned their ties with their mother-country nor with one another.

At the time of the great reforms in dogma, the Nubians played a part about which too little has been said. They enjoyed exceptional privileges at the court of Malkata. It was ruled by a queen almost certainly of their own race, as some portraits of Tiye, such as the little ebony head now in the Berlin Museum (72), show her to have been. Her southern looks are even more pronounced in the portrait on a pendant (the *Menat* counter-poise) which was found during the excavations of her palace at Malkata, and another similar portrait found at Tell el Amarna. Finally there is little room left for doubt when one studies the small sardonyx tablet, now in the Metropolitan Museum, which depicts the queen as a female sphinx. The face clearly betrays her origins; it was recently compared with another image of her still to be seen at Sedeinga in Northern Sudan in the ruins of the temple, dedicated to Tiye. Even the wigs of the royal ladies at Malkata as well as at Tell el Amarna were inspired by the short neat coiffures of the Nubians.

Nubian influence at the palace was offset by the marriages the king contracted with several oriental princesses whose suites accompanied them to Egypt; for example, in year 10 of his reign, Amenophis III issued a historic scarab announcing the arrival of Gilukhipa, daughter of Shuttarna, king of Naharin, escorted by three hundred and seventeen women of her harem. But she was a secondary

62. *The "Divine Father" Ay and the "Nurse" Tey receiving their rewards in Akhetaten (Cairo Museum)*

61. *Statue of Amenophis III executed in the Amarnan style (Metropolitan Museum of Art, New York)*

wife, as were most of the foreign princesses sent to the pharaoh's court as tangible evidence of his alliances (one recalls the three Syrian princesses who were secondary wives of Tuthmosis III). They must have led obscure and rather dull lives in the shadow of the formidable Tiye. Little interest was apparently taken in them, and foreign sovereigns who sent ambassadors to Egypt for news of their daughters or sisters often had to wait some time for an answer, as the wives of foreign origin lived in the utmost seclusion: Kadashman Enlil, brother of a Babylonian princess at the court of Amenophis III, sent a number of emissaries before he could obtain any information at all.

In short, at Pharaoh's court there were royal children with the warm blood of Nubia in their veins, but also princes and princesses in the palace harems whose physical type was that of the light-skinned northern races.

In the year 30 of his reign Amenophis III prepared to celebrate his first jubilee with his favourite, Tiye, and his other wives and princesses. Confident in the strength of his armies, he had gradually lost interest in his foreign empire. As the most pampered and indulged of monarchs, living in the greatest refinement of luxury ever known in Egypt, he enjoyed a life which his viziers and ministers assiduously kept free from care. At the time of the jubilee he was probably already showing signs of the loss of vigour which rapidly overtook him during the following years.

Despite the care taken at court to portray only the princesses (64), there are still sufficient traces of the presence at court of the crown prince (the future Amenophis IV) and several of his brothers. Among these was probably the king's eldest son who died prematurely, and who is mentioned on a monument found near the Serapeum of Memphis—Dhutmose, the young captain whose whip with his name on it was found in Tutankhamen's burial treasure.

Although the contemporary inscriptions are practically silent on the subject, it seems that about year 30 the crown prince, soon to share his father's throne,

63. The god Nile in the form of the king Ay
(Museum of Fine Arts, Boston)

was Amenophis, already married to a young woman of great and subtle beauty called Nefertiti. To this day no one can say exactly who she was. For a long time she was thought to be identical with Tadukhipa, the daughter of King Tushratta of Mitanni whose letters from Tell el Amarna inform us of her presence there. But it is known that Tadukhipa reached Malkata in year 36 of Amenophis III's reign, and at that time Nefertiti had already borne her husband Amenophis IV-Akhenaten his first four or perhaps five daughters. Some authors suggest that she might have been the daughter of Tiye and Amenophis III, or of Amenophis III and a secondary wife, but there is no evidence to support this. As usual, when dealing with the heretical period, we are thrown back upon conjecture. Her only relative of whom we know anything was her sister Mutnedjmet, whose portrait is in the tombs of five of Akhenaten's courtiers at Tell el Amarna. As Mutnedjmet does not bear the title of princess, Nefertiti cannot have been of royal birth. Was she even Egyptian? There is no evidence to the contrary, and her beauty was of the noble Theban type seen in the necropolis paintings; but the coloured bust now in Berlin shows the rosy tint of her complexion, which suggests that she was careful to avoid sunlight or, alternatively, that she was of northern stock.

The other apparent link between her and Egypt is provided by her "Nurse", Tey, wife of the "Divine Father" Ay. But who were Tey and Ay? They appeared at Tell el Amarna, and are shown in their joint tomb as fervent supporters of the Amarnan reform, and extremely close to the heretical king (62). What was their background? Here there is a curious coincidence to be noted: on comparing the names and titles of Ay (or Aya) with those of Yuya, the father of Queen Tiye, one finds an almost perfect parallel between them. Some have even suggested that they were one and the same man. He would, however, have had to live to a great age for one of his daughters to be old enough to marry Amenophis III; to have survived the reigns of Amenophis III, Amenophis IV-

64. Eight royal princesses making libations to Amenophis III and Tiye. Theban tomb of Kheruef

Akhenaten (including the period of co-regency with Smenkhkare) and Tutankhamen and subsequently to have ruled himself for a short time. Yet there is a striking resemblance between Yuya's mummy, which was found in the Valley of the Kings, and a splendid portrait of Ay as king depicted as the Nile-God, at the base of a statue now in the Boston Museum (63). Indeed, in a recent attempt to find the link between the two, it has been suggested that they might have been father and son, which would account for similarity of names, titles, physical features and family connections with the town of Akhmim, where Ay had a chapel dug for the god Min, and where later Tutankhamen, his *protégé*, and he himself after his coronation, were to worship that god and make it fashionable to include his vocable in the composition of given names.

Ay was definitely Akhenaten's man, his most faithful supporter in the city of the Globe, Commander of the King's Horse, and Lieutenant-General of his Chariots, Personal Scribe to the King (the great *Hymn to Aten* was engraved in his tomb), the Royal Fan-Bearer, and above all *it-neter*, "Divine Father" or "Father of the God". Was he perhaps Pharaoh's father-in-law?

It has been suggested recently that he may have been the widowed father of Nefertiti, remarried to Tey, who would then have been the nurse, or at least the stepmother of the future queen. But Ay is never described as "father" of the queen; the theory is scholarly and attractive, but not proven.

Immediately before the jubilee (or feast of *Sed*) of Amenophis III, the crown prince's courtiers organized festivities during which Amenophis IV was to be appointed co-regent. It was at that time too that to confirm his theological stand-

point the prince planned the dedication of a new temple to the Rising Sun—
Re Harakhti—to the east of the actual Karnak sanctuary, with the intention of
becoming its high priest. He defined the new aspect of the divinity as he saw it
and wished it to be seen at Karnak: "*Re Harakhti-who-rejoices-on-the-horizon-
in-his-name-of-Solar-light (Shu) which-appears-in-the-Solar-Globe (Aten).*"

Thus the jubilee of Amenophis III corresponded to the jubilee of the god,
who, like the king, after a long span of life, was to be reborn on the horizon at the
conclusion of the *Sed* mysteries. During the ceremonies, Amenophis III was to
go through a simulacrum of death, reminiscent of the barbaric ritual murders
of the chieftains of prehistoric Egypt, on the approach of senility. He would
wear the shroud of Osiris, the god whose murder was followed by the birth of
his son Horus, guarantor of eternal existence in all things. He would then be
seen to reappear, like Horus, the rising sun, to begin a new cycle. At his side, his
son, Amenophis IV, now his co-regent, would symbolize his rejuvenated powers,
and later would officially undertake the work of theological reform in an attempt
to define anew the true nature of the god.

This essential phase of divine pharaonic life was symbolized by certain
changes within the sanctuary and the erection of new monuments. On this
occasion, Amenophis III decided to build or enlarge a temple to Amun at
Soleb, in Sudanese Nubia. In elegance it rivals that of Luxor. The work was
planned and supervised by Amenophis who gave the sanctuary its harmonious
floral columns, installed the temple priests, and organized the ceremonies of
Sed. Other high officials, including Ramose, vizier of the south, travelled to
Nubia for the festivities. In honour of the jubilee Amenophis had delivered to
Thebes two monolithic statues forty cubits high, quarried from the Red

65. *Rupestral drawing from Aswan depicting the two sculptors Men and Bak, heads of the
schools of art of Amenophis III and Amenophis IV*

Mountain, the Gebel el Ahmar in northern Egypt. These are the famous colossi of Memnon which still stand by the pylons of Amenophis III's funeral temple at the entrance of the Theban necropolis. The artist responsible for them was probably the king's chief sculptor Men, in charge at the Gebel el Ahmar, whose impeccable taste and style are beyond dispute. His son Bak, also a sculptor, joined the ranks of the co-regent, whose personal instructions he scrupulously obeyed. The classical style, in which human shapes were idealized, suggesting by a serene and elegant synthesis the features and forms of royalty (65), had to be abandoned in favour of total, almost harsh, realism; the whole truth was to be preserved in stone so that art itself might express the revised idea of divine incarnation. Bak was probably commissioned to carve the impressive pillar-statues of Amenophis IV for the temple to the east of Karnak, which the prince dedicated to the sun at the beginning of his reign (66). Such a reform could obviously only succeed if a general consensus of opinion was in its favour and if the elite was convinced of its necessity. The innovations of Akhenaten, who has been described as the "greatest mystic of antiquity", brought in their

66. *One of the Osirian pillars from the sun temple of Amenophis IV at Karnak (Cairo Museum)*

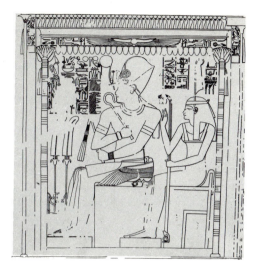

67. *Amenophis III with the Maet enthroned beneath the double canopy of his palace, in the Theban style*

68. *Amenophis IV and Nefertiti, the sovereigns of Amarna, shown in the style of the new school*

wake profound modifications at every level of Egyptian society. To simplify a theology inaccessible to the masses; to reconcile people and god by showing the latter as the orb shining impartially upon all; to proclaim what the priests had known "ever since the time of the gods": that men were born equal and that only their "wickedness differentiated them"; to unite mankind by bringing it close to all other life, and reminding it of the intimate relationship between all mineral, vegetable, animal and human elements; and to suppress the practice of magic which could only paralyze moral progress—such were the leading ideas of Amenophis IV's great design.

By the same token he set out to liberate the townsmen from a stifling tradition, to broaden their vision and even force them to look beyond the rigid formulas which had governed their thoughts for centuries. During the first three years of his co-regency the prince and his supporters made a determined attack upon set ways and ideas. The most immediate and tangible result, apart from the new art forms, was the adoption of the spoken language for official documents, hitherto prohibited by religious and civil authority. Such radical changes must certainly have encountered major obstacles and objections. Indeed, the experiment could only have been attempted during a co-regency, with the elder king remaining in his Theban capital and continuing to control the affairs of state through his senior officials. This allowed the younger king, with the support of his family and faithful friends, to establish a new city and, in virgin soil, to sow the seeds of his whole reform. The new spirit prevailed more slowly at Thebes, but Ramose, the vizier of the south, had his tomb decorated in both classical and modern style (67, 68). Elegant and stylized reliefs and paintings shared the walls of his burial chapel with the almost aggressively realistic double portrait of the young royal couple at their palace window.

For his experiment Amenophis IV selected the region near Hermopolis, the city of Thoth, god of thought, in the XVth nome of Upper Egypt. This area on the eastern bank of the Nile, for a length of about six and a half miles, is protected by the Arabic Chain at a point where it forms an immense circle. Within a few years he turned this barren site into a dream-city of palaces and small houses, nearly all surrounded by superb gardens. He named it Akhetaten, or "the horizon of the globe". Today it is known as Tell el Amarna, a contraction of two names: that of the modern village to the north, el Till, and that of the tribe of the Beni Amran who inhabited the region. Fourteen majestic steles hewn out of the cliff-sides defined the boundaries of the new capital. Eleven of them marked the rock on the right bank, and three others, against the numulithic limestone of the Libyan chain to the west, defined the cultivable area intended to supply the temple, palaces and private dwellings.

The three first frontier-steles (one at the extreme north of the town and the two others to the south) date from the fourth year of the co-regency. Upon them, Amenophis IV formally declared that he had vowed never to go beyond "this pure place", neither to the north nor to the south. He swore that no one, not even the queen, could induce him to seek elsewhere a more propitious place for the veneration of Aten. He proposed to erect five sanctuaries and two main palaces, one for Pharaoh and one for the queen. He also proposed to have a tomb built for himself in the eastern mountain, one for Nefertiti and one for the princess Meritaten, adding that if one or the other of them should die in another Egyptian city they must be brought back to Akhetaten for burial. He also ordered the preparation of a tomb for the sacred bull Mnevis, one for the high priest, and others for members of Aten's clergy, high officials and other subjects.

All this was on the eastern side of the town, certainly a deliberate reversal of the centuries-old placing of necropolises on the west bank of the Nile, where the sun disappears with the dead who, thanks to the Osirian ritual, are reborn after slow and mysterious transformations. The heretical king vigorously opposed practices he considered as magical; according to him, after sunset nothing survived and everything slumbered in a kind of cosmic sleep, the "breath of life" barely reaching the nostrils.

This new dogma was linked with a new conception of the goddess Maet, daughter of Re. She was the very quintessence of the Egyptian pantheon protecting the crown, and represented law and order. Any attempt to weaken her attributes could undermine the very foundations of monarchy. Some authors regard this revolutionary interference with the goddess as one of the greatest dangers ever to have threatened Egypt and the Empire. But Amenophis IV was bound to make the attempt, for above all it was essential for him to bring outdated concepts into line with the new spirit of the times.

Maet was not only law and order—as Re's daughter, an emanation of the sun, she was also the breath of life, and perhaps even light itself. Amenophis III, in his coronation name and in the names of several of his temples, had already

69. *Amenophis IV-Akhenaten and Nefertiti, accompanied by a princess, make offerings to the globe of the god Aten (Cairo Museum)*

tried to stress the importance of this aspect of the goddess by using the formula *Khaemmaet* which means "appearing (or rising) at the same time as Maet". In other words, the king and this celestial force of which he was both the guarantor and the proof, were but one.

To be convinced that, initially, Amenophis IV was content to follow the lead given in his father's reign, we need only enter once more the funerary chapel of the Theban vizier Ramose, where the wall illustrations convey a single idea presented in two styles. First, one sees Amenophis IV in traditional regalia, seated upon a platform beside the goddess Maet, who wears an immense ostrich plume on her head, shaped in the hieroglyph of her name but also, by the faint movement of its feathers suggesting the movement of the breath of life. In front of the king two hieroglyphic emblems always held by the gods at all periods of pharaonic Egypt, those of life (*ankh*) and divine power (*ouas*), represent flail holders, with the feathers of the flails pointing at the king and symbolically directing the flow of divine current towards him. The inscriptions call him "he who lives by Maet" (67). In contrast, another scene, a little further on, shows the co-regent at the window of his palace, with Nefertiti; both of them are portrayed in the new manner, the chief preoccupation of which seems to be absolutely accurate delineation of expression and features. The Amarnan globe shines over the couple, with its rays ending in tiny hands, those nearest the royal face holding the hieroglyphs of life and divine power which in the other group represented flail holders. Light, the dispenser of life, from the globe, is thus transmitted to them (68).

By the fourth year of his reign Amenophis IV had outlined the basic tenets of his heresy. It was far more a question of expressing in up-to-date images ideas long since fossilized into archaic forms than of radically transforming these ideas. Not only did he make the spoken language official currency, but he also launched a bold, naturalistic and readily apprehended symbolism to express his religious concepts (69).

In the winter of the year 6, Amenophis IV became Akhenaten "the servant of Aten", and drove in his electrum-plated chariot to eleven new steles on the western and eastern cliffs marking the limits of his great new capital. Here he made appropriate offerings and publicly renewed his vow never to overstep the boundaries of his city. He was now permanently installed in the city of the Globe (70) and his vow, which he repeated again in the year 8 at the fourteen frontier-steles, suggests that while the old court still ruled, he as co-regent was not free to act as he wished elsewhere in Egypt.

The main buildings of the city were predominantly religious; the second jubilee of Aten's name had been celebrated shortly after the second jubilee of Amenophis III at Malkata, and family events drew the co-regents even more closely together. In the city of the Globe the sovereigns had just celebrated the birth of their third daughter Ankhesenpaaten when, at Malkata, Queen Tiye's last daughter, Baketaten, was born about year 33. This name seems to have been chosen to affirm publicly that the Atenist religious experiment had the sympathy and approval of the senior branch of the dynasty. This little princess was born barely two years after the death of her maternal grandparents, Yuya and Thuya, who had recently been re-buried in a small tomb in the Valley of the Kings. Aanen (71), the Second Prophet of Amun, Heliopolitan High Priest of Re Atum and brother of Tiye, officiated at their funeral. The funerary equipment included, in addition to precious chests presented by the sovereigns, armchairs given by their eldest daughter Sitamun. Her father had married her a few years before and the chairs depicted the king's favours to her. However, if one agrees that the dead couple were the parents of the "Divine Father" Ay, it is surprising that there were no gifts from the Amarnan court.

Shortly after this, the Second Prophet of Amun, Aanen died and was immediately succeeded in year 34 by Simut; Amun's temples at Karnak were

XXVII. *The goddess Isis on one of the double doors of the gilt shrine, reminiscent of a chapel of the South*

therefore still flourishing, and there was no persecution of the dynastic god—indeed, the queen mother's brother had even been a most eminent priest of Amun. At the same time the temples begun in Aten's domain at Karnak by Amenophis IV before the year 4 of the co-regency, were still being built in year 6 of the Amarnan king's reign. Four of them were of sandstone of which one contained a single obelisk of the same material. The foundations of a fifth in a different stone were also laid in the great domain of "Aten of Heliopolis" in the south (that is Karnak at the period of the heresy). Finally a small pavilion had probably also been built in the immediate neighbourhood of the sacred lake at the time of the third double-jubilee of the two kings and the Globe, in the year 4 of Akhenaten, that is the year 36–7 of Amenophis III.

We can place Tutankhaten's birth between the years 34 and 35 of Amenophis III's reign, but intensive study of his burial treasure and of the remains of monuments erected during his brief reign, has produced few references to the identity of his parents. Genealogical records seem to have been systematically neglected at the time of the Atenist heresy, both at Malkata and at Tell el Amarna, where nothing but the Globe as creator of all life had any importance. Only in one inscription upon a lion consecrated in the temple of Soleb and later taken further south to Gebel Barkal in the Sudan does Tutankhamen call Amenophis III his father. Many authors refuse to take this literally and regard it simply as a general reference to a royal ancestor. Indeed, among the many theories put forward, one suggests that Tutankhaten may have been the son of Amenophis III and princess Sitamun (i.e., the son of his half-sister and aunt), and another that his parents were those of Smenkhkare and Nefertiti. Some concede the paternity of Amenophis III, but believe the mother to have been an unidentified secondary wife. Another recent suggestion is that Tutankhaten's father may have been a hypothetical son of Ay and Tey (Nefertiti's "Nurse"), who would have been the queen's foster-brother, and later married to a daughter of Amenophis III and Tiye. Or his mother might have been Meritre.

Many Egyptologists point out the striking resemblance, observed when the bandages were removed from the head of Tutankhamen's mummy, between Tutankhamen's features and those of Amenophis IV, familiar from his many portraits. On the other hand, the similarity in cranial formation and general aspect of Tutankhamen's mummy and the body found in Queen Tiye's pseudo-tomb at Thebes, successively believed to be that of Amenophis IV and Smenkhkare, convinced scholars that Tutankhamen was the brother of one or the other of these two kings. This seems more than probable; almost certainly Amenophis IV and Smenkhkare were brothers, or at least half-brothers. The latter must have been born at Malkata shortly after Amenophis III's first jubilee.

Let us return to the few known facts which may be helpful. It has been suggested that Queen Tiye was barren at the time of Tutankhamen's birth, but in view of the renowned vigour of Egyptian and Nubian women, and the fact that

XXVIII. *Head of one of the funerary couches in the form of a cheetah*

70. *Group of Amenophis IV-Akhenaten and Nefertiti; painted limestone (Louvre)*

71. *Aanen, brother of Queen Tiye, priest of Heliopolis, Second Prophet of Amun (Museo Egizio, Turin)*

hardly two years earlier she had borne the little princess Baketaten, it is quite likely that she gave birth to the prince when she was about forty-eight (and Amenophis III about fifty-two), assuming that she was married at thirteen.

Other clues must be sought in Tutankhamen's tomb. Not only did he bear a great resemblance to Amenophis IV and Smenkhkare, but also to Queen Tiye, a most important point (72, 73). In addition to this, to bear out the inscription on the lion found at Soleb, there was in the child-king's tomb a small golden statuette showing Amenophis III crouching in the attitude of the solar child (IIIa), as if to show his oneness with the son in whose flesh he would be reborn. This statuette, wrapped in linen and laid in a tiny coffin, was found beside a lock of Queen Tiye's hair touchingly enclosed like a mummy in its own little sarcophagus. It seems futile to refuse to make so obvious an inference. Other objects in the tomb also allude to the king's parents, such as the alabaster pitcher bearing the pharaonic names of the Malkata couple.

There were also several objects in the tomb which had belonged to other members of the royal family: an ivory palette with the name of Meritaten (the king's sister-in-law and wife of Smenkhkare); a small box-lid with the picture of another sister-in-law, Neferneferure, in a crouching position, which had been part of Smenkhkare's burial treasure; a box with the twin cartouches of Akhenaten and his co-regent, Smenkhkare; and the whip of prince Dhutmose (the king's elder brother?). And there were the tributes of several close relatives and those of faithful servants and friends, such as Nakhtmin and Maya who had dedicated statues to the king. But only the statuette of Amenophis III and Queen Tiye's lock of hair seem to prove his parentage.

Without wishing to be rash, it does therefore seem probable that before the

72. *Head of Queen Tiye in inlaid ebony (Ehem. Staatliche Museen, Berlin)*
73. *Tutankhamen's profile from his funeral mask. Solid gold (Cairo Museum)*

end of the year 35 of Amenophis III, the Great Royal Spouse Tiye gave birth to her last child, Tutankhaten, in the harem at Malkata. Egyptian custom decreed that the child's birth name should be chosen by his mother from words she had uttered when she was delivered—in the case of a prince destined for the throne this name was used until his coronation. Later a second name was added to his style. When he uttered his first cry and the "breath of life" entered into him, Tutankh*aten* was stamped with the mark of the Atenist heresy, and his young sister, born a year or two earlier, had also been dedicated to the Globe, ruler of Akhetaten, the capital where they were both soon to be taken to live with their young nieces.

Since an element of doubt is always dominant in this strange period, it is not surprising to learn that scientific circles still disagree about the meaning of the young prince's name. For all Egyptian names were short sentences, intended to place the newly born under the protection of a god. Only the seven fairies of Hathor who welcomed the infant into the world could tell us what Tiye really meant by the words which, more than 3,000 years later, everyone knows. Some say the meaning is "powerful is the life of Aten" or "gracious of life is Aten"; yet others say "living image of Aten" and finally, a recent theory suggests "all life is in the hands of Aten". Thus philological opinion remains divided upon the name which the Egyptians ceased to use from the day of the young king's coronation as *Nebkheprure*.

(*see page 263*)

5 Tutankhaten and the two capitals

1361–1359

At the time of Tutankhaten's birth, the paragon city of Thebes, then at its apogee, was a rich and free capital open to oriental influences and in touch with all the known world. Akhetaten (74), the heretical city, represented the quintessence, so to speak, of refined Theban civilization, where peace and prosperity following upon the national victory favoured an unprecedented flowering of the arts, where the nobility and the middle classes lived in greater luxury than ever before and even humble folk enjoyed comparative ease. Old-fashioned habits of austerity had vanished altogether: on festive occasions men wore magnificent, elaborately curled wigs and women long plaited artificial tresses falling below the shoulder (a fashion more popular than the short, round, Nubian wig preferred for its exotic quality by the ladies of the heretical city). Men and women now wore loose pleated linen robes, with wide sleeves often trimmed with fringes and elegant bows. Sandals had not yet acquired the long up-turned toes *à la poulaine* of the XIXth Dynasty but were often decorated with leather patterns and some of the king's footwear was gold-tooled, or of an original design with open fronts but protected heels. This taste for luxurious comfort was again the keynote in aristocratic dwellings: on the outskirts of the town they were set in large gardens but in the central built-up areas where space was limited, some houses had as many as three stories. At Akhetaten, however, which the royal couple from Malkata often visited, there was plenty of room for Akhenaten's architects to build the immense and lavish houses admired and envied by every Egyptian (75).

Palaces and hovels alike were built of unbaked brick; limestone was only used for thresholds, column-bases or lintels and door- and window-frames. Doors and columns were of wood. Around each estate was a high wall with a watchman's lodge near the gates from which a path led at right angles to the main building. This was always rectangular in shape and divided into three essential parts. A large reception hall was followed by the largest living-room of the central part of the house. Its ceiling, higher than those of the adjacent rooms, was supported by columns of which wealthy homes had four, and there was often a small hearth in the centre. A large flat stone with a shallow rim by one wall served as a basin to receive the lustrations poured over the hands and feet

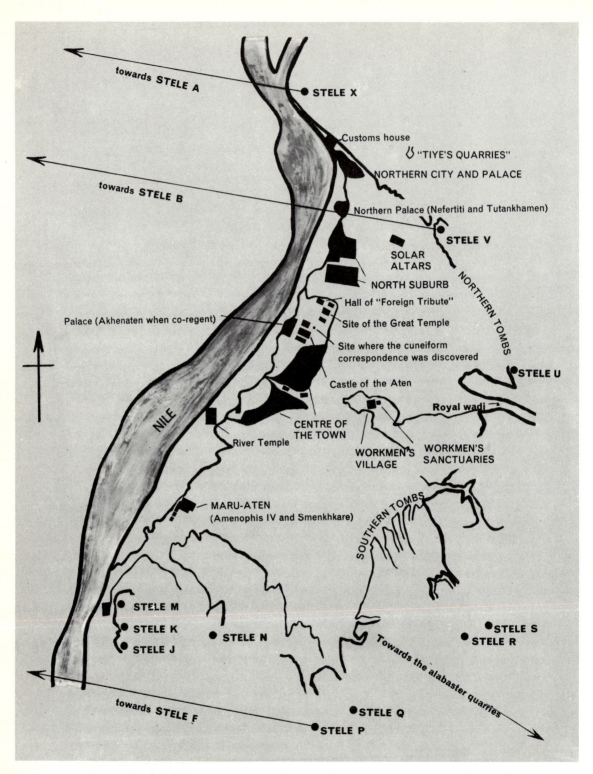

74. *Town plan of Tell el Amarna covering six miles of the eastern bank of the Nile*

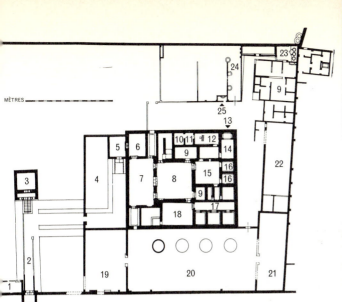
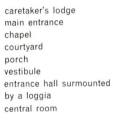
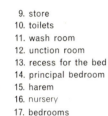

MÈTRES

caretaker's lodge	9. store	18. west loggia
main entrance	10. toilets	19. servants' entrance
chapel	11. wash room	20. yard and grain
courtyard	12. unction room	silos
porch	13. recess for the bed	21. stable
vestibule	14. principal bedroom	22. servants' quarters
entrance hall surmounted	15. harem	23. kitchen
by a loggia	16. nursery	24. cattle
central room	17. bedrooms	25. kennel

75. Plan of an Amarnan house belonging to a high official

76. Reconstruction of the central room from vizier Nakht's house at Tell el Amarna

of the family and their guests. Against the opposite wall was a platform for seats. The narrow stone-barred windows were set very high to temper the harsh daylight. Sometimes the columns were decorated with plants and animals, and in the palaces so were the ceilings. On either side of the central room were the master's study and his office; a stair-well led to a loggia over the entrance hall. The third portion of the building was private, and its main square drawing-room usually reserved for the lady of the house. On either side of this were the bedrooms, all usually very plain and each with a small alcove. The sanitary arrangements were most refined, generally even equipped with seats. The Egyptians were not acquainted with the bath-tub before Graeco-Roman times, but always, it seems, had shower-rooms. As in most warm countries, they took particular care of their skins after washing, and all the private apartments had "unction" rooms for oiling and massage. Drains and conduits were of pottery. The residences of the sovereigns of Amarna and Malkata were built on similar lines although naturally with more luxurious appointments (76).

Behind the house lay the servants' quarters, the kitchens and the bakery, the home brewery and the cellars with the wine-jars marked with the source and vintage of their contents: the wines of the "Domain of Aten" were mostly from the western river, that is from the delta, near modern Alexandria. At the back of the house also were the stables, the cattle-sheds, the kennels and the workshops for carpentry and spinning. A well provided water, and numerous silos shaped like sugar-loaves housed the grain. Naturally there was also a pleasure-

77. Reconstruction of the commercial quarter of Tell el Amarna

garden with sycamores, palm trees, willows, sometimes acacias, pomegranates and great clumps of flowering shrubs: tufts of papyrus, opium poppies, cornflowers and even mandragora bushes grew thickest round the central rectangular lily-pond where the blue lotus grew. At the entrance to the garden was a small open-air chapel with an altar upon which, on a sort of flat stone, the solar globe with its rays ending in tiny hands shone over the Amarnan royal family. On either side of this slab was a diptych with the portraits of the master and the mistress of the house. Possibly this was a forerunner of the Christian triptych, showing church benefactors.

In the centre of the heretical city were the palaces, the main temples and the ministries. Immense buildings with courtyards adorned with statues and colonnaded porticoes constituted the official palace precincts, and over the central street of the town was a great arch, the first Egyptian notion of a bridge, connecting the two parts of the pharaoh's domain.

The private palace was set upon a height, reached by a three-terraced garden. The grounds sloped down to the river where a long portico led to a private harbour with a landing-stage on the flower-decked banks of the river for the royal barges bringing the Malkata sovereigns some 220 miles down the Nile to share for a few days the radiant life of the city of the Globe. None of the echoes of outer bustle and worry seemed to penetrate and the only preoccupation was with implementing the religious reform.

When Tutankhaten was about three years old, between years 37 and 38 of Amenophis III's reign—that is towards the end of year 9 and beginning of year 10 of Akhenaten—he accompanied his parents and his elder sister Baketaten to

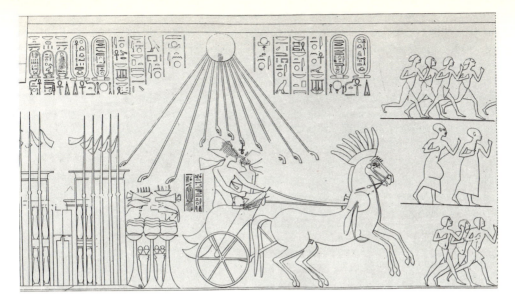

78. *The royal couple embracing while leaving the temple of Aten* (*Tomb of Mahu*)

Akhetaten. It was after the third jubilee of the Theban king which had also been celebrated in the City of the Globe at the same time as the twin jubilees of Aten and his servant Akhenaten. Before tying up, the barge sails past the commercial district where the grain silos loom over the dazzling white parapets of the docks (77). Nearby is the shop of the Mycenean merchant whose octopus-patterned pottery is so fashionable at the moment.

The little prince is then driven in the chariot of one of the Amarnan princesses, thoroughly enjoying the parade of which he is himself a part, following the other royal chariots through the city and watching the puffing court dignitaries, even the vizier, trying to keep up with them on foot as they pass the huge temples (78). The procession halts within the outer precincts, before two great pylons similar to those of the temples at Luxor and Karnak. But the masts before them from which flutter long ribbons (symbolizing the breath of life) are in two groups of five, the sacred number of Khmunu (Hermopolis) and of Akhetaten, instead of being in twos or fours as at Karnak or Memphis. The two royal couples cross the great roofless halls with their numerous brick stands—one for every day of the year—erected to receive the daily sacrifice and the food offerings made during the feast of Aten's jubilee. After consecrating choice plants to the sun on the open-air altars, reached by a few steps, they leave the first building, the *Perhai* (House of Jubilation) to enter another, separate one, the Gem-Aten (Aten has been found) (79, 80).

The next visit is to the almost completed temple known as *Shuyet-Re* (Fan-Screen of Re) dedicated to Queen Tiye. This sanctuary is shaped like a huge kiosk, a sort of peripteral temple whose screenwalls allow cooling draughts of

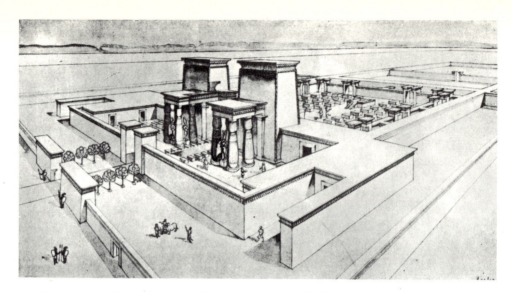

79. *Entrance to the sanctuary of the great temple at Tell el Amarna*

air to circulate in the shade. As is the case with all the sanctuaries connected with the active role of the royal women, it is inhabited by the divine breath of life which they transmit to the sovereign to invigorate him, as Isis's wings had done for the inanimate Osiris. While their elders inspect the progress of the work, the child and the little princesses gaze at the painted sandstone statues of Amenophis III and Tiye, of Akhenaten and Nefertiti, which Mutnedjmet, Nefertiti's sister, explains to the children whom she often escorts.

But official visits had to be curtailed as far as possible because of the increasingly poor health of the Malkata king. Indeed in year 36, when his ally, King Tushratta of Naharin, yielded to Amenophis III's insistent demands and sent him one of his daughters, the princess Tadukhipa, as a bride, she found awaiting her at Malkata an almost exhausted monarch. Tushratta, informed of this by his ambassadors or at the request of the pharaoh himself, agreed to lend the Egyptian ruler his miraculous statue of Ishtar the Great, mistress of love and war. The goddess apparently lived up to her reputation; and the pharaoh kept her in his palace and was most reluctant to part with such a miraculous remedy. Nevertheless Tushratta, his ally against the Hittites, his friend who had showered him with gifts of gold, lapis-lazuli, weapons, precious stones, chariots and harness, and quite recently even thirty women, would not part with his statue permanently. Amenophis III had prudently left it at Thebes, fearing for its safety in the city of the Globe where Aten reigned. A much more tolerant attitude reigned at Malkata, where shortly before year 36 Amenophis III had felt free to order sacrifice to Amun and the goddess Hathor at Sinai.

But let us rejoin the procession which now winds past the ministry of foreign affairs (the office of "Pharaoh's correspondence") at the gate of which, bowing low, stands the minister Tutu, in charge of all letters addressed to the king by

142

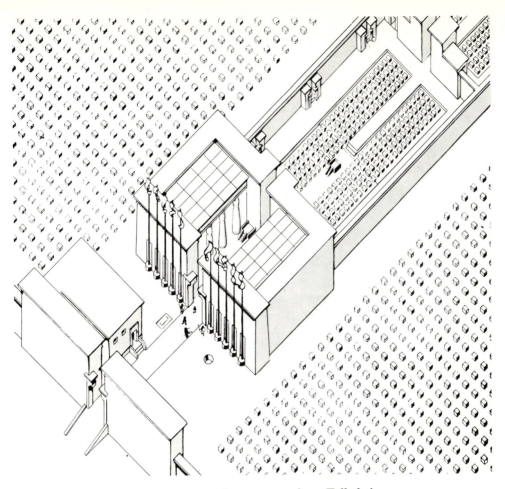

80. Reconstruction of the entrance to the great temple at Tell el Amarna

his allies. During the co-regency period, it seems that copies of the letters were also passed to Akhenaten in his city. Thus more than 360 tablets in cuneiform were found in the ruined office of the archives.

Policemen on raised and shaded traffic-boxes calmly hold back the crowd impatiently awaiting the passage, in their electrum-plated chariots, of their sovereigns, living emanations of the sun. On this occasion the young students of the house of life—the university—with its laboratories and a scriptorium for copying the sacred books, enjoyed a holiday and some of them were even admitted to the inner courtyard of the palace where courtiers and high officials were assembled to see their sovereigns appear at the great state window (81).

A few years later the princess Ankhesenpaaten, who had always lived at the heretical court, reminded Tutankhamen of the near delirium which swept through the crowd when Akhenaten and Nefertiti, from that same window, had distributed the "gold of reward" to the "Divine Father" Ay. On such occasions

143

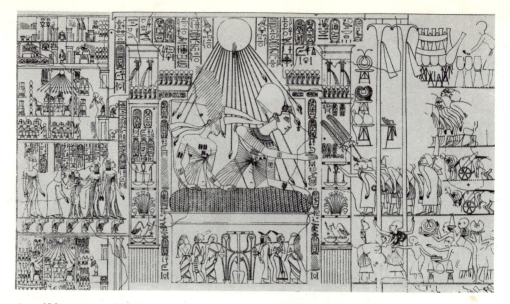

81. Akhenaten and Nefertiti at the "Great State Window" of their palace. On the left are the royal princesses and a plan of the palace (Tomb of Pernefer)

the ceremony of "the appearance" had taken place on the immense palace balcony—apparently a heretical innovation. Gold necklaces were clasped round favoured necks; precious goblets, plate and jewels tossed to the privileged. But Ay, as Master of the King's Horse probably valued most highly his award of red-brown leather gloves (82) which he proudly displayed to all before being borne home in triumph. The festivities and pageantry of this occasion were even more impressive than those which rewarded Pernefer, master of the pharaoh's household.

The procession now passed the residence of Panehesy, the high priest, and the office of public works. From the barracks came detachments of troops of the pharaoh's "pacific" and international army, led by cornets: first a body of Egyptian infantry, then another of Bedouins and men of the Shardanes contingent, and finally a third of Nubian archers (83).

Whenever he visited Akhetaten, Amenophis III used his own palace there, *Splendour of Aten*. This particular visit of the parents of Akhenaten and Tutankhamen gave Huya, the queen's major-domo in the city, the idea of having a double lintel, which had been made for his funeral chapel, decorated with two parallel views of the royal couples (84). On one side, Akhenaten and Nefertiti, seated close together in an affectionate attitude, receive the homage of their four eldest daughters. On the other, Tiye, accompanied by her last daughter, Baket-aten, faces her husband. Some Egyptologists believe the child's gesture to signify worship of her deceased father, but there is nothing to support this view. In any case, there is no portrayal of Tutankhaten, who is never shown in these royal family groups (any more than the other royal princes), since under Aten's

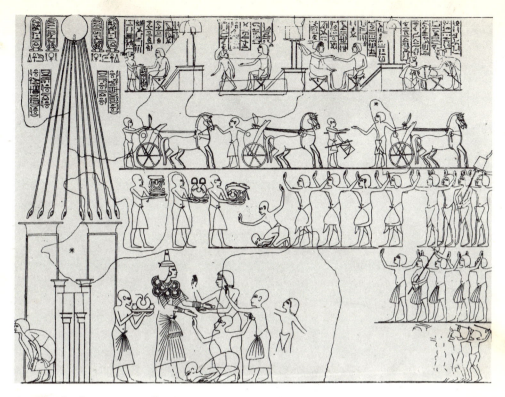

82. The final scene: awarding honours to the "Divine Father" Ay. Celebrations at Amarna

rule (probably for ritual reasons) only feminine members of the family are shown with the kings. Even the courtiers obeyed this law in the decoration of their tombs; for instance, Panehesy, the high priest, is depicted sharing a meal with his wife and three daughters.

Clearly, within the fourteen boundary steles of his city, Aten seemed to reserve his blessing for the royal daughters, thus stressing the importance of the maternal line of descent. Moreover, certain chapels were specifically dedicated

83. Procession of the international military guard at Tell el Amarna

84. The double lintel from the tomb of Huya. The two families of the co-regency at Amarna

to the queens and princesses—the "Fan-Screens of Re" (*Shuyet-Re*). Their symbolism was composed of the ostrich-feathers of the fan used in the hieroglyphic representation of their name, evoking the breath of life which they passed on through the intervention of the solar globe. Near the great official temples of Tell el Amarna, excavations have revealed several "Fan-Screens of Re" for Tiye, Nefertiti and Meritaten. The ruins of this last show that it was oriented on a north-south axis, the better to catch refreshing breezes so welcome in a torrid land. Another *Shuyet-Re* was built upon the left bank of the Nile near Hermopolis, which Amenophis IV dedicated to the little princess Ankhesenpaaten Tashery.

Another record of this same royal visit shows Akhenaten's deferential welcome of his father, the younger sovereign himself pouring a drink for the Theban king (85). There is no need to search the contemporary diplomatic correspondence for evidence of the precise ailment which the goddess Ishtar had been asked to cure: Amenophis III's physical debility is only too obvious in the illustration of the Amarnan stele shaped like a vine-trellis with grapes hanging from the top, under which the two Malkata sovereigns are shown before a table of offerings (now in the British Museum). The king is portrayed as he must have been shortly before his death—obese, heavy-featured, his expression as listless as his stance, in striking contrast with the vital and energetic profile of Tiye still discernible beside him although the stone has suffered damage (86).

Shortly after this first visit to his elder brother's capital, little Tutankhaten started to attend school at the palace where his studies were to benefit by emulating the sons of the nobility and the foreign princes of the *Kap*. Children's education began very early in Egypt at that time, and although they were breast-fed for what seems to us a very long time, they began learning to read at the age of four. In the mornings, they were taught to recognize and pronounce the several hundred hieroglyphs representing everything alive and real. These signs were divided into separate categories, a means of introducing the children to an idea of hierarchy. When they could read the basic signs, had learned to conjugate verbs and to set pronouns in their proper places; when they could make agreements in number and gender, use figures and do mental arithmetic,

85. *An unfinished relief on which*
Amenophis IV is pouring a drink
for Amenophis III. Limestone
(Staatliche Museen, Berlin)

86. *A chapel-stele showing Amenophis III in the Amarnan style (British Museum)*

they were then taught the hieratic script used on papyruses and *ostraca*. After this they were introduced to the literary language, its specialized vocabulary and the system used for transcribing foreign, mainly Asian, nouns. For his exercises the little prince was privileged to use papyrus, manufactured in Egypt from the time of the Ist Dynasty of fibres from the great marsh-reeds, which ordinary schoolchildren could not afford—this royal material was most expensive and generally used for making scroll-books. Schoolchildren wrote on calcareous slivers or potsherds, known today as *ostraca*. The teacher corrected the young prince as strictly as his schoolmates, and when their copies of phrases from popular fables or books of social instruction were faulty, marked them in red ink. The greatest stumbling-block was the joining of words, a hard task for a child accustomed to the spoken tongue and suddenly required to use unfamiliar, archaic language.

Tutankhaten was equipped for school like a little scribe: his palette (IV*b*)

147

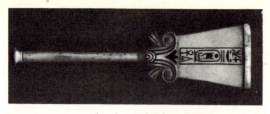

87. *Tutankhamen's ivory
"papyrus-smoother"*

was a rectangular board (the simplest of these were wooden and the most elaborate of ivory or even gold-plated) with two hollows at the top to hold solid blocks of colours—black and red (soot and ochre mixed with gum). A slot in the middle of the palette held the little marine reeds used as pens—the *calami*, whose ends were not trimmed to a point like goose-quills, but crushed by chewing into a tiny miniature paint brush. A small hollow column, topped with a floral capital, served as a "pencil box" for these fragile writing instruments. The little pupil also had a smoother for restoring a non-absorbent surface to the papyrus after erasures (87). The eraser itself was a small scraper of very fine sandstone, kept in a small leather bag with a drawstring top. For rubbing out mistakes on *ostraca*, a small sponge fastened to a string was used. The small bowl for moistening the brush often had an inscription on the outside, reminding the scribe that before beginning work he should sprinkle a libation of a few drops of water in honour of Imhotep, the deified sage who built the stepped pyramid at Saqqara in the IIIrd Dynasty. But most of the scribes' palettes were under the protection of Thoth, the god of letters, measure and wisdom.

The young prince and his friends devoted the afternoon to physical exercise: swimming or wrestling. He also learned archery and probably to ride the thoroughbreds sent as gifts to his father by sovereigns of the East. But riding was not an Egyptian pastime, and his lessons were exceptional. Normally when a pharaoh is shown with his horses, they are drawing his chariot.

When his primary studies were over, the little prince began to study composition; the wisest and most learned scholars impressed upon him the importance of letters:

> What you gain in one day at school is for eternity—the work done there is as lasting as mountains.
> Do you not carry a palette? That is what constitutes the difference between you and him who wields the oar.
> Plunge into a book as one plunges into water.
> Poverty awaits him who does not go there.

In spite of his apparently delicate health, it was at this time that he was taught by his "master of arms" to hunt hare, gazelle, ibex, antelope and even ostrich in the desert, according to an ivory bracelet decorated with pictures of an ostrich hunt found in his tomb. But the young prince much preferred running with his dogs or sitting quietly under the palace arbour playing *senet* (XLIX*b*) or the serpent game with his companions or making sparks fly from a sort of lighter which he even took with him to his tomb (177).

XXIX. *Head of a funeral couch in the form of a sacred cow*

He had not quite finished his first cycle of studies when a great ceremony took place in the capital of the Globe. The sovereigns of Akhetaten with their six daughters gave an audience to all the foreign ambassadors in a building specially constructed for this sort of parade where the envoys presented their tributes to the king. For some time past pessimistic rumours had been circulating at the court of Malkata, where Queen Tiye was implored by her courtiers to save the threatened throne by intervening with the co-regent. Amenophis III was dying (his mummy showed a serious state of dental decay with complications) and had lost interest months before in everything that went on around him. The high priests of Karnak had again become arrogant. The Asian situation, too, was serious. Letters from his allies to Amenophis III and to his co-regent remained unanswered. The court seemed indifferent to the Hapiru invasion in Palestine encouraged by Labaja, Prince of the Caravans, and to the regular incursions into Syria of the Hittite king, Suppiluliuma. In the Syrian North certain provinces had already acquired autonomy through the treachery of the king of Amurru, Aziru, son of Abdi-ashirta. The tribute which Egypt's Asian vassals had regularly paid since their subjection by Tuthmosis III now only arrived sporadically. Tiye anxiously watched her husband fading away and realized that some action by her heretical son was required if criticism was to be silenced and the precarious situation of the empire concealed. No doubt very few Asian delegates arrived with many gifts and the treasury intendant loaded them up with part of the tribute which the king of Mitanni had just sent. On the other hand, the Nubians remained staunchly faithful, proving once more, if such proof were needed, the devotion of the southern peoples to Yuya and Thuya's descendants.

This ceremony, sometimes called the parade or scene of tribute, of the year 12, which, if the inscriptions have been correctly read must have taken place on the eighth day of the second month of winter, is considered by some authors to mark the real accession of Akhenaten to the throne immediately after his father's death (88). A letter (No. 27 Knudtzon edition) from King Tushratta of Mitanni to Akhenaten (Naphuria) in which he seems to allude simultaneously to Amenophis III's funeral and Akhenaten's accession was registered in the archives with the date of its arrival in Thebes. To make full use of this document, as we have already mentioned, we have to accept the restored reading of year 12, but this is contested by, among others, Sir Alan Gardiner who reads it simply as year 2. In this case, the funeral of Amenophis III would have preceded the parade of the foreign tributes, and the ceremony might simply be part of a coronation scene. But then it is difficult to explain how the princess Meketaten is shown with her five sisters during the parade and how at her death, probably at the end of the same year, her sarcophagus could receive the joined seals of her grandfather and her father.

XXX. *Head of a funeral couch in the form of the hippopotamus goddess*

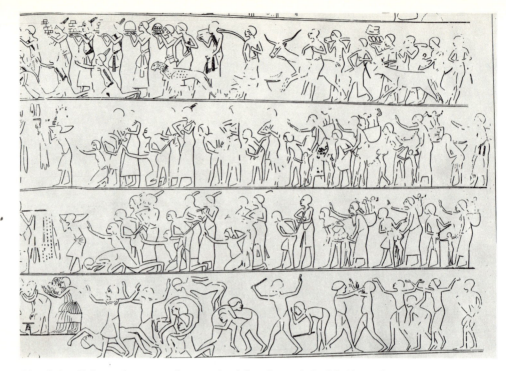

88. A detail from the processions and celebrations of the Nubians during the "Parade foreign tribute" in the year 12

This is the most obscure period of Tutankhamen's life, dominated by those two basic enigmas: was there a co-regency of Amenophis III and Amenophis IV? And is Napkhuria still used to transcribe the coronation name of Amenophis IV in Akkadian, or is it sometimes used for *Nip*huria, Tutankhamen's coronation name? Again one is forced to wonder whether at the death of Amenophis III, the Thebans, hostile as they were to Akhenaten's heresy, did not deliberately choose the child Tutankhamen as his father's heir, and systematically ignore the heretical master of Akhetaten.

This theory would explain why Akhenaten in his turn took a co-regent (Smenkhkare) to emphasize his new pre-eminence as elder king. One cannot consider the problem of Tutankhamen objectively without taking these possibilities into account, and without stressing the doubts attendant upon collation of scattered documents, some of which are often contradictory.

But without drawing conclusions, let us at least note that although Smenkhkare's palace is mentioned once in the Amarna excavations, Tutankhamen's is not. Yet Tutankhamen and Ankhesenpaaten are often referred to in the north of the town in Nefertiti's domain.

One might provisionally assume that at the time of the famous Amarna parade, the king succeeding Amenophis III, presumably Akhenaten, may, in spite of his vow never to leave the heretical centre, have visited the southern

89. Scene of grief and lamentation in the palace at the death of Princess Meketaten

city, Malkata, and resided there in his palace, which is called in the Tell el Amarna letter No. 27 "the castle (*Pabekhen*) named Rejoicing in the horizon (*Hai-em-akhet*)". This visit might have been for his father's funeral. If Akhenaten had incurred the hostility of the Malkata court, he certainly encountered no opposition from his mother Tiye, who always seems to have acted as a go-between for the two courts and, diplomatically, to have kept Tushratta of Mitanni friendly towards her eldest son. Indeed, it was to Tiye that Tushratta sent presents, and to her that he turned on hearing of Amenophis III's death, asking her to strengthen the bonds between their two countries. Therefore the princess Tadukhipa was sent to the harem of the new king (Naphuria: Akhenaten).

Akhenaten had already married before year 9 of his reign a secondary wife called Kia, but his perfect understanding with Nefertiti still seemed unquestionable after the parade of foreign tribute at the end of year 12, when the couple are depicted together mourning over the inert body of little Meketaten. The reliefs which twice show these heartbreaking scenes in the royal necropolis of Akhetaten are unique in the history of Egypt. They are even more revealing in the death-chamber: while the royal parents and their suite mourn over the dead princess, a woman leaves the room holding a newborn child to her breast, suggesting that Meketaten died in childbirth, having married her father, as his third daughter was to do some years later (89).

If Amenophis III had his own palace in the city of the Globe, Tiye also had

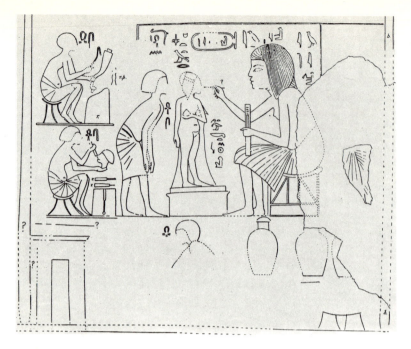

90. *The workshop of Yuti, sculptor of Queen Tiye. The artist is finishing a statue of
Princess Baketaten (Tomb of Huya)*

hers, which is often mentioned in the ruins of Tell el Amarna. One might therefore assume that she stayed there fairly often after the death of her husband,
although still continuing to reside at Malkata. But she had numerous estates
throughout Egypt, and it was not only to Tell el Amarna that she took Tutankhamen after his father's death. The existence, however, of a palace assigned
to little Baketaten at Akhetaten suggests that the queen mother may have liked
to stay in the Amarnan city. It was in this palace that she encouraged the
sculptor Yuti from whom she commissioned portraits of her youngest daughter,
Baketaten (90). The Amarnan couple always showed the powerful Tiye all
possible respect, and the banquets given for the dowager queen were noteworthy
enough to be recorded in the tomb of Huya, her intendant at Tell el Amarna.
Facing the sovereign heirs, is Queen Tiye with her small daughter Baketaten
(91). One has to imagine the presence of Tutankhaten with them, since, in strict
obedience to the rules, he is not shown. On the other hand, beside Nefertiti,
sharing the lavish meal, is his close cousin, and future bride, Ankhesenpaaten.
Tiye raises to her lips a goblet from which she drinks, but when it came to
showing her eating, Theban decorum prevailed, and the sculptor did not dare
portray her in such a free attitude. Only Akhenaten, Nefertiti and their small
daughters are seen biting heartily into pieces of meat and roast duck. Although
the presence of the young prince is referred to in odd inscriptions scattered in
the ruins, he is never actually shown at any phase of Amarnan life either in wall-

154

sculptures in the tombs or on the steles of the heretical family in Akhetaten, or even with Tiye and Baketaten when the queen mother was led by her eldest son into the temple he had built for her—the Fan-Screen of Re—which she had seen nearing completion on her last visit with Amenophis III (92).

In the Theban city the little prince had returned to school. If some of the Nubian grandees wore plain gold earrings, their children seemed to prefer great tasselled eardrops and Tutankhaten, like his little cousins of Tell el Amarna, wore these even before the age of puberty; in his tomb similar earrings were found, the ornamental insignia of which show that he still wore them after becoming pharaoh (111a). But then, he was a child-pharaoh, who still probably had to do his lessons. He had good friends, older than himself, among whom were two "children of the *Kap*", who figure on the monuments of the period; Khai, portrayed on the walls of the temple of Kawa in the Sudan, and Hiknefer whom we know from his picture on the tomb walls of Huy, viceroy of Nubia, and from that in his own tomb at Toshka, opposite Aniba in his princedom of Nubia.

Tutankhaten now dated his exercises in red ink, and as he was certain to reign, being a prince of the blood, his teachers were especially vigilant and strict with him. He would soon be required to solve problems which had defeated the presumptuous scholar, the scribe Hory. He could calculate the number of men needed to transport an obelisk sixty yards long and give the proportions of the ramp needed to raise it. Soon he would be asked to plan a military expedition

91. The royal banquet in honour of Tiye (Tomb of Huya)

155

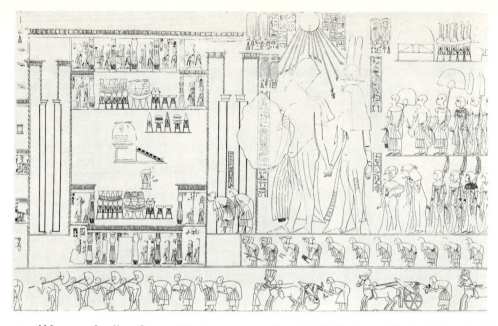

92. Akhenaten leading Queen Tiye into the temple called "Shadow of Re" which he had dedicated to her (Amarnan Tomb of Huya)

and to answer precise questions on the geography of Syria. He could now add and subtract whole numbers and fractions, and to multiply he used duplication as European students still did in the Middle Ages. Naturally he knew how to calculate the area of any triangle, but there was no question as yet of asking him to work out the volume of a truncated pyramid. He was a good pupil, approaching the end of his second cycle of studies with the prospect of becoming "a scribe who has received the writing case"—or what we should today describe as graduating with honours.

For several reasons, Tiye, the queen mother, was increasingly worried about the unrest and the threat of revolt, both in Tell el Amarna and in Thebes. Since the death of Amenophis III and of Akhenaten's second daughter, there had been hard problems to face in the city of the Globe. In the first place, Akhenaten's right to the throne was contested throughout the country. Tutankhaten had his partisans in Thebes where, under Queen Tiye's wing, he was still considered as the rightful heir of Amenophis III. Amun's priests rallied to him, and it was even said that they tried to gain the sympathy of the beautiful Nefertiti. Then, no sooner had Akhenaten completed the building of a kiosk to Aten near the sacred lake of Karnak, than he unleashed a violent offensive against most of the gods of Egypt, especially Amun and his associated deities, whose clergy constituted a threat to his own rule and his ideal.

From the delta to the Sudan he despatched teams of workmen to disfigure the statues of the deities and hammer out their names, and, worse still, to erase every mention of the word "god" in the plural. In the sacred cartouches con-

156

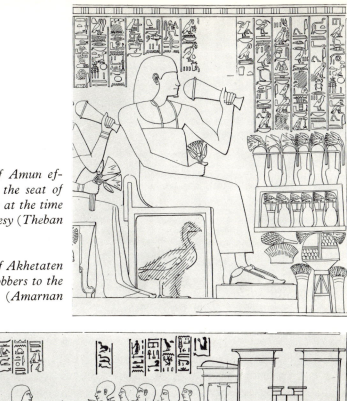

93. *The sacred goose of Amun effaced from beneath the seat of the vizier at Thebes at the time of the Amarnan heresy (Theban tomb of Ramose)*

94. *The chief of police of Akhetaten handing over two robbers to the vizier of Amarna (Amarnan tomb of Mahu)*

taining his father's names he left only his coronation name of Nebmaetre, which did not contain the vocable of the hated god, but that of the goddess Maet, daughter of Re. To her he always showed respect and stressed the new interpretation of this deity as "breath of divine life", twin of the god Shu who animates all beings. He even ordered the removal from noble Theban tombs of the image of Amun's sacred goose (93). At Hierakonpolis he attacked the vulture goddess Nekhabet and in Nubia the silhouette of the god Min. Open warfare was thus declared, and although Akhenaten could congratulate himself on the efficiency of Mahu, his chief of police, in protecting the town from thieving Bedouins and political rebels (94), he was betrayed in nearly every other quarter; and if the army did not actually rise against him, it remained passive in Asia and seems to have been far less loyal than was supposed. The minister of foreign affairs at Akhetaten, Tutu, continued to leave unanswered the letters of allies in Asia who might still have been helped, those who were later to succumb for lack of support. The saddest and most dramatic of these cases is that of the faithful prince Rib-Addi, king of Byblos, who paid with death for his patient loyalty to the pharaoh; whereas one suspects the duplicity of Aziru, simultaneously fearing and hoping for the Hittite king to invade against Tunip (Aleppo). That was the beginning of the great Syrian war embarked upon by the prince of the Hati (Hittite).

In year 15 of his reign, Akhenaten ceased to appear with Nefertiti in the streets of Akhetaten, and he no longer dedicated steles for his favoured servants to be placed in their domestic chapels as guarantors of perpetual life. For more than eleven years, however, the royal pair had personified the ideological reform he had struggled to get accepted (96). When the people, courtiers or humble villagers, saw passing through the great streets the luminous chariot of Aten, in which the king and queen rode, often locked in each other's arms, they understood the inference that as long as Aten's beloved couple lived, all else would endure with them. If on the wall of every burial chapel the sun shone not only on the king and queen, but also on palace and temple, this was not simply an imaginative representation, but a deliberate statement that the creator inhabited the noblest of his creatures. Upon the household steles the theme was even clearer: as with the temple pylon from which the sun rises, on the left, is the king, the masculine element, corresponding to the south tower, and on the right, the queen, the feminine element, evoking the north tower. Above them, the globe spread *for them alone* its rays ending in tiny hands holding the symbol of life. Around them are the little princesses, the fruit of a union inspired by the divine breath (95). The two principles were inextricably bound to each other and neither could alone ensure the eternal cycle of Egypt's life.

Then, abruptly, Nefertiti no longer appears as one of the royal couple. Did Akhenaten desert her? Or, on the contrary, did the queen forsake the heresy which was leading the dynasty to disaster? She joined Tutankhaten's party, realizing that therein lay the only hope of a return to the eternal Egypt of her childhood for which she passionately longed. Perhaps this was just after Tiye's death at Malkata, and Nefertiti, aided by the "Divine Father" Ay and her "Nurse" Tey might have decided to save the Egyptian crown by giving it to Amenophis III's youngest son, Tutankhaten. This was year 15 of the Amarnan reign. From this time onwards a strange situation prevailed in the southern district of Akhetaten—Maru-Aten—where the heretic settled with a prince, Smenkhkare, perhaps the son of Amenophis III and of Sitamun or another of his secondary wives. He married the young man to his eldest daughter, Meritaten, and gave to each of them one of Queen Nefertiti's two names: Neferneferuaten.

XXXI. *Serket protecting the canopic shrine*
On the two following pages: XXXII. *The alabaster canopic shrine which was contained within the double coffer of gilded wood*
XXXIII. *Stopper from one of the four canopic urns in the form of the king's head*

He also had Meritaten portrayed instead of his wife Nefertiti. At this time he shunned magic more than ever, and the tiles of his southern palace now show brightly coloured bushes of flowers with flights of wild duck (no longer threatened by boomerangs since they no longer represent demons), and young calves frolicking against a gay sylvan background (97).

Nefertiti withdrew to the northern end of the town near the police station in her palace "Aten's castle", or *Hat-aten*. It was a most elaborate building, complete in every detail down to an aviary decorated with the most beautiful "naturalistic" murals ever found in Egypt's ruins, showing gentle turtledoves at rest in a papyrus thicket, contrasting with the swoop of kingfishers diving toward the water. Apparently, her three youngest daughters lived there with her; the eldest, Meritaten, was married to Akhenaten's co-regent, Smenkhkare (98). The king himself had so far yielded to his mystical propensities that, deprived of Nefertiti, his feminine counterpart whose famous tiara echoed the red crown of the North, he now had himself portrayed on steles in the company of his co-regent and half-brother (or brother) in an equivocal attitude which has sometimes been cited as proof of a relationship as scandalous as that of Hadrian and Antinous. In fact, Akhenaten was simply carrying to the extreme his pursuit of a dream-ideal, and insisting upon perpetuating this symbol of life passing from the Globe to the double-principle of the couple, itself essential to the enduring omnipotence of the Globe (99).

The queen's third daughter, Ankhesenpaaten, had just been married to her father—she must have been about eleven—and towards year 16 of his reign gave birth to a little princess, Ankhesenpaaten Tashery, to whom a "Fan-Screen of Re" on the left bank of the river near Hermopolis was at once dedicated. Akhenaten had thus made of his daughter a potential future sovereign of Egypt.

Had he finally realized how much his intransigence of the last few years had hastened his failure? Smenkhkare's investiture probably did not take place at Thebes but at Akhetaten, for the coronation hall to the south of Akhenaten's great palace was built for this occasion, when he was given the coronation name of Ankhkheprure. Did the senior co-regent then send him on missions throughout the country in an attempt to recoever some of his lost power? There is little to support this possibility save for the fact that at Memphis Smenkhkare dedicated a temple to the god Aten.

The very few documents mentioning Smenkhkare do little to dispel the mystery which surrounds the Amarnan family. One can only assume, from the evidence of wine jars bearing his name, that Smenkhkare spent the first part of his three-year co-regency in a pavilion in the north palace. At that time the break with Queen Nefertiti was not yet complete—some even say that she concealed her dislike of the new co-regent and tried to persuade him to go to Thebes where his murder had been arranged. But that too belongs to the realm of conjecture.

XXXIV. *One of the four small gold mummiform coffins placed*
in the canopic urns, containing the king's viscera

95. *"Manifesto" of the solar cult of Amarna. The sovereigns and the three princesses beneath the beneficial influence of the Globe. Limestone (Staatliche Museen, Berlin)*

96. *A fragment of the stele showing the Amarnan couple, symbol of creation by the Globe. Limestone (Staatliche Museen, Berlin)*

97. Pieces of glazed terracotta bricks decorated with Amarnan motives (Louvre)

It seems clear, however, that the last two co-regents of Tell el Amarna tried to preserve a last link with Thebes. Was it a desperate attempt at reconciliation with the clergy of the dynastic god? Or was it founded for ritual reasons because of the origin of Smenkhkare who was attempting thereby to assert his rights to the throne as superior to those of Tutankhaten? In any case, that some conciliatory gesture to Thebes was made seems proved by the existence of a temple —possibly funerary—in the name of Smenkhkare, mentioned in a graffito of the Theban tomb of Pere, dated year 3 of Smenkhkare's reign and alluding to the recitation of prayers to Amun in this temple at Thebes. The yellow soapstone group which Smenkhkare may have ordered to be made of himself with Meritaten, a fragment of which is in the Louvre, is probably of this period (100). The sovereign wears the distinctly Osirian *nemset*, or wig cover, which seems to preclude the possibility that this portrait was intended for the heretical city.

However, Smenkhkare's sojourn at Thebes, if he had indeed been sent there, did not affect his continuing worship of Aten, since he retained the epithet of Neferneferu*aten*, "beloved of Re's One and Only", which we know was formerly reserved for Queen Nefertiti herself.

It is very difficult to say today where he died—whether at Thebes or at Tell el Amarna. However, the pseudo-tomb of Queen Tiye (No. 55 of the Valley of the Kings) might be regarded as a temporary and hastily equipped burial place for the young king. At any rate it contained, among other royal relics, burial furnishings which came from Smenkhkare's sepulchre and which may well have been pillaged for subsequent use in Tutankhamen's tomb. For among the objects of the famous treasure, upon the small gold sarcophagi containing the viscera of Tutankhamen, were still visible traces of the name of Smenkhkare. Who can explain why the gold bands binding Tutankhamen's shroud should also have come from Smenkhkare's burial equipment? It is possible that certain

98. Study showing probably Smenkhkare and Meritaten (Ehem. Staat. Mus., Berlin)

pieces of funerary furniture may have been usurped, but it is hard to see why anyone should have chosen for Tutankhamen things so intimately associated with the mummy and viscera of his predecessor, and which the young king, whose treasure was so vast, had no need to steal from a corpse, a sacrilegious act if ever there was one! What motive had prompted the "Divine Father" Ay who was responsible for his burial?

Some light may be shed on the Amarnan problem by solving the enigma of this tomb, at first believed to be that of Queen Tiye. But to the difficulties of

99. *An unfinished Amarnan stele probably depicting the two co-regents Akhenaten and Smenkhkare. Limestone (Staatliche Museen, Berlin)*

interpretating its other contents must be added the major one of identifying the mummy.

For Theodore Davis, the wealthy archaeologist who discovered the tomb in 1907, failed to record the details of his find with the requisite scientific precision. At the time of its discovery, the portrait of Queen Tiye and her son on a gilt wooden panel found in the tomb, and, on preliminary investigation, the feminine shape of the mummy's pelvis, led to the assumption that it was indeed the body of Queen Tiye. This was later disproved when the specialist in royal mummies, Elliot Smith, identified the bones as being those of a man apparently no older than twenty-five, showing signs of hydrocephalus. In 1933, Dr Derry re-examined the skeleton which, since Elliot Smith's verdict, had been accepted as that of Akhenaten. In Dr Derry's view, there was no sign of hydrocephalus, but the platycephalic skull, like that of Tutankhamen, must have been that of a man no more than twenty-three years old. This lent added weight to the theory held by certain archaeologists that the mummy was that of Smenkhkare, Tutankhamen's brother. Since 1947 this view has again been contested and new arguments advanced in favour of the mummy being after all that of Akhenaten. Opinions still remain divided.

100. A statuette thought to be of Smenkhkare (Louvre)

One point however seems beyond doubt: the sarcophagus itself was indeed that of a lady, a royal princess, though not of a queen. It was probably destined for princess Meritaten, Akhenaten's eldest daughter, before her marriage to Smenkhkare. Similarly, the canopic urns used for the king were also originally intended for the princess: the pharaonic serpent had clearly been added to the brow of their wigs. The sarcophagus, too, had been adapted to the personality of its new owner, a king of the heretical period. But which? Smenkhkare or Akhenaten? The inscriptions and the jumbled contents of the tomb do not give us positive evidence of the identity of its last occupant.

To return to the mummy, the very broad and apparently feminine pelvis was an argument in favour of attributing the corpse to Akhenaten. It seemed to call to mind the heretic king whose famous "Osirian statues", erected in the early part of his reign, showed such markedly feminine characteristics. But is this enough? One could use a similar argument to establish the mummy as Smenkhkare's. For this royal corpse showed another anomaly; the position of the arms gave it the attitude of a royal female: the left arm bent on the breast and the right alongside the body. This of course reminds one of everything about Smenkhkare which shocked the first Egyptologists. I therefore suggest that this position may confirm Akhenaten's efforts to transfer to Smenkhkare the mystical role of Nefertiti as half of the royal couple. It would not be too daring to suggest that the young co-regent's limbs were so arranged in death to eternalize the symbolic

168

role that Akhenaten, in his mystic folly, had wished him to play.

The death of Smenkhkare was preceded or followed very closely by that of Akhenaten, probably year 17 of the latter's reign at the earliest, although some authors prefer year 18 or even 21, but this is as doubtful as the king's age when he died. Some say Akhenaten was then forty-seven, but others, the very ones who believe the mummy in Tomb no. 55 to be that of the heretic, agree with the latest medical opinion that he was between twenty-five and twenty-six years old! According to this last theory, which we have mentioned before but do not believe, he would have launched his reform at the age of nine!

The young co-regent may have been buried in the necropolis of the southern city, but not necessarily in the sort of storeroom where Davis found the mummy. On the other hand, no one knows yet where the heretic died. The fragments of his great sarcophagus, discovered in the tomb he was building for himself in the royal necropolis of Akhetaten, show that on its four corners were images of the queen instead of the four tutelary goddesses of Egypt, and that the four sides of the sarcophagus were decorated in high relief by the Globe darting forth its rays. If the king's oath is to be believed, nothing, not even death, would part him from his city, and the only tomb prepared for him was in Tell el Amarna. To bury him elsewhere would therefore mean using an improvised tomb. For lack of evidence, no final conclusion can be reached, but one cannot help wondering about the source of the *ushabti* of Akhenaten which have been appearing sporadically on the market for some years now.

The pharaohs of Amarna, then, both died in the same year. The queen mother, Tiye, "the lady of the empire", must have been buried with great pomp in the Valley of the Kings, and her body probably laid in the burial chamber built for her by Amenophis III in his own tomb; a sepulchre perhaps plundered later and its remaining contents removed to Tomb No. 55 of Thebes.

There remains the most famous and least-known of queens—Nefertiti. One cannot be sure of the date of her death, nor even of a single event of her life, except for her separation from the king and her move to the northern district of the town. It is known that she owned a palace there in which Tutankhamen is frequently mentioned; it is certain that he lived within her orbit for several years and was with her when he married her third daughter Ankhesenpaaten, his niece and also his sister-in-law, who must have been about two years older than himself. In the previous year she had given birth to a daughter by her own father from the marriage contracted when she was eleven.

At Nefertiti's side were the "Divine Father" Ay, her presumed father, and her "Nurse" Tey, the powerful *eminences grises* of the court. Their main preoccupation was to maintain direct succession to the throne, by which they hoped to spare Egypt a religious war or bloodthirsty reprisals against the worshippers of Aten once the heretic was dead. At the death of Amenophis III his frenzied mysticism had broken out, and he had destroyed images of the gods as he had destroyed their priests, so that he was no longer called anything but the "great scoundrel".

Amenophis III's last surviving son, Tutankhaten, was perhaps still resident in the southern city, and his legitimacy was beyond doubt. With such a young child on the throne, the priests of Amun would be enabled to regain their lost power, and, from the time of the old king's death, they had regarded Tutankhaten as the new son of the sun, despite the presence of Akhenaten at Tell el Amarna. This attitude was so generally accepted that even certain foreign rulers preferred to correspond with Tiye, his mother who lived at his court, rather than write to the heretic.

Tutankhaten thus became a pawn in the great game the "Divine Father" Ay was playing. After the funeral of the last heretical sovereign, it was certain that the new king would be crowned at Thebes, where he was entitled to sit on the throne of Horus, since he had done his final duty by his father Osiris, and assured his immortality by the ritual of "the opening of the mouth and the eyes".

The shrewd vizier, Ay, had probably long foreseen the situation and laid his plans accordingly. Amun's priests could not yet rule as absolute masters without the support of the army, which was desperately needed to guard the frontiers and protect Egypt's trade with the whole oriental world. Ay's position as lieutenant-general of the chariotry, the most distinguished corps of the period, gave him great power over the officers, and there is no doubt that he was in tacit agreement with General Horemheb, the official defender of Egypt's possessions in Asia. Ay, while firmly establishing his prince on the throne, was thus in a position to protect the interests of the last and most far-seeing allies of the Amarnan family.

In order to invest the putative pharaoh, aged nine, with at least the appearance of the virility expected of "the Bull of Egypt", the little boy was married to a royal princess whose divine origins had been duly confirmed by her recent marriage to her father. With Ankhesenpaaten married to Tutankhaten, Thebes prepared to crown her new king.

XXXV. *One of the many ushabtis of Tutankhamen, here shown wearing the red crown of the North*

6 At Thebes, Nebkheprure-Tutankhamen, the king who "spent his life making images of the gods"

1352-1343

SINCE TUTANKHATEN'S coronation was vital to the official reinstatement of Amun's supremacy, there was no question of the court moving to Memphis as in the past. Indeed, during his father's life-time, before the break and the departure for Akhetaten, Amenophis IV had also been crowned ("taken the crowns") at Karnak, the Heliopolis of the South.

No doubt after ritual fasting and preliminary purifications, the nine-year-old boy stood by the pylon of the great temple of Karnak, built by his father Amenophis III. Bareheaded, naked to the waist, his feet unshod, he wore only a simple pleated loincloth. He was escorted by the highest dignitaries of the court, foremost among whom were the scribe-general of the army, Horemheb, and the "Divine Father" Ay, lieutenant-general of the chariotry. For days before the ceremony, architects, intendants and innumerable workmen toiled frantically to banish from the temples traces of their humiliation during the persecutions which followed Amenophis III's death, but time was too short and many of the copper-plated and gold-knobbed timber gates which had been ravaged by fire were still unrestored.

The procession had not completely passed the first pylon (now the third) and only the senior officials had followed the prince beyond the first courtyard where the obelisks of his ancestors Tuthmosis I and Tuthmosis III stood. Priests, masked as the gods they impersonated, came to meet him; one of them, Horus of the Horizon, wearing a falcon's mask, took the prince by one hand and led him towards a chapel-screen built by Tuthmosis I in front of the gate of the second (now the fourth) pylon. Ever since the Sesostrian period, this gate-way had been the main entrance of the temple known as *Ipet-esut* and before its magnificent lintel where a statue of Tuthmosis I used to stand beneath the festive double canopy of *Sed* (jubilee), Tutankhamen could have read the inscription recording that the great gate was twenty cubits high and had been hewn from the finest white limestone.

Assisted by another priest, disguised as the god Atum and holding the king's other hand, Tutankhamen performed the first rite of enthronement which led

XXXVI. *Pectoral in gold cloisonné decorated with semi-precious stones and glass-paste: in the centre is the winged scarab, symbol of resurrection*

173

him into a hall of the temple where his body was to undergo a first transformation, and the guiding priests handed him over to others for "purification". The future pharaoh then stepped into the centre of a shallow pool on the low rim of which four priests stood at each of the four cardinal points, recalling the division of the world into four parts according to the ancient liturgy of Heliopolis. Their masks were those of Thoth of the ibis beak, Seth of the curved muzzle and erect square ears, falcon-beaked Horus of Behdet, and another falcon god called Dunawy. They "baptized" the prince, by pouring a lustration over his body from their four tall gold ewers. As soon as it left the vessels the holy water carrying divine life (represented by the hieroglyphs as a cross with a crook and the hound-headed sceptre) modified the nature of the son of kings, who was then deemed fit to appear before the gods.

He was then led to a special part of the sanctuary set aside for coronation rites, possibly known as "the house of the king" and situated between the second and third (now fourth and fifth) pylons in a hall of jubilation in which stood the two vast electrum-plated obelisks erected by Queen Hatshepsut. It contained two rows of papyrus-shaped columns and its walls were partially hidden by "Osirian colossi" dating from the reigns of Tuthmosis III and IV. For the act of coronation which took place there, the essential part of this hall consisted of two basic pavilions (or chapels), reminiscent of the two primitive temples of Egypt: the "house of the flame" (*Per-neser*), the archaic Northern sanctuary, and the "great house" (*Per-wer*), the primitive temple of the South. In the first were the priests impersonating the most august deities, including Nekhabet, Buto, Neith, Isis, Nephthys, Horus, Seth and others completing the Ennead. Their exaltation reached its climax when the young prince entered the southern chapel where Amun's daughter, the snake-goddess, the "great-in-magic" awaited him, raising her expanded royal cobra's hood: she rushed to "embrace" him, as the ritual formula tells us, coiled around his head and raised her own head above his brow. The prince, who had for some years been initiated into the language of serpents, was thus formally acknowledged as the heir to the throne as Amun's invisible hand guided his daughter to the sovereign's face.

Then the priest Inmutef ("pillar of his mother", recalling the assistance rendered by Horus to his mother Isis), wearing a leopard-skin and a wig of plaited hair drawn to one side and ending in a great curl, approached. Aided by his assistants, he placed one after the other upon the head of Amun's chosen one, the many crowns investing him with (and enabling him to assume) all the powers and duties of a pharaoh: the white mitre and red mortar-shaped cap, which together formed a third head-dress known as the Two Powerful Ones or *Pasekhemty*, which the Greeks called *pschent*: the *atef* crown of the god Re, the *seshed* headband, the blue leather crown or *khepresh*, the *ibes* crown, the diadem of two tall plumes, and the various linen wig covers. These sacred objects, the age-old insignia of royalty, were kept in the temple and had eventually to return there: only the headband could be worn by the god's son when he died and was called to rejoin his father. No doubt that is why no crowns or royal

101. Head of the king from a coronation group where the god Amun is placing his hand on Tutankhamen's head-dress (Metropolitan Museum of Art, New York)

headgear were found in the young king's tomb. Perhaps an exception was made for the "crown of office" symbolizing the son of god's supremacy over the earthly realm: the blue leather helmet or crown, the *khepresh*. This may have been placed in the tomb in the hatbox and stolen later by thieves. The king left the chapels wearing this *khepresh* as well as the (giraffe?) tail of the primitive clan chieftains which would henceforth hang from his belt, and sandals upon the soles of which were portrayed the nine defeated hostile peoples.

Now he had to pass through the essential phase of his enthronement, crossing the threshold of the third (now fifth) pylon. Before reaching the fourth (now sixth) pylon, built by Tuthmosis III, he had to turn to the right and be led into a side chapel to the south of the great antechamber in front of the fourth (now sixth) pylon. He was led before a shrine hewn from a single rock of rose granite resting on a sandstone base and flanked to the east and the west by "Osirian colossi". In the eerie gloom of the shrine, dedicated by the warrior king Tuthmosis III and called "Menkheprure-who-takes-the-crowns", Amun confirmed upon the head of Nebkheprure the *khepresh* which gave him sway over all the domains of the sun. The little king kneeling with his back to the lord of Thebes felt the hand of Amun touch the nape of his neck (101).

In a long magico-religious ceremony he received his "great name", consisting of the five "titles" selected by the scribes of the House of Life—the epithets accompanying these titles varied with each king, but their basic elements were immutable. There was first the *Horus* aspect, the earthly incarnation of the god, to describe the new king; then, to express his double nature, the image of the two tutelary goddesses of Egypt, the *vulture* and the *cobra*, whose perpetual reappearance evoked eternity. The third name was that of the *Golden Horus*, the principle of good and of eternal life prevailing over evil and annihilation. Then came the coronation given name, always preceded by the terms "king of the South and of the North" (*Nesut-Byt*). As the god's earthly incarnation, shining from the meridian upon the world of the living, the pharaoh must be above all the embodiment of vitality and dynamic energy. He was "the one of the South" and then only "the one of the North", in that order, not because of early political struggles at the time when the chieftains of Upper Egypt may have founded the monarchy, but because these names had a cosmic and religious significance. Tutankhaten, on his coronation day, therefore, became king of the South and of the North, Nebkheprure ("the master of transformations is Re"). The king's fifth name was his solar name, that of his birth, which in the list of his titles was preceded by the term *Son of the Sun*—Queen Tiye had called him Tutankhaten.

Having acknowledged his son, Amun was then asked to grant him for eternity Re's jubilees and like Horus the accomplishment of his earthly tasks as king.

Preceding the others, the king left the sanctuary with the *aura* of Amun, the Hidden Wind, about him; on his head was the *khepresh*, the royal head-dress worn on almost every royal occasion. He had received it from the god and was certain to dedicate a statue to record this event for the sanctuary—its fragments are in the Metropolitan Museum. But in his tomb, between the golden chapels recalling his coronation, two gold and silver walking sticks were also laid. Those metals, symbolizing flesh and bone, day and night, were designed to perpetuate the image of a nine-year-old king wearing the *khepresh*, which conferred upon him authority over "all that the solar globe circumscribes" (*p.* 136). The prince invested with his powers could now return to the sanctuary and perform the holy office for the first time. He could now appear as a king before all classes of his people and masked priests performed again, in public this time, the coronation scene. Seated upon an ancient throne, he again received the two crowns of the South and the North as the *pschent* was placed upon his head. Before him, priests impersonating the cardinal points or the spirits of the Nile, twined lily and papyrus, the plants of the Two Countries, around a symbolic pillar in the ceremony of the Sma-Tawy (102), after which the king simulated the archaic rite of running round the wall of the sanctuary of Memphis, which represented the whole of the god's domain.

On the eve of their coronation or at the conclusion of the festivities, future kings customarily displayed their hunting prowess—taming wild horses, baiting savage bulls, or wrestling with lions who could not resist them since they themselves were lions. It was impossible to expect such feats from the child-king and

XXXVII*a. The king's pendant in gold cloisonné depicting the vulture-goddess of the South, Nekhabet*
b. Pectoral decorated with the vulture of Upper Egypt. Gold cloisonné inlaid with glass paste

for Tutankhamen's coronation such a show had to be dispensed with; but the unforgettable exploits of his glorious ancestor, Amenophis II, whose arrows pierced several copper targets, and who mastered a lion which became like a lamb in his hands, are recalled on a votive shield in Tutankhamen's tomb (XV), and were probably imitated by certain ritual gestures of the young king's in the temple courtyard.

The king held the two traditional sceptres of the great Osiris, the crook or *heka* of Southern royalty, and the flail or *nekhekh* of the North; in his tomb two sets of sceptres were found, the smaller of which, more suited to the grip of a child, bore the names of Aten (104). Amun had crowned the king at Thebes, but worship of the Globe was not on that account banished from the new sovereign's beliefs. Throughout his reign the name of Aten and that of the Theban god are to be seen, side by side, apparently in harmony, on the king's throne, as well as on his dalmatic and his sceptre for consecrating offerings.

Still wearing his *khepresh* in which he had manifested his divine presence, he returned to the central aisle of the temple and entered the sanctuary of the sun-barge before which the two heraldic pillars of Tuthmosis III appeared to spring from the ground like flowers. After he had passed the hall of offerings, he reached the holy of holies. To "contemplate at last the countenance of the god", he had crossed the great hall of celebration, to arrive before the "gates of heaven" or the "gates of the horizon of Amun". And it was here that, for the first time, he was initiated into the ceremonies of the cult.

After his investiture, he entered a temple courtyard in which, most carefully tended (a replica of that at Heliopolis), grew the sacred persea upon whose miraculous fruit the ibis-headed god Thoth would write his coronation name, that he might enjoy innumerable jubilees (103).

Now invested with full powers, the king of the South and North left the temple once more by way of the great pylon of Amenophis III. Before returning to his palace at Malkata he had to make a public appearance standing in his electrum-plated chariot upon both sides of which had already been engraved the divine titles which he had just received. It was also decorated with the entwined plants of the South and the North. On its body, surrounded by decorative motifs of Asian influence, were cut in relief the vassal peoples of Egypt, kneeling and bound, as if the artists had wished to defend the child-king against evil and ensure the peace of which he was the prime defender (XIX). At the front of the yoke pole, over the rein-holder, was a gilt falcon on top of whose head rested an immense solar disc upon which, in relief, was engraved the king's coronation name.

He drove southward through the many villages of this Theban region, to the great capital of the right bank, the supreme city Nō, probably the most important of all antiquity at that time. The procession came to a halt in the temple of

XXXVIII. *The king's pendant in the form of a boat, showing the symbol of the god's resurrection, flanked by two royal serpents*

102. *"Sma-Tawy", union of the Two Countries for Ramesses II (Abu Simbel)*

103. *The god Thoth, before the god Harakhti, inscribes the coronation name of Ramesses II (Ousirmaat-re-Setepenre) on fruit from the Ished tree (persea) (Abu Simbel)*

Ipet-resyt, the modern Luxor, after wending its way through the dense crowds already sated with the food and drink, distributed since early morning, and singing the praises of the new sovereign of whom it was said that he would restore Thebes to her former prosperity. For the coronation, an amnesty had been declared, religious differences set aside and even many convicts released from prison—Thebes had not known such rejoicing in seventeen years.

Back at Malkata, Tutankhaten and his young wife prepared for their return to the northern district of Akhetaten where Nefertiti awaited them, anxious to learn from the "Divine Father" Ay how successful the official encounter with Amun's priests had been. During this time Ay and Horemheb had ordered the immediate consecration in Amun's domain of a black granite group stressing Tutankhaten's right to the throne of his ancestors, which Amun had just bestowed on him, and in the Karnak workshops a great effigy of Amun (now in the Louvre), showing his characteristic motor-shaped cap with the two tall plumes and their seven ritual sections was being carved. The god held Tutankhaten, standing before him, by the shoulders, the king wearing a leopard-skin in which he had attended the royal funeral. The statue constituted a vigorous statement of Tutankhaten's legitimate right to rule—divine, because granted by Amun. Perhaps the remains of a garment found in the tomb sewn with tiny stars like the spots on the pelt of an animal of the cat family, with a gilt wooden cheetah's head attached to it, was the one he had worn when, child

180

though he was, he officiated as the last scion of the royal family in the role of the *Setem* priest at the funeral of his predecessor. His great-uncle Aanen had worn a similar vestment (shown in the statue at Turin) at the funeral of Thuya and Yuya when they were permanently buried in the Valley of the Kings.

Ay accompanied Tutankhaten to Akhetaten where, as his tutor, he soon became vizier, which enabled him to speak in the king's name. Since the young king was now set on the path of Amunite orthodoxy, Horemheb seems to have decided upon more regular residence in Thebes, which he apparently ruled as the king's lieutenant, a sort of viceregent, at the head of the country. His army career seems to have been successful more through diplomacy and astuteness than through dazzling feats of arms. In his own coronation inscription he alludes to powers vested in him by the king himself (whom we must probably take to be Tutankhaten's predecessor) and enlarges upon the part he played at court when discord (or madness?) prevailed. "He had but to open his mouth and answer the king to calm him with his speech." Could this be an allusion to Akhenaten's last years and the mystical madness into which he seems to have sunk? We learn further that Horemheb acted as viceregent of the Two Countries over a number of years, during which he enjoyed an uncontested authority that some Egyptologists do not hesitate to qualify as dictatorial.

One can hardly imagine the life of a young and probably frail boy called upon at the age of nine to wear such a heavy crown. He was taken to the garden city where his young queen awaited him, surrounded by the flowers and the romantic, almost morbid, charm of an isolated court at which it was forbidden even to mention the name of its dead creator, whose heresy was now condemned on all sides. What can the child's conception of Amun and Aten have been? What was he to think after the pomp of his coronation, and the obsequiousness of the Theban priests in the solemn and grandiose city of temples in Karnak, when he found himself once more in the solar chapels or visited the almost deserted temples of Aten? What he had heard decried only a few years before, he now had to accept as the power to which he owed his own sudden transformation into a living god.

Although apparently he kept his name of Tutankh*aten*, at least in Tell el Amarna, during his first few years as king, he was already being called Tutankh-*amen*, as he had been called at the time of his enthronement in Amun's great temple. In the heretical city where there are traces of his presence in objects he owned and inscriptions mentioning him, there is evidence that he sacrificed or prayed to a whole pantheon: Isis, Atum and the god Shed were revered; Amun and Mut received his offerings of flowers (stele now in the Berlin Museum). It is beyond doubt that he lived in Akhetaten at that time, but no palace bearing his name has been found. He may have lived in that of his wife, Ankhesenpaaten, or on one of the great estates with palaces dedicated to royal ancestors, such as Tuthmosis I whose coronation name was *Aakheperkare*. More likely the latter, which is mentioned in Tell el Amarna as his residence, and not the building in Memphis of the same name mentioned during the reign of Ay. It was also probably thought desirable to strengthen the young king's influence in Thebes before installing him at Memphis, Horemheb's favourite city, where while still a general he had already built his own tomb.

The solemn inscription on a tall quartzite stele (now in the Cairo Museum), intended for the north-east corner of the great pillared hall at Karnak (a copy of which was also erected in the temple of Amenophis III, north of the great temple) recalled the name of the king's palace at Tell el Amarna at the time when he was persuaded to order the restoration of the temples, cult and clergy of all Egypt (105). The programme was grandiose and indeed worthy of a king, and was defined by Horemheb who composed the text. On the stele, too, in its arched top, were representations of the young sovereign, twice repeated, making offerings and libations to the divine couple of Karnak, Amun and Mut. In the inscription which tells of his own coronation Horemheb declares himself the author of the plan, and when he later usurped the young king's stele and replaced the names of his predecessors by his own, he was, after all, only giving credit where it was due.

Horemheb speaking in the young king's name, announced that after his coronation, joyfully accepted by the country, he was now in his palace in the domain of Tuthmosis I, at Tell el Amarna, and must congratulate himself upon the works he had undertaken as soon as he was crowned. He would suppress evil in all the land and cause the ruins to "flower again" and become once more "monuments of eternity". This would be an immense task as there was not one temple in good condition from Elephantine to the confines of the delta. The shrines had fallen into desolation and weeds grew over the monuments; sanctuaries and halls were used as public footpaths. The country had been wretched since the gods abandoned it: when an army was despatched to Djahy (generic term for Syria) "to extend the frontiers of Egypt", it failed miserably and the gods were deaf to all entreaties.

The situation was desperate. "Meditating in his heart" as to what might please his father Amun, he had decided to build him an "august image of pure gold" inlaid with lapis-lazuli and all sorts of rare and precious stones—the largest ever to be made since it would have to be carried "on thirteen stretchers" and no statue yet made of the god had required more than eleven. He had also decided to make a slightly smaller one for the god Ptah of Memphis but this would only require eleven stretchers. He also undertook to rebuild the sanctuaries, setting up foundations for the offerings. But this was not all—he had to re-establish the clergy and select its new members from the core of the nobility which he said had remained the elite of the country:

"he gathered in priests and prophets, children of the notables of their towns, each the son of an eminent man whose name is known; then he endowed the temple with treasures and filled the warehouses with slaves, male and female."

He then turned his attention to the god's barges which were to be rebuilt of prime quality cedarwood, and he vowed to gold-plate them so that they might again illuminate the river. This would again require male and female workers

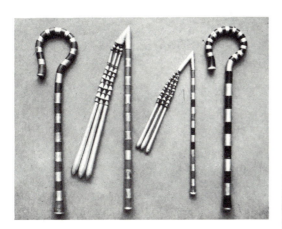

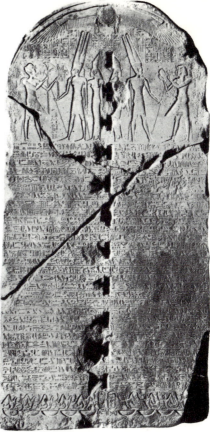

104. The king's two sets of sceptres: the smaller set bears the name of Aten and the larger the name of Amun

105. Stele of the "Restoration of the Theban temples" appropriated by Horemheb. It shows signs of having been intended for re-use (Cairo Museum)

and singers, who would be paid out of the royal coffers. This programme was carried out for the delight of the gods and goddesses of the country, whose favour the king acquired, for his deeds filled them with delight. A flourishing era began. The gods repaid the king a hundredfold, and "Amun loved better then ever his son Nebkheprure, Lord of Karnak, Tutankhamen, him who satisfies all the gods".

The vast scale of these undertakings shows the extent of Horemheb's determination to restore order and reinstate the clergy in all its prerogatives. Just as the traditional religious machinery was again set in motion, so the normal activities of the country were to be resumed according to a set course. Young as the king was at that time—probably about twelve years old—it was not desirable that he should continue to live in the city of the Globe, far from the active life of the country and utterly remote from the dynastic sanctuaries. Of course, there was no question of persecuting or suppressing Aten: the king was expected to relegate him to the secondary and innocuous role he had played before the heresy. But to do so Tutankhaten had definitely to abandon the ephemeral capital. Although some of his furniture, such as the throne of his youth, bore the name of Tutankh*amen*, the principal scenes upon its back were dominated by the heretical Globe with the tiny hands at the end of each ray. The king's name had permanently to be stabilized, and from year 4 of his reign he

106. Tutankhamen's hat- or wig-box   107. The king's "camp bed": a. as it was found

was to be known exclusively as Tutankhamen, in order that Thebes might once more see in her king the confirmed son of the imperial god. It was at the end of year 4 that, leaving Akhetaten where Nefertiti had died, accompanied by his young wife (henceforth to be called Ankhesenamun), the king became Tutankhamen and probably never revisited the heretical city. The royal barges were loaded with much of the beautiful furniture in the Amarnan style which reflected some of the poetic brilliance of Akhenaten's dream-city. Some of the pieces found in Tutankhamen's tomb may have accompanied him on this return voyage to Thebes: a wig-box (106), a folding bed (107), and of course the triangular lidded chest, an ancestor of the present-day chest-of-drawers, which for convenience was carried on two poles serving as a sort of stretcher (*p.* 58).

The palace he chose to live in has not been identified with any certainty, but he would have preferred Malkata which he had known as a very young child. Like all Egyptian sovereigns he must have had official residences in other cities, and it is easy to imagine the luxury of the royal palaces renovated for the young king's visits, which were organized with great pomp and ceremony by the "Divine Father" Ay. From the outset of his reign the main object of these visits was to start restoring the temples and reviving the worship of the gods, which simultaneously reaffirmed the salutary role of the crown. Memphis, where an Apis bull was buried during the young king's reign; Medinet Ghurab, where Tutankhamen seems to have added his stone to the temple of Tuthmosis III; Abydos; the Faiyum—all were visited by Pharaoh. Though he did not desert the god of the heresy, Aten, and continued to add to his temple at Karnak itself, he did however, on the advice of Ay, revive the tradition of his ancestors who particularly revered the great sphinx at Giza. At that time Egypt extended her hospitality to many foreign gods; the Asians, for instance, worshipped Haurun, whose name was soon associated with Horus-in-the-Horizon, Harmakhis of the necropolis, the king-maker-sphinx. Traces of inscriptions show that Tutankhamen and Ankhesenamun had made sacrifices to this god on the Giza plateau.

b. unfolded

Naturally, however, the young king was urged to devote most of his efforts to Thebes. The ruins of Karnak, so often sacked and troubled by revolutions, wars and rebuilding, let alone earthquakes, have not yet yielded up all the evidence of that period. But scattered blocks and architectural fragments even from the interior of the pylons convey some idea of what was being built in Tutankhamen's name, and of what his successor Ay added. The latter adhered so closely to the original plan that the cartouches of the two kings, found near one another, even encouraged the belief that there had been a third co-regency at the end of the heretical epoch.

Tutankhamen's buildings grew apace, and, as we know, his mentors did not hesitate after his death to take the credit for them—often the names of Ay and of Horemheb conceal the young king's cartouches. At Luxor, although Horemheb's signature replaces most of those of his predecessors, there is no mistaking the royal features of Tiye's son on the two interior walls of the famous bell-shaped colonnade began by Amenophis III.

Tutankhamen's contribution to the Theban temple provides us with some most vivid and important information. Perhaps there too it was the young king's personal wish to honour the god he had been taught to regard as pre-eminent, which caused him to endow the temple with a permanent image in stone of Amun's most beautiful feast. Every year in the month of Paophi, the second month of the floods, came the period of eleven days during which the capital celebrated the feast of Opet. Ipet(Opet)-resyt was the name given to the temple at Luxor which nowadays is considered to be the god's harem, but this is a dubious interpretation. Ipet(Opet)-esut was the name of the temple at Karnak. At any rate, it was to this temple that Amun and his spouse Mut, accompanied by the god Khonsu proceeded ceremonially at the time of this "divine emergence", giving the crowd a glimpse of the triad of its three great gods. With the return of the royal family to Thebes, the feast of Opet recovered its lustre, and the majestic and festive spectacle it provided on the banks of the Nile and round

the temples so impressed Tutankhamen, that he had all its phases sculpted on the inner walls of the portico at the eastern and western limits of his father's colonnade.

The western wall was devoted to an evocation of the procession from Karnak to Luxor, following a north-south axis; on the eastern wall was the return of the procession from south to north to its point of departure. On the Nile a full flotilla including the king's boat prepared to escort the sacred barges of the Theban gods. Before leaving the temple Tutankhamen himself performed the first rites of the ceremony, sprinkling a libation over flowers and other offerings, and blessing them with incense (108). The procession then left the temple to strains of military music, escorting the priests who bore, shoulder-high, tiny sacred boats containing the chapels of the gods, which in turn were to be borne by great river barges. The king walked to his own vessel and gave the signal of departure for the whole fleet which was then towed southward by sailors on the towpath, preceded by their pennants, and urged on by musicians and singers. The banks, of course, were lined with admiring and applauding crowds, the holiday spirit prevailed, and the young king so enjoyed the popular riverside songs that, as was the custom in the heretical city, he had them inscribed on the temple walls beside the pictorial record of the splendid pageant:

> There is a welcoming inn,
> Its awning facing south;
> There is a welcoming inn,
> Its awning facing north;
> Drink, sailors of the pharaoh,
> Beloved of Amun,
> Praised of the gods.

XXXIX*a. The king's pectoral made up of the sacred eye flanked by the serpent-goddess of the North and the vulture-goddess of the South. Gold cloisonné with glass-paste*
 b. Pectoral decorated with the winged scarab protected by the two goddesses Isis and Nephthys. Gold cloisonné with glass-paste

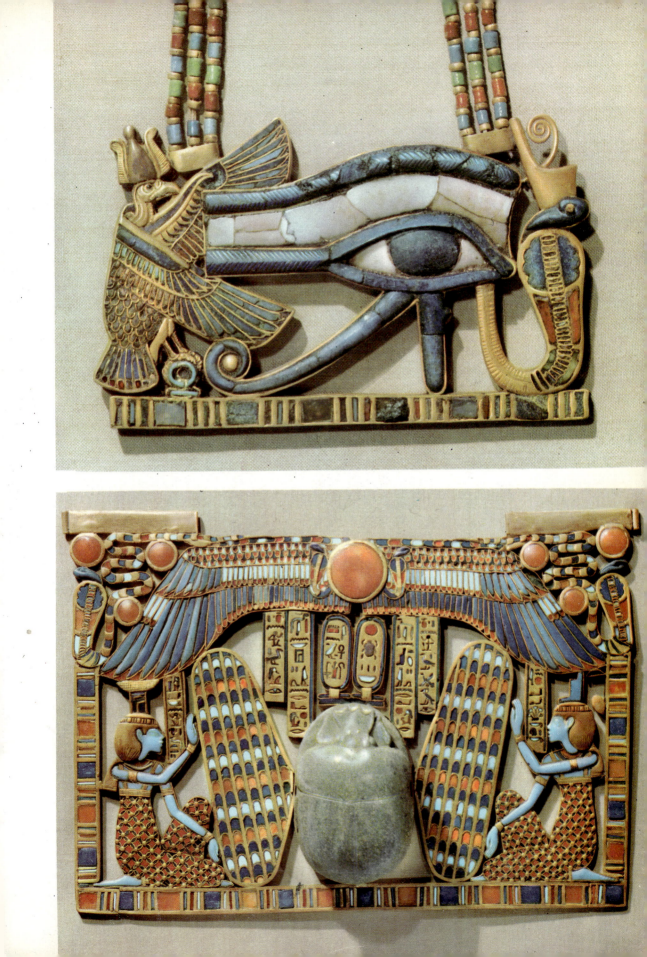

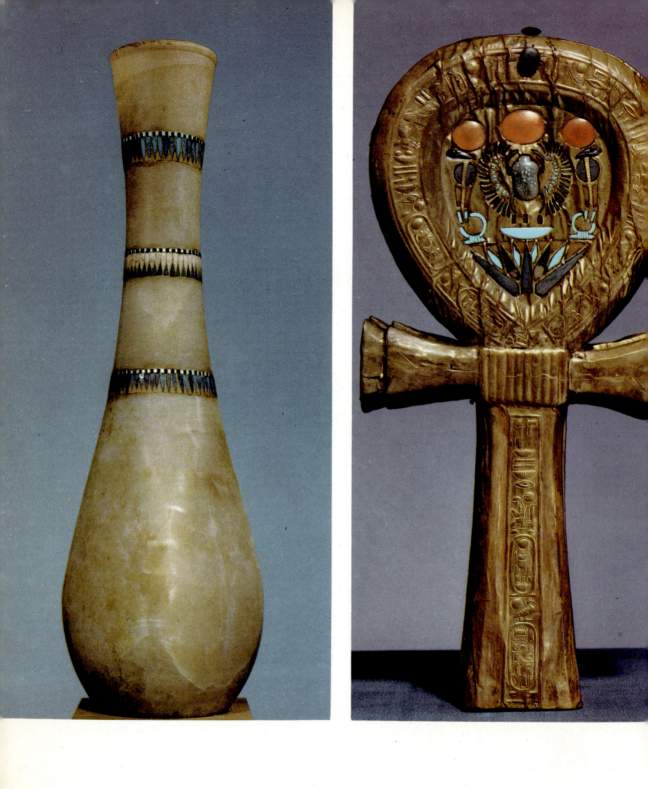

109. Procession of fat oxen during the great feast of Opet

During the voyage from Karnak to Luxor, the king had symbolically to seize an oar to show that he was assuming full responsibility for his journey on his father the god's behalf. Soon Amun's great barge, called *Woserhet-Amun*, tied up at Luxor, and the god's small barque was carried in a great procession to the temple. The priests struggled to force a passage between the heaped tables of offerings, overflowing with food, and the vendors' temporary stalls set up around the temple esplanade. During one pause the king stopped to watch with amusement some female acrobats as they danced to the rhythm of the sistrum, the castanet, and the eternal *darabukka*. But this childish frivolity had to be cast aside as the procession wound onward to enter the temple by the pylon and vanish from the eyes of the crowd. Then the real holiday began for the people, and until dawn songs and popular concerts echoed through the narrow streets of the southern city.

Eleven days later the river parade retraced its course northward. Tutankhamen had returned to Luxor to fetch his god whose barge, this time, would not be towed. The fat oxen—welcome gifts of the Nubian grandees—whose twisted horns were treated as fantastic ornaments even on the beasts themselves, had been sacrificed close to the temple, ensuring that the current, extremely strong at the time of the floods, would bear the barges swiftly down to Karnak (109). The king, at the head of his troops, which included foreign auxiliaries, would escort them along the banks at the river's own pace. This concluded the festivities, which would be echoed thousands of years later in European carnivals, and indeed by the annual procession of the local saint's barge, Abu el Haggag, that takes place to this day between Karnak and Luxor (110).

Not all the ceremonies the little king had to attend were so enjoyable, but he

XL*a. Alabaster vase with a long neck inlaid with floral garlands*
 *b. Mirror-case found in a large coffer. In the form of the sign
   of life, it is made of gilt wood inlaid with glass-paste*

110. The procession during the present-day feast of the Moslem saint, Abu el Haggag

dutifully played his royal part. As soon as he had been crowned, he had been asked to approve the site selected on the left bank of Thebes for his funerary temple, and on the day the priests demarcated the outline of the foundations with string he came to make the ceremonial act of foundation. He then had to appoint the staff of this domain, some members of which already ministered to his father's funerary property, such as Woserhet, "accountant of all good things of the house of Nebmaetre", who was named "first prophet in the house of Nebkheprure".

Few Egyptian kings ascending the throne as young have left their mark by so many foundations in a limited number of years. In the region of Thebes statues of Amun with Tutankhamen's features sprang up everywhere. The sovereign himself was depicted within the circle of the gods, and the most moving of these portraits is a trio of Karnak (now in the Cairo Museum) showing the adolescent wearing the *atef* crown, standing between Amun and Mut, who have their arms on his shoulders, and the young king clasping them round the waist and gently urging them forward (111).

There is a complete return to Amunite dogma in these portrayals, and if the faintly morbid grace of the divine and royal features inevitably reflect the aesthetics of the period, the themes treated are once more severely traditional. On these official statues the royal spouse is never shown, and the king alone appears in the company of the gods. In one case only, at Karnak, did Tutankh-

190

amen erect a monument, framing a doorway, of Amun and Amunet, which may have been a discreet allusion to the royal couple.

The close bonds linking the Amarnan family to Nubia seem to have endured throughout Tutankhamen's reign, and the temple founded by Amenophis III at Kawa, then Gem-Aten, in the region of the third cataract, was the object of renewed attentions from the time of Tutankhamen's accession. The cult of Amun and of Atum, the sun god of Heliopolis which had been practised there, was revived. The king himself, both forms of whose name (mentioning both Aten and Amun) are still there, is depicted offering flowers to Amun-Re after exulting in the rehabilitation of his father's monuments. Thus Tutankhamen carried his great scheme for restoring all the empire's sanctuaries as far as Nubia and built a small temple there, with a four-columned courtyard, later usurped by Ramesses II. Gem-Aten (or Gempaaten) had its own governor, "scribe of the temple in the house of Re", "pasha of Gem-Aten:" Panakht. Faras, south of Abu Simbel, on the east bank was another very important foundation by Tutankh-amen in Nubia. This centre must have been in close touch with the temple at Kawa, and their respective officials paid each other numerous visits. The most picturesque was at the time when the fat oxen were to be despatched to the

III. The "trio" composed of Amun, Mut and Tutankhamen who appears here as the divine son (Cairo Museum)

metropolis for the feast of Opet. The "children of the *Kap*", remembering their upbringing at the court of Egypt, undertook themselves to select the tribute to be delivered to the viceroy. Khai, "superintendent of the lands of the South" under Tutankhamen, had himself portrayed taking part in this ceremony on a wall of the temple at Kawa. No doubt it is he who appears at Faras as first prophet of the deified King Nebkheprure (Tutankhamen).

On this side, too, the king erected a sanctuary for Amun-Re, Atum and Re Harakhti, but it is noteworthy that this temple was mainly dedicated to the king himself as lord of the city. In antiquity the township was called Sehotep-Neteru, "he who appeases or contents the gods", and these terms figure in the young king's formal titles as an epithet of one of his five names. It would not be surprising if Tiye's Nubian origins were eventually traced to the region of Faras. At any rate, during the king's lifetime an image of him in divine form was made there, adopting a custom endorsed by his father Amenophis III when he ordered an image of himself as a god to be made for his temple of Soleb, further south.

Faras was the headquarters of the viceroy of Nubia, and among Tutankhamen's contemporaries we should mention his viceroy Huy, the paintings in whose tomb give us a comprehensive account of provincial administration in Egypt's southern possessions. The sister (possibly the wife?) of this senior official, Taemwadjsi, seems to have been the first lady in the social and official life of Egyptian Nubia at the time, as her titles conclusively prove. Not only did she more or less deputise for her brother in the temple of Faras, but she was also the "matron of the harem" of Tutankhamen! This probably means that she recruited the handsomest girls of Nubia to brighten court life at Thebes. The magnificent paintings of Huy's tomb show some of the pretty princesses his sister charged him to escort to the metropolitan capital (112).

During the XVIIIth Dynasty, the southern province of Nubia extended to the district of Napata in the Sudan of today and included two distinct regions. The first began near the town of Hierakonpolis, south of Thebes, and ended near the second cataract: the land of Wawat or Lower Nubia. The other, Higher Nubia, or the Land of Kush, reached to Karoy. The viceroy, whose importance was even greater now that Nubia had become an associate of Egypt and a thoroughfare for the traffic of African produce toward the Mediterranean, was seconded by two deputy-governors or lieutenants, each in charge of a province. From a graffito in the little rock chapel of Ellesiya, facing Aniba, the modern capital of Egyptian Nubia we have the name of Amunemipet, one of Nubia's two lieutenants under Tutankhamen. Upon being appointed, the viceroy was greeted in his Nubian capital, Sehotep-Neteru (Faras) by senior officials led by his two lieutenants bearing offerings of food and bags of gold-dust. With them were the

XLIa. *Funerary headrest in opaque blue glass-paste. Gold frieze decorated with two recurring signs of divine life*
b. *Folding headrest in painted ivory decorated with the two heads of the protective spirit Bes*

mayor of Khaemmaet, Soleb, in charge of Amenophis III's great temple; the mayor of the town in which he was to reside, his namesake Huy; the first prophet of the temple of Tutankhamen in that city, accompanied by the second prophet, Mermose; the priests of the temple, and, naturally, the lieutenant of the fortified garrison of the town, Penno.

Huy, the new viceroy, son of a high official under Amenophis III and a faithful, although much older, friend of the young king's, was born of an ancient and noble local family. At the outset of his career he may already have served under Merimose, Amenophis III's viceroy in Nubia, as "scribe of the correspondence", and his knowledge of the country was extensive. His diplomatic duties, dating from the beginning of the reign, in the capacity of the "sovereign's messenger in all foreign lands" had brought him prestige, and given him above all great insight into the human mind. When he was sent to Nubia, he already wielded exclusive power at court since, in addition to his rank of "Divine Father" he was also one of the "fan-bearers on the king's right", "intendant of Amun's cattle in the Land of Kush" and "intendant of the lands of gold of the lord of the Two Countries". To this was added an aura of glory probably acquired during the disappointing battles waged by the pharaoh's troops in the rebellious possessions of Asia at the end of the heretical reign; he bore the title of "his majesty's brave in the cavalry".

For the installation of his viceroy the king decreed the most elaborate ceremonial over which he himself presided in his palace, seated on the ancestral throne under a canopy. He was formally dressed in a great robe of pleated linen, wearing the *khepresh* helmet and holding in one hand both the crook and the flail of royalty; in the other he held the sign of life. This official regalia was completed by a long animal tail and sandals. He appeared on a platform below which a very simple scene took place in the great throne-room: Huy was led in wearing his pleated robe and carrying the flail, attribute of one of his functions. Escorting him, bowing low, were the members of his court. Speaking in the king's name, the "head of the treasury" welcomed Huy with these words: "[The region] from Nekhen (Hierakonpolis) to Nesut-Tawy (Napata) has been handed over to you." Huy replied: "May Amun of Nesut-Tawy grant all that you have commanded, my lord sovereign." Whereupon the courtiers echoed in chorus: "You are the son of Amun, O Nebkheprure, may he send you the chiefs of all foreign lands bearing choice goods from all their countries."

The introduction and speech of welcome were followed by Huy's investiture with the gold ring of office. Although the inscription accompanying this scene is very worn, the vizier Ay seems to be mentioned in it, and may well himself have handed the viceroy his seal (113).

Huy now left the palace with his two sons, one of whom was "master of the horse", Pesiur. He carried bunches of flowers in both hands and received an

XLII. *Head of a "dummy" of the young Tutankhamen, wearing a compromise between the crown of the kings of Lower Egypt and the head-dress of Nefertiti. Stuccoed and painted wood*

112. Procession of the young Nubian princes in the tomb of Huy, viceroy of Nubia

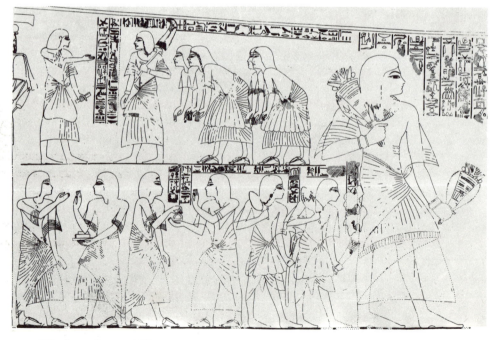

113. The investiture of Huy

ovation from the administrative officials, the *rudus*, or civil servants who were to work under him in Nubia. His attendants, employees and the crews of his barges, praised him loudly, waving flowers and leafy branches, and escorted him to the temple of Amun where he gave thanks. On leaving the sanctuary, Huy was to sail for Nubia to take up his appointment. His fine barge was ready, very similar to the king's vessel. It had a large central cabin, decorated in warm colours, just forward of which were the boxes where the thoroughbreds were already quartered (114). Fore and aft were cabins adorned with images of the four Horuses of Nubia. The hull itself showed the pharaoh as a sphinx vanquishing a Negro. All Huy's family was on the quayside—his two sons, his mother, the lady Wenher, and the women of his household led by a singer of Amun. There was dancing for the viceroy's departure, and the vessel weighed anchor as soon as the last gifts and provisions for the voyage had been loaded.

Settled in his Nubian headquarters, Huy at once set about collecting the taxes. The court, much impoverished by the heretical king's experiments, had chosen this administrator with particular care, for his shrewdness and high repute were well known, and swift results were expected from his appointment. The choice was indeed justified: he was to be seen everywhere, inspiring new confidence in the peasantry and the workmen, organizing expeditions to the mines and supervising cattle-breeding. He sent emissaries to the extreme south to urge the hunters of elephant, giraffe and panther to greater efforts. He had ebony and mahogany cut and shipped down between the cataracts along the Nile. He exploited every resource of Sudan and Nubia to the full, and relying

114. Huy's river boat

115. *Huy paying homage to his sovereign, Tutankhamen*

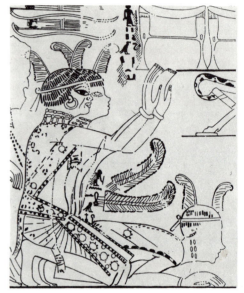

116. *Hiknefer, the prince of Aniba in Nubia, accompanied by two of his compatriots, paying homage to the viceroy*

117. *Tutankhamen's folding stool, probably of Nubian workmanship*

118. *Nubian tributes being presented to the viceroy*

on the authority of the Nubian nobles who had been brought up at the pharaoh's court, he established so stable a government that even art flourished and gold-smiths and cabinet-makers produced some real masterpieces. If a small rebellion broke out in a remote village, Huy was instantly informed and the "lost sheep" at once put to work in the prisons.

He was aided by a tried team of officials: the scribe Kha and the "accountant scribe of the gold", Harnefer; and he also placed great trust in the "chief of the stables", Hati. Soon the vice-regal palace received men and occasionally women bearing gold tribute, sometimes in rings, and sometimes in the form of gold-dust in small bags. Watched over by the viceroy, sceptre in hand, the revenue was counted, weighed in the scales presided over by the god Thoth, and registered by the scribes. Huy was soon in a position to inform the king that he would shortly proceed to Thebes with all the tribute of the South. Loaded to the gunwales, the many boats and barges amounting to a veritable fleet escorted him down the Nile in the most picturesque water procession. From the banks one could see the stalled cattle, the roped bundles of exotic produce, and guess at the piles of gold in the cabins under military guard. It was also known that princes and princesses of Wawat and Kush sat sheltered by awnings on the bridge of one splendid vessel. On the cabin roofs squatted rebels whose ardour had cooled in jail and who, with their wives and children, were going to Thebes where they would be employed as servants in noble households.

For weeks Tutankhamen had been impatiently awaiting the arrival of these wonders which had suddenly filled his life with new interest. Dressed somewhat as he had been for his coronation, he was to sit once more under the canopy with the lotus-shaped columns from which, in the fashion of the day, hung a frieze of stylized bunches of grapes. Over the cornices were rows of sacred serpents with solar discs resting on their heads. The base of his throne was entirely covered with a frieze of birds with human hands, symbolizing conquered vassals in abject adoration of the lord of the land. The canopied platform had been set up in the main palace courtyard, as an impressive procession and much produce were expected. Huy, holding the flail as well as the crook—one of the emblems of Southern royalty and the main attribute of the vice-regal office—was to conduct the grandees of Kush in person to make their offering to Pharaoh. These princes, however, were preceded by those of Wawat, first among whom was the prince of Miam, Hiknefer, "child of the Kap" and an old schoolfellow of Tutankhamen's. He prostrated himself before the king, as did the two princes with him, who also wore the official dress of the chiefs of Wawat: a pelt hanging down the back, and two ostrich plumes set in a short wig and held in place by a white headband (116). They presented the pharaoh with superbly wrought furniture, eminently fit for his palace, folding stools of precious woods with fur cushions (117), armchairs, beds, shields covered in animal skin, and bows and arrows. At his feet their attendants laid gold rings and bags of gold-dust, cornelian heaped up in bowls, jasper, elephant tusks, ebony boomerangs and even a gold-plated chariot (118). There were also a golden shrine and a master-

119. *The work of Nubian gold-smiths*

piece of Nubian craftmanship—a sort of stool upon which a long tray held a complete representation in gold of a characteristic landscape of Wawat, centred around a sort of pyramidal hut, surrounded by trophies. In a forest of date palms with tall clusters of leaves, two giraffes reached up to the fruit, and Nubian figures gave life to the foreground. Below the tray hung animal skins and rectangular panels adorned with gold discs. It was the pride of the Nubian goldsmiths, their finest achievement (119). Two other similar but smaller pieces were also presented to the king.

The Wawat chieftains were followed by a young Nubian princess and princes, with very delicate features, in Egyptian dress but adorned with the Nubian tassel-earrings and wild-cats' tails tied to their arms. Their servants followed bearing yet more gold and more animal skins, and escorting an ox-drawn cart in which rode a very handsome princess with a parasol to shield her from the sun, and a young female slave as driver. She was indeed a beauty worthy of the pharaoh's harem, and the special choice of the lady Taemwadjsi. With her she brought slaves still in manacles, followed by their pendulous-breasted wives, surrounded by children, the smallest of whom hung on their backs in leather sacks. The princes of Kush also sent ahead piles of gold and red jasper; they raised their hands to Pharaoh in respectful greeting, and knelt before him. Two rows of their attendants, laden with gold rings, animal skins and giraffe-tails, possibly destined to adorn the royal loincloth, followed them. There was also a giraffe, and some of those astonishing fat oxen of the Kush countryside whose curiously-shaped horns were a feature of masquerades (120), as for instance during the feast of Opet, when false hands were tied to the ends of the horns and a dummy head placed between them. When the animals lowered their heads, the

200

120. Nubian tributes presented to the viceroy

whole of Nubia bowed to the king. At the end of the procession, the viceroy turned again to his master and lowered his flail before him in token of homage and gift offering (115).

Tutankhamen had maintained a dignified attitude throughout the ceremony and his interest had not flagged for a moment. The spectacle enthralled him. He was eager to descend from the platform and actually touch all the entrancing objects, and talk to the Nubian princes with whom he had so much in common. He was not accompanied by the queen any more than on other official occasions. The archaic protocol, from which Amenophis III had earlier freed himself by insisting upon having Tiye by him on all formal occasions, had been restored.

The viceroy had been successful, and the royal treasury was greatly enriched: it would now be possible once more to cast gold statues of Ptah and Amun. The last phase of the ceremony now took place in the courtyard where Tutankhamen rewarded his representative with a profusion of gold necklaces which entirely covered the viceroy's neck and breast. When the latter left the palace to return home his household greeted him with cries of joy, waving leafy branches and shaking rattles.

These diversions at the Theban court came all too seldom for the young king whose difficult profession he was learning from the two imperial officers, Horemheb and Ay. Of the two, he seems to have been fonder of the latter, who was probably his great-uncle. At the palace, Ay seems to have been the epitome of power itself, and nothing could be undertaken without his express agreement. This was officially recognized to such an extent that he did not hesitate to have himself portrayed in ritualistic royal scenes, in an unexpected place, and quite against all the rules. A fragment of decorated gold found in the first cache of Tutankhamen confirms this: he stands in the place of Amun—or Re—before his young master Tutankhamen, who, holding his *harpee* (Syrian war sickle),

121. A fragment of a sheet of gold showing Tutankhamen, escorted by his wife, performing a ritual act in the presence of the "Divine Father" Ay (Cairo Museum)

makes the traditional gesture of annihilating Egypt's enemies. For once Queen Ankhesenamun escorts her husband, and is shown behind him during the ceremony. But Ay's boldness in thus usurping the place of the supreme god was quite without precedent (121).

It was already some time since the little king had been initiated into the ceremonial of the cult of which he had officially become the high pontiff. He knew when to take his place on the massive rectangular throne copied from the seats of the earliest kings; he understood the protective virtues of the wild animals depicted with tied limbs upon the seat of his stool, and knew that when he used the armless liturgical chair with its folding base, that as supreme pontiff he must be flanked by the flail and ostrich-feather fans (123); he knew the magic part played by the skull-crushing sceptre adorned with sacrificial animals, and that the mere touch of this sacred object converted the tangible goods of this world into divine offerings (122). When he was handed the tall crook, carved with a Negro and an Asian reduced to impotence by the bonds of servitude, he knew that dragging their bodies in the dust established an invisible barrier around his frontiers protecting them from invasion (XVIII).

The sun had not been removed from the galaxy of gods he was required to worship—far from it. Indeed, a favourite ring of the little king's with probably the most elaborate bezel known, which was buried with him, showed upon an oval flanked by the vulture and Horus spreading their wings, the kneeling king between the images of two baboons capped with the lunar disc, and worshipping the falcon-headed sun-god Horus upon his throne (xxvb).

With Tutankhamen's accession the expression of the dogma was to be re-interpreted, since the path laid down by the heretic was not to be followed. However, the last players in the Amarnan drama had been so closely concerned with the reform that the new religious attitudes which they had absorbed were too deeply implanted to allow a complete return to the past. A point to note in this context was the celebration of the cult with its final act in which the god

123. Tutankhamen's fan

122. Tutankhamen's sceptre used for consecrating offerings

was offered his beloved daughter Maet—Equipoise, Law and the Breath of Life.

The heretic's interpretation of this symbol was slightly different: when the Globe shone in splendour it received the supreme offering of the daily sacrifice. The king and queen, instead of raising to the creator the tiny crouching statuette of Maet, wearing an ostrich-feather on her head, presented to the god not his divine daughter, but the emanation of the god himself in the form of his names, contained in two cartouches. On either side, however, the princesses wearing three plumes on their heads were reminders of the goddess Maet. When the queen took part in the ceremony, she was depicted crouching on either side of the cartouches she held up. Then the god showed himself over the altar, giving life with his all-powerful breath, symbolized by the almost horizontal position of the windswept ribbons at the back of the royal headgear.

How could these rites possibly be carried out after the return to orthodoxy? In Tutankhamen's burial treasure, between the golden chapels and amongst the furnishings closely linked with the monarchy, was a box which the diggers described as an "unguent container", carved in the shape of a double cartouche (XIII). Its shape and decoration are highly evocative and we might well consider it as the object used by Tutankhamen in the celebration of sacrificial rites.

Rather than being a proof of total rejection of the religious reform, it seems to suggest the process of adaptation which must have taken place. First of all the goddess Maet of the classical ritual is no longer shown, but is replaced by the double cartouche of the heretical cult. She is, however, still present in the form of two tall ostrich plumes, flanking the disc over each of the sacred rings. Within the cartouches, on both sides, the king's coronation name is illustrated by hieroglyphs for the sun (*Re*) and the basket (*neb*), but replaced in the case of the scarab (*kheper*) by images of the little king crouching. On one side is a boy with the curl of childhood, on the other the same boy in the same attitude wearing the royal *khepresh*. On this liturgical object the king's name probably replaces that of the god: the god's son is now presented as an offering for the supreme sacrifice. This is not the only example among the elements of the royal treasure to suggest an affinity with Christian liturgy and the symbolic pomp which still encompasses a pope. But it was the first time in Egypt that the king, son of the god, offered up his own name to the god. After Tutankhamen, the precedent was established and later Ramesses II was to adopt this innovation as his own.

When the court returned to settle in the capital, a new trend developed in Theban art. At its peak of gracious elegance and enhanced by the luxurious taste of the day, it was brutally shaken by a current of expressionism which saved it from dullness and decadence. At first shocked and aloof, the artists of the old school gradually yielded to the demands of an altered vision and, absorbing the new tendencies, revitalized their style and strengthened an idiom which could once more depict things as they were. Charm and prettiness remained, but a taste for detail and anecdote, tending to transform traditional subjects into *genre* scenes, invaded the whole artistic field, including official portrayal.

Amarnan influences are obvious in the structure of the compositions, the attitudes of the characters, the evocation of events and gestures never previously depicted. The young prince did not give impetus to the revolutionary work of the royal artisans as his elder brother had done, but a rather new, distinctive, "Tutankhamenesque" style marked the first years of his reign and set an original stamp upon the famous reliefs of the feast of Opet in the temple at Luxor, as well as on the truly enchanting pictures painted on ivory or inlaid with glass-paste on the gold-plated wooden chest in his tomb (v) or on the back of his throne (vi). The paintings convey all the charm of Tiye's youngest son, with the delicate slightly hooked nose and prominent wide-arched brows shading the eyelids.

Fashion continued to favour wigs and ever more finely pleated linen loincloths and tunics, enlivened by bands and belts of brilliant colours, matching the immense necklaces which covered nearly half the breast. Some of the palace furnishings indeed were over-elaborate, in particular certain vases and alabaster lamps. But they may have given pleasure to the little king and queen. There is no record of any surviving children of their marriage, and nothing is known of their tastes. Despite the luxury and variety of Tutankhamen's funerary equipment, (124, 125, 126, 127) there is nothing to indicate their private idiosyncrasies. Though everything the country could provide was his, the treasure in the king's

125. Tutankhamen's drink strainer

126. Nefertiti strains a drink for King Akhenaten

124. One of the king's decorated sandals

tomb reveals his people's degree of evolution, their customs and rites, but is silent upon Tutankhamen himself.

Nor should one draw hasty conclusions from the arms, the battle- and hunting-scenes surrounding him after death. Did he really race after ostriches in the desert in a chariot drawn by spirited mares (xx)? Had his arrows transfixed hyena and ibex? He cannot in any case have been strong enough to face up to the royal lion, so that the jointed gold corselet (ancestor of the coat of mail) (128) which was made for him was no doubt only worn for peaceful parades when, driving his chariot through Thebes with foreign captives in his train, he was officially credited with feats he could never have physically accomplished. Indeed, there is no material evidence of Tutankhamen's ever waging war, and it was surely not on the battlefield he heard his armies' trumpets, but on the river-

127. Tutankhamen's wine-jars: a. Syrian pottery; b. Egyptian pottery

side during the great festivals, far from the Asian world that was always a latent danger to his empire.

Egypt's increasingly ineffective armies had to be bolstered up by the subtleties of diplomacy, in which the "Divine Father" Ay deferred to the pharaoh's ambassadors, especially to Horemheb, the "scribe of the army", who, from the very beginning of the reign, had succeeded in collecting the Lebanese and Palestinian taxes. Thus, as his majesty's envoy abroad, Huy had ushered in to the palace the grandees of Retenu who, like true merchants, without undue humility, arrived at the head of an impressive column of wares which they offered as "gifts" to the king, though with the tacit understanding that they were barter for goods of almost equivalent worth. The correspondence exchanged between the oriental chieftains and the Egyptian kings during this period leaves no doubt as to the interpretation of that scene which some prefer to regard as the conclusion of the young king's Asian campaign and others as an episode during his coronation.

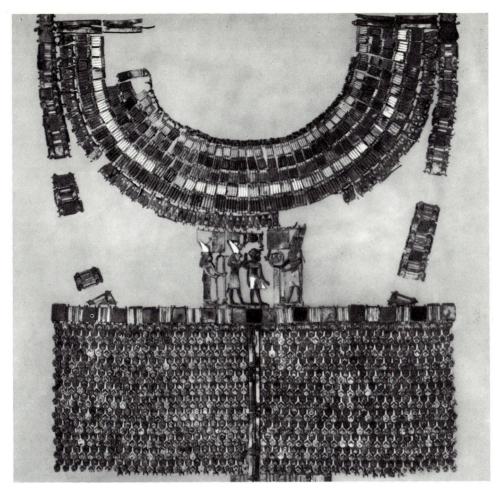

128. A fragment of Tutankhamen's "chain mail"

At the beginning of the reign, Horemheb for his part had managed to collect all the tribute of Palestine; perhaps he overstated its importance. Upon the walls of his first tomb built at Memphis, an impressive procession of all the Asian races, escorted by their cavalry, delivers the famous tributes to the pharaoh (preserved in the Leyden Museum). In fact, the royal army's power at that time was negligible, and it was constantly defeated in Asia Minor. The inspirer of the "stele of the restoration of the temples" erected in Tutankhamen's name, in other words, Horemheb, made no secret of it:

> If one [army was] sent to Djahy (a generic term for Syria) to extend the frontiers of Egypt it would encounter no success at all.

This was a direct criticism of Akhenaten's policy of peace which Horemheb openly attacked. However, all the mistakes made were not attributable to the heretic alone, for his father Amenophis III had ignored the complaints or requests for assistance he received from his allied vassals as the Amarna correspondence shows only too clearly. King Akizzi made complaints. The citizens of Tunip (Aleppo) recalled that for twenty years they had begged for assistance to no avail; Amenophis III would take no military action. One remembers also the entreaties from Rib-Addi, king of Byblos, Egypt's ally, who finally succumbed to the attacks of Aziru of Amurru, ally of the Bedouins and the Hapiru *Sa-gaz* (the cut-throats). Throughout this period merciless war was waged between the Mitannians and the Hati (the Hittites of the Bible), but Egypt was content with her more or less enduring alliances and never even attempted to defend them against outside aggression. Officially she even maintained apparently friendly relations with the different powers warring amongst themselves. Tushratta of Mitanni had married his sister and daughters to the pharaoh, yet Suppululiuma who threatened the Mitannian empire seems to have ingratiated himself with the Egyptian crown. He could only attack Mitanni gradually, prudence being imposed upon him by the opposition he encountered in Anatolia itself, but he managed to cement alliances which so often in the unsettled orient served to play a double game.

It seems improbable that Horemheb, during Tutankhamen's reign, really waged great battles in troubled Asia, and even though he may have been moderately successful in Palestine, he was mainly preoccupied with the defence of his own national frontiers. In his tomb at Memphis are depicted Palestinian refugees, hunted by Trans-Jordanian Bedouins, arriving famished with their flocks at the Egyptian border and imploring the general to intercede with the king for their right of asylum:

> The barbarians have taken their land, their dwellings have been destroyed, their town devastated and their crops burnt. Their country has been so hungry that they lived in the mountains like goats. Now they come to beg the Powerful to send his victorious sword to protect them, saying: "We few Asians who do not know how we may survive, have come to seek refuge in the land of Pharaoh as we did in the time of the fathers of his father, since the beginning."

In fact, during the nine years of Tutankhamen's reign, though one suspects the gradual weakening of the empire's hold on her Asian protectorates, one cannot point to any real war. Horemheb was there to deal with the country's business and the vital interests of the nation. The accumulation of titles the king was said to have bestowed upon him is significant: "the king's deputy in all countries" (that is, vice-regent); "the king's elect"; "president of the Two Countries" (for administrative purposes); "the two eyes of the king of Upper and Lower Egypt"; "the greatest among the favourites of the lord of the Two Countries"; "the true scribe, well-beloved of the king"; "chief intendant"; and "the confidant of the king's especial confidants". When one remembers the king's age, it is easy to understand Horemheb's power, not only over the prince, but also over the "Divine Father" Ay. In spite of the typically oriental overstatement of those titles, they give an idea of Horemheb's ascendency over the royal family and how he could obviously sway the palace attitude even at times of bitter internal dissension, as had happened in Akhenaten's day; but it undoubtedly took a somewhat dictatorial form: "the greatest of the great; the most powerful of the powerful; high lord of the people" were his self-appointed titles.

Far more useful than his military strategy, his scribe's art and his love of law had made him an experienced legislator apparently dedicated to stamping out corruption. Once enthroned, he was to promulgate an edict against prevaricators which enables us to imagine the state into which the country had sunk at the end of the Amarnan epoch. Already in the inscriptions officially attributed by him to his young king, or even on the texts of his statues as a general, placed under Amun's protection (Metropolitan Museum), one can sense the germ of the

129. *Presentation of gold necklaces to General Horemheb: fragment from his Memphite tomb (Rijksmuseum, Leyden)*

counter-reform which he intended to impose upon the country, "to suppress evil-doing throughout the Two Lands, so that the truth may be established and falsehood be an abomination in the country as in the beginning". (*Stele of the restoration of the temples.*)

In the sixth year of his reign the young king was fifteen and maturing. The palace of Malkata on the left bank was not far from the Valley of the Kings, and on the same side of the river the inspectors of the necropolis were beginning to find traces of grave-robbers' depredations. The day came when his majesty had to be told that some of his ancestors' sepulchres had been desecrated. In this particular instance the bodies had been fairly recently buried, and belonged to actors in the Amarnan drama. But we have not enough detailed information to reconstruct the events. Did the new king, on leaving Tell el Amarna, respect the wishes of his brother who wanted to remain after his death in the necropolis of Akhetaten? Or did he decide, on leaving the city, to bring his dead and their treasure back to Thebes? Again one encounters the mystery of the famous Tomb No. 55 in the Valley of the Kings and all one can state with certainty is that at some time various objects belonging to the Amarnan family were stored in it: Queen Tiye's golden funerary chapel, canopic urns and a sarcophagus belonging to the princess Meritaten, and the mummy of a pharaoh who died before Tutankhamen—Smenkhkare or Akhenaten?

It was probably shortly after this that the king ordered the restoration and repair of what had been spared from the pillage, but still another problem arises: the archaeologists found in the rubble fragments of clay seals bearing Tutankhamen's name. They also found a jar containing linen embalming bandages inscribed with a line of cursive hieroglyphs stating: "the living god, lord of the Two Countries, Nebkheprure, beloved of Min: woven in year 6". Tutankhamen had indeed ordered the depredations to be made good. But now a new difficulty is encountered: though the names of Aten are not hammered out everywhere, the silhouette of Akhenaten on the fragment of his mother's gilt chapel has been effaced; the heretical king had therefore been attacked, but this fact ill accords with what we know of Tutankhamen's and Ay's tolerance towards the memory of the heretic. There are objects bearing Akhenaten's name and even Smenkhkare's in Tutankhamen's burial treasure, and these would not have been placed in the tomb with their names still intact if these kings had already been persecuted in Tutankhamen's lifetime. The enigma therefore remains unsolved.

At any rate, if the body of Smenkhkare had indeed been reburied in this sepulchre, someone at the palace had certainly appropriated pieces of his burial furnishings, to place them shortly afterwards in Tutankhamen's tomb and even around his corpse.

Between his fifteenth and eighteenth years Tutankhamen developed a taste for religious matters and, apparently, politics. From childhood he had been

XLIII. *Unguent jar: hunting scene dominated by the figure of the king as a lion. Painted alabaster*

aware that disagreements and rivalries had finally been settled between his father, his brother and the kings of Asia Minor by the almost magical effect of little clay tablets covered in nail-shaped signs and borne by brave and swift messengers. His mother Tiye, a queen of unusual erudition, who possessed a library of literary and scientific works, had explained to him quite early the workings of these international exchanges. As soon as he was old enough to do so he followed the correspondence with his country's allies and studied the tactics of balancing influences, dividing adversaries, and strengthening alliances. He had noticed that Burnaburiash, king of Karaduniash (Babylonia) greatly feared a rising of the Assyrians who were still his vassals. Therefore Tutankhamen did nothing to discourage the advances the Assyrians made to him, and accepted the visit of a commercial delegation to Egypt to adjust trade between the two countries. At the same time he postponed the despatch to King Burnaburiash of the presents he had requested. The ruse was successful and the king of Karaduniash reacted as Tutankhamen-Nebkheprure (the Niphururia—or Niphuriria—of the Babylonian letters) had expected: the anxious Burnaburiash wrote him the only letter in the royal correspondence surviving today which can be ascribed with certainty to his reign (Knudtzon No. 9):

To Niphuria, king of Egypt—
Thus speaks Burnaburiash, king of Karaduniash, thy brother.

All goes well for me. All hail to thee, thy house, thy wives, thy children, thy country, thy nobles, thy horses, (and) thy chariots.

When my fathers and thy fathers established between themselves friendly (relations) they exchanged rich presents and (never) refused each other, the one to the other, whatever beautiful thing they desired.

Now my brother has sent me as a gift (but) two minas of gold. If now gold is abundant (with thee), send me as much as thy fathers (did) but if it is scarce, send me [at least] half of it. Why didst thou send me (only) two minas of gold?

Now the tasks I have (to carry out) in the temple are great, thus have I undertaken them with zeal to accomplish them: send me (therefore) much gold.

As for thee, whatever thou desirest of (the produce) of my country, write to me and it shall be brought thee.

At the time of Kurigalzu, my father, the Canaanites all [together] wrote to him: "We [are going] to the frontier of the country in order to cross it, that is why we wish to enter into relations with thee."

Here is what my father replied to them: "Abandon (any idea) of making an alliance with me! If you perform hostile deeds against the king of Egypt, my brother, in league with others, is it not I who will have to go and punish you since he is allied to me?"

It was for thy father's sake that my father did not listen to them.

Now [concerning] the Assyrians, my vassals, I have written nothing to thee as they claim. Why have they gone to thy country? If thou lovest me, they must not (be allowed to) buy anything at all, let them return here empty-handed!

It is as a present [of friendship] that I send to thee three measures of beautiful lapis-lazuli stone and also five teams of horses (?) for five wooden chariots.

(Translated from the Akkadian by M. Kanawaty)

The young sovereign of Thebes was beginning to learn his royal trade.

XLIV. *Unguent jar in the form of an ibex. Inlaid alabaster.*
The remaining horn is natural

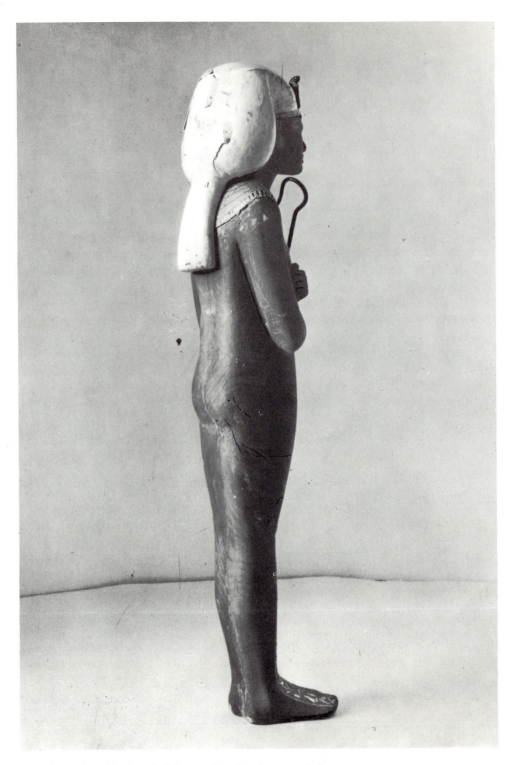

130. One of the king's ushabtis wearing the afnet head-dress

7 The death of the king and preparations for immortality

1343

ANALYSIS OF HIS mummy shows that Tutankhamen was between eighteen and twenty years old when he died. This allows one to set the approximate date of his coronation in his ninth year, since there is no date mentioned in connection with him after year 9 which appears on wine-jars found in his tomb.

It is impossible to say whether the king was the victim of illness, accident or assassination, and his body provides no clues, but considering the early deaths of his two predecessors and brothers Amenophis IV-Akhenaten and Smenkhkare (the latter was probably under twenty-five when he died) it seems probable that Tuthmosis IV's last heirs were physically frail and hence short-lived.

One can at least try to deduce the approximate season of Tutankhamen's death from the fruit and flowers buried with him, in particular the mandrakes and cornflowers which in Egypt reach maturity in March and April. His funeral, therefore, must have taken place at this time, and his death must have occurred some seventy days before, since this was the length of time required for mummification. Thus Amenophis III's last son died some time in January 1343, to the immense distress and apprehension of his family, his friends and the Malkata court. His young widow refused to select from among her entourage a successor to her husband who would wield the sceptre of Egypt. In the interim, the "Divine Father" Ay who had guided and supported the sovereigns from the time of the heresy, had to support Ankhesenamun in her royal duties.

In the meanwhile, there was the king to be buried; this son of the god, this "divine flesh" must be helped to rejoin the Globe which had created him. Ay was familiar with the ritual and wanted to supervise the preparations for Tutankhamen's "voyage of eternity" himself, rather than let the priests of Amun do so. But although he had been able to arrange the coronation of his young prince and enable him to reign as his ancestors before him, it was less easy to ensure his immortality. Ay had not forgotten the dramas that marked the deaths of Nefertiti, the heretic Akhenaten, and finally Smenkhkare.

Tutankhamen who was among the founders of temples at Kawa and at Faras in Nubia, and of sanctuaries at Karnak and Luxor, had also, from the time of his accession to the throne, considered building his own funerary temple to the west of Thebes, which would simultaneously allow him to erect a private palace adjoining it—this was customary as we see from the ruins of the funerary monuments of Ay, Horemheb, Ramesses II and Ramesses III in the region.

Although it cannot be definitely proved, it seems that one of the two anonymous temples, traces of which still exist behind Amenophis III's burial domain, belonged to Tutankhamen. At any rate, two magnificent statues still showing signs of multicoloured paint, and carved from the red quartzite of Gebel el Ahmar, near Memphis, probably come from this lost sanctuary. Resembling the young king, they were successively usurped by Ay and Horemheb, in whose funerary temple the American archaeologists found them; one is now in the Cairo Museum, the other in the Metropolitan Museum.

But had Tutankhamen really thought seriously about his tomb, for at eighteen does one contemplate the possibility of death? For every Egyptian, however, death was a desirable transformation, the passage to the true and eternal life. It was not considered as an end but as an inevitable, almost a welcome, transition, requiring only that great care be taken to smooth the path to immortality by correct observance of the ritual. For this reason the tomb and its contents were of supreme importance. Perhaps the young king, or one of his courtiers, did in fact choose a site in the Valley of the Kings and prepared it for a long syrinx. Certainly one was built, reminiscent of Akhenaten's at Tell el Amarna, plunging straight into the mountain in a row of rooms and corridors in such a way that the sun would penetrate into and illuminate the burial chamber. But it was Horemheb who was buried in it.

Or again it is possible that the tomb, intended for him but unfinished at his death, was subsequently occupied by Ay, although it was no doubt ravaged on Horemheb's orders; the faces of the elderly monarch and his wife Tey have been entirely mutilated.

Whether the one or the other of these hypogea was prepared for the young king, work upon them ceased abruptly on his death and the workers' efforts were diverted to a far more modest sepulchre, the general plan of which echoed the main design of the royal Tuthmoside tombs, the digging of which was already well advanced. It is more than likely that this was the prospective hypogeum of the "Divine Father" Ay, who thus enjoyed a right occasionally granted to certain "royal relatives". No doubt it was necessary to complete the work on it, but the seventy days of the mummification were sufficient.

Ay asked the intendant of the treasury, Maya, chief of works in the necropolis, to supervise the installation personally, and Maya, who seems to have been very close to the young king, went to work. Since he was "the servant of his majesty, seeking what is useful to his master", he ordered one of his most skilful artisans to make his own funerary gift, which would bear eternal witness to his own merit and his devotion to the royal person.

This gift was a miniature of the king recumbent upon a bier decorated with

XLV. *Tutankhamen on a papyrus raft, in the attitude of a harpooner. One of the funerary objects used to evoke the mystical pilgrimages during the funeral. Gilded wood*

lions' heads (LIV). It was an exquisite piece of work. Touches of colour accentuated the features of the sovereign and of the two bird-effigies flanking him, each spreading one of its wings over the body's folded arms, as if taking affectionate possession of it. The bird on the right had a human head, in common with all images of the souls of dead Egyptians. The left-hand bird was a falcon. Around the bed were inscriptions recalling Maya's names and titles. In the king's tomb few such personal gifts were found. However, Maya was not the only friend whose present was buried with the king: five little *ushabtis* (or burial statuettes) depicting the dead king in several of his customary styles of head-dress were among the objects presented by the "royal scribe, fan-bearer on the right of the king", General Nakhtmin (130).

Little is known of these two men whose names are permanently linked with Tutankhamen's ephemeral existence, but several monuments, now in the Leyden and Berlin Museums and in the Louvre, help us to understand the part they played at the end of the Amarnan epoch. We meet Nakhtmin later as the henchman of Ay when he was king; and after three thousand years we can still trace the development of Maya's career: he became one of the wealthiest noblemen and Horemheb's powerful minister of finance.

At all events, they are the only two non-royal Egyptians whose names are to be found among nearly two thousand objects in Tutankhamen's burial treasure. Both provide precise information among a mass of objects which are far from being completely explained.

Maya's gift, by itself, epitomises the whole drama from which the funeral rites enabled the deceased to emerge victorious. The supine form is the dead man preserved from corruption by embalming; his earthly and visible projection is flanked by the two principles binding him to eternity: yesterday and to-morrow. The human-faced bird is Osiris, the first god to be incarnated on earth, who died that the divine race might perpetuate itself; and the falcon, glorious and dynamic image of the young Horus of the horizon, represents new life. Together they embody the dual principle of the "two souls" of the deceased, that of the eve and that of the morrow, those two notions of the succession of days and nights of which the Egyptians, with so many different symbols and this plurality of attitudes, strove to find an explanation. Maya deserves remembrance if only for this, this tangible expression of a philosophy of eternity.

General Nakhtmin's contribution is quite different. Perhaps he was related to the "Divine Father" Ay or even to Tutankhamen himself, for one of his statuettes dedicated to the king still bears this inscription: "the servant who makes his master's name live". The act of reviving the name of the dead during the funerary rite is the prerogative of the eldest son, and when there is no male heir, of the daughter. It seems probable that, as Tutankhamen died childless, the person to accomplish this duty would have been his closest relative, or at

XLVI. *The king wearing the red crown of the North and holding the royal insignia. One of the funerary objects used to evoke the mystical pilgrimages during the funeral*

least his most faithful friend. In any case, the inscriptions show that strong bonds of affection bound Nakhtmin to his king. And yet, on the day of the burial, another general made the final magic gestures over the mummy: Ay, the "Divine Father", master of the king's horse, assumed this role for reasons of state.

When the pharaoh's death was announced, all Egypt went into mourning. The news spread rapidly along both banks of the Nile and the people said "Horus has rejoined the Globe". In palace, ministry and noble household, work ceased and the Egyptians crouched in lamentation with their heads upon their knees. The queen and the royal princesses uttered shrill cries of despair, and then, as soon as the body was taken to the "golden hall" under the liturgical tent where the priests and their assistants would proceed with the embalming, the whole country entered into ritual observance of the period of silent grief and fasting, during which all rejoicing was proscribed. Men of the king's immediate circle ceased to shave until the day of the burial.

The workshops on the west bank of Thebes, where the craftsmen of the necropolis lived, were plunged into frantic activity, for everything had to be ready by the date of the funeral. Naturally among the many objects to be buried with the king some came from the palace itself and included family souvenirs, jewellery and furniture used during the king's childhood, as the funerary rites demanded. The equipment specifically required for the burial and for the different phases of the transformation to the other world figures there for the same reason. Nothing so far seems to indicate that it had been necessary to the king during his reign. The craftsmen were therefore hard pressed during the period of mummification.

However, detailed study of the treasure by its discoverers and by Egyptologists who subsequently studied the problem of Tutankhamen, has brought to light that some of Smenkhkare's burial furnishings found their way into Tutankhamen's tomb. The little golden sarcophagi containing the royal viscera, for instance, and certain inscribed bands found on the mummy show that Smenkhkare's name had been scratched out. Several experts agree that Smenkhkare's tomb was partly stripped of its contents by Ay some nine years earlier, to the benefit of Tutankhamen.

The pharaoh then had not broken with the Amarnan reforms when he settled in Thebes, and more than any other his reign was a period of transition during which Aten and Amun co-existed without apparent friction. Officially Amun had again become the supreme master. In practice Aten continued to be so, as can be seen from the king's mummy which, unlike those of most Egyptian sovereigns, had not been desecrated by the robbers of antiquity.

The cellars of Malkata contained wines from Aten's vineyards, and the best vintages were selected to be placed in the tomb. The linen-mills of Tell el Amarna had been most prosperous and had furnished the palace with great fringed scarves, marked with the years 8 and 10 of Akhenaten's reign. These were used for wrapping the statues of gods afterwards placed in coffers of blackened wood. There was a scarf with long fringes dated year 7 which

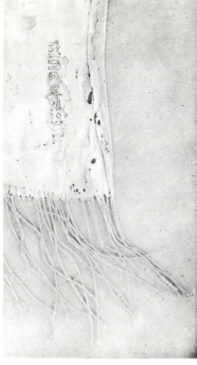

*131. Tutankhamen in the form of the god Anubis
during the course of his transformations*

*132. Inscription on the linen scarf
round the neck of Anubis*

adorned the magnificent statue of Anubis on his golden shrine at the entrance
of the Treasury (131, 132).

But all the preparations made for eternal life, according to classical rites
established "at the time of the gods", and reverting to traditions which had
probably been abandoned during the heretical reign, could only serve their
purpose if the body itself, the earthly mainstay of the deceased, was transformed
into a divine and incorruptible image. Then, in the invisible world, all the
constituent parts of the king's personality would unite with this sublimated and
imperishable material projection, which possessed the properties necessary to
take part in the harmonious movements of the cosmos.

The ritual, technique and amulets of mummification would therefore transform the royal corpse into a god, dead to the earth (Osiris) but resuscitated or
reinvigorated (*Ounen-Nefer*) for eternity. Indeed, the embalming workshop
was called the "House of Vigour" (or "of Vitality") (*Per Nefer*), and the process
of embalming could be called *senefer* or restoration of vigour or vitality. The
ceremonies concluded, the dead man would rise like the sun at the dawning of
the world, emerging from a blue lotus-flower (the nenuphar or water-lily, *nefer*)
dominating the waters of primeval chaos. Thus the final phrase of the mummification ritual would be his passport to eternity: "You live again, you live again
forever, here you are young once more for ever."

For seventy days the body was treated by priests and technicians, the former performing anew the work that Osiris' escort had executed over the dismembered body of the first king of Egypt slain by the Evil One. The "Reader" priest supervised the work and recited the appropriate formulas in the presence of the "Official of the Secret of the Embalming Workshop". The "Embalmer of Anubis" (the black god with the head of a young dog, black being the colour of rebirth), and the "Chancellors of the God" also took part in the operations which involved the handling of many valuable objects, while the majority of officiants around the body were called the *Ut* or *Wet*.

After withdrawing most of the brain through the nostrils, they dissolved what was left in the skull with certain aromatic lotions. The viscera were then removed through an opening cut in the side of the body with a "stone of Ethiopia", according to Herodotus. The abdomen was then filled with crushed myrrh, cassa, and various aromatics, after being washed out with palm-wine and soaked with aromatics. Incense, however, was not allowed to be used. Thus nothing remained in the body, no putrefiable matter, organs or fats.

The organs once extracted were immediately prepared for storage in the round-bellied urns with lids sculpted into human faces (XXXIII). These urns took the form of the idol of Osiris later erected in Aboukir harbour, a sort of vase which the Greeks revered as an evocation of Canopus, Menelaus' pilot, supposed to have died there. The excavators found four of these urns in the rich alabaster coffer (XXXII) with its four compartments (133). They contained, wrapped in linen, small coffins of gold cloisonné, portraying a dead sovereign, in which were the embalmed organs (XXXIV). Magical inscriptions were carved on the inner surface.

The body, now deprived of everything corruptible, and entirely shaven, was plunged, for a period of seventy days, into dry natron which absorbed all its remaining humidity. After this, it was washed, and then set to dry on beds of animal shapes with very tall legs so that the officiants could handle it without having to bend down. Perhaps the three golden beds in the tomb were used for this purpose, though there is nothing to prove it (XXVIII, XXIX and XXX).

Then came the bandaging, the last stage of embalming. Hundreds of yards of very fine linen were used, so that the king's body was totally enveloped in protective layers. First each finger and toe was bandaged separately, then each limb and finally the whole body. During the bandaging prayers were recited and magic formulas pronounced while unguents were poured. Too many of these were lavished on Tutankhamen, burning away nearly all the tissues and attacking the bones. Only the parts protected by gold were preserved: the face covered by the mask and the hands and feet guarded by finger stalls. The larger bandages of the outer wrappings were also impregnated with unguents.

The mummy was literally covered with treasures and it is an irony of Tutankhamen's fate that its deterioration was not due to theft but to the superabundance of oils destined to give it new vitality. However, the hundred and forty-three precious objects tucked between the bandages were in an excellent

222

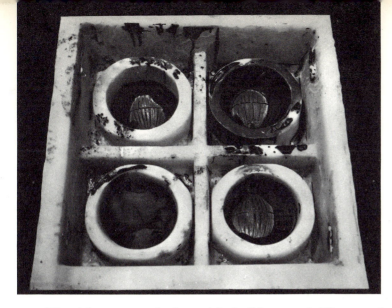

133. *The alabaster canopic chest with the lid removed. The tops of the sarcophagi immersed in unguents and resin are visible*

134. *Tutankhamen's mummified head*

state of preservation: golden finger-stalls, sandals, gold rings, necklaces, bracelets, diadems, daggers, pendants, pectorals and amulets cut out of gold leaf. The incorruptible metal endowed the protected creature with its own power, and everything united to make a god of the mummified prince.

There is one very important detail which might pass unnoticed and which is still not entirely explained: the two plain straps of golden leaves placed on the breast of the body and decorated with a knot. On the bas-reliefs and statues of every period the Egyptian kings wore the small corselet with a single strap of this kind. But the gods' corselets were always held by *two* straps. Tutankhamen, wearing two in death, was therefore considered a god as soon as he entered the embalming workshop where his corpse was transformed into an eternal body.

In preparing the mummy the embalmers shaved the skull like that of a high

135. The bead uraeus on the king's skull

136. The monarchic animals adorning the skull of the king's mummy

priest (134). Some day it may become clear why Tutankhamen's head was prepared in a totally different manner from those of most of the other sovereigns found in the cache of Deir el Bahri. Those other great kings of Egypt still have almost living heads of hair; but on Tutankhamen's head there was only a small skull-cap of very fine linen decorated with woven bands and beads of gold and glazed terracotta shaped like a bandeau on the brow, from which rose four sacred cobras whose sinuous bodies adorned the crown of the head (135).

Although Tutankhamen officially worshipped Amun, and although Osiris—whose legend could not be mentioned during the Atenist heresy—had resumed his place as master of the funereal domain, the young king's deep faith had probably never enabled him to cast off entirely the beliefs of his childhood. Naturally, the "Divine Father" Ay insisted upon all the Osirian rites for the pharaoh's corpse and the pomp of the obsequies observed for great kings faithful to their ancestral religion. But the last descendant of the heretical epoch could not be allowed to depart without bearing in the place where the royal crowns had been set the mark of the well-beloved Globe. The four sacred cobras—or *uraeus*—were inscribed in several places with cartouches bearing the names of the Solar Globe Aten as they were quoted during the later years of the Amarnan king: "Re-of-the-horizon-who-rejoices-in-the-horizon-in-his-name-of-Re-the-Father-who-comes-in-the-Aten". At his rebirth the king would appear at dawn as the one who dispensed the breath of life. To hold this skull-cap in place, a broad golden band—wider at the temples in order to protect them—encircled the whole head and covered the brow. Upon this was laid a linen coif

224

137. *The same gold animals after cleaning*
138. *The head of the mummy ready for the funerary mask*

ending at the back in a sort of pigtail. A vulture with widespread wings cut from a sheet of gold adorned the front of the skull. This royal vulture, the goddess of Upper Egypt, was joined to the serpent of Lower Egypt, the sacred *uraeus* erect above the forehead (137). All these pieces were held in place by a second golden bandeau broadening between the temples and the eyes. Over many more wrappings of fine linen, lay the king's diadem, consisting of a small golden circlet decorated with discs of cornelian; in the centre of each was a golden nail, surrounded by a border of inlaid glass-paste imitating lapis-lazuli and turquoise (1). Four similar ribbons hung at the rear, the two which came over the ears entwined with the long undulating bodies of two cobras, their heads raised towards the king's face. All the pharaoh's headgear had to include the *uraeus*, symbol of his supreme authority. In funerary portrayals, the serpent was accompanied by the head of Nekhabet, the vulture of the South. These two essential elements of the diadem were supposed to be very close to the body of the king, but they may have taken up too much room under the bandages wrapped around the skull, and the priests set them along the thighs of the mummy, paying the greatest attention to their correct orientation (139). The geographical distribution of all the elements of a man's life, especially that of a king, was essential and nothing was left to chance during the preparations for the eternal voyage. In the tomb the mummy was to lie with its head to the west and feet to the east. When it rose it would face the rising sun. It was therefore logical to lay the long *uraeus* against the left leg close to the north of which it was the symbol. Conversely, the vulture's head rested by the right thigh, facing

225

south. The encircling bandages again enwrapped the head and when it was entirely covered, a final ornament was laid upon it—a double roll of fibres and cords, possibly a forerunner of the Bedouin headgear of today. A modern observer might be inclined to see in this a precautionary measure taken by the officiants to prevent the burial mask which was put in place at the end of these operations from weighing directly upon the mummified face (138).

Everything that was done to preserve the face was equally done at each stage for the body, and the different layers of bandages held within their elaborate network jewels and amulets of predetermined categories. The king's neck, upon which the safety of his head (seat of his re-animation) depended, was especially protected. The safety of this most vital part of the body was assured by two sets of necklaces and twenty amulets grouped in six rows (140). Nearest to the neck was a necklace of four rows of round beads, and, after several more layers of bandages, images of vultures and of cobras (one of the latter having out-stretched wings and a human head) cut from incised sheets of gold and certainly made for the mummification (141). They formed a magical net, to reunite the two parts of the world which the king would find again in his eternal empire. More linen bandages covered these sacred images. Then, in four successive layers, each separated by bandages, came very fine amulets of gold and precious stones, hung round the neck on threads of gold. Infinitesimal fragments of papyrus, still

XLVII. The lid of the alabaster jar decorated with a small bowl showing a bird in its nest having just emerged from its egg

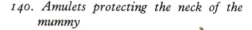

139. Objects on the torso of the mummy (note the long serpent by the left leg)

140. Amulets protecting the neck of the mummy

bearing the names of deities, such as Isis and Osiris, seem to prove that a sort of small prayerbook had been put there with the following symbols: the serpent's head in cornelian, images of the papyrus column in feldspar which conferred sexual vigour and eternal youth, and the cornelian knot guaranteeing protection by Isis and Horus, and a welcome to the kingdom of Osiris. The seated images of Thoth, the ibis, of Horus, the falcon and Anubis, the young dog appeared with them. The ritual of *The Book of the Dead* indicates that the amulet of the *djed* pillar, the emblem of Osiris, had to be of gold, and placed at the neck of the dead man to help him through the portals of the other world, and allow him to rise and live as a perfect soul in the beyond. Two of these pillar-shaped amulets were indeed hung round the king's neck, one of solid gold and the other inlaid with blue glass-paste. Finally, on the last layer of objects, a gorget of beaten gold represented the necklace of Horus, showing the sacred falcon with its curved wings spread; the counterweight at the back served as fastener.

Thirty-five more objects were laid in thirteen layers between the neck and the abdomen; over a few thicknesses of bandages, almost upon the skin, was a real collar of several rows of tiny gold and blue glass beads in a pattern of yellow zig-zags and blue waves. Golden pendants completed the ornament at both ends of which were golden falcon-heads.

The next two layers consisted of jewels which the king must have worn in his lifetime, since they showed signs of wear. They were nearly all necklaces and pectorals. The pendant of the finest was an image of gold cloisonné, encrusted with cornelian, lapis-lazuli and glass-paste, of the Southern goddess, Nekhabet, the vulture (XXXVIIa). On the back of the jewel, carved in the gold, a little pendant-necklace hung from a chain around the bird's neck, with the king's coronation name in a cartouche. The long necklace from which this jewel hung had a counterweight fastener made of two miniature falcons. But this piece was admirably restrained in comparison with others overburdened with symbols and colours. First came the three pendants which lay over the bandages concealing the blue and gold collar; the central one had a magnificent sacred eye (*wedjet*) flanked on the left side (of the mummy) by the serpent of Buto dominating Lower Egypt, and on the right by the vulture of Upper Egypt (XXXIXa). Near the serpent hung another pendant, made of a winged scarab poised on a basket and holding in its forepaws a disc set in a crescent moon: this ornamental combination of the three hieroglyphs of Tutankhamen's name was on the left side of the mummy, that is, the northern side, the domain of night ruled by the moon. Symmetrically opposite, on the right side, was another jewel showing the solar falcon crowned with the disc.

Another layer of bandages and then, lower on the breast, below the magnificent vulture pendant, lay a very heavy pectoral consisting of a triple set of the king's hieroglyphs, again with three scarabs. Floral tassels completed this jewel which hung upon rows of beads fastened with an image of the king's name up-

XLVIII. *Head of the sacred cow. Used to evoke the mystical pilgrimages during the funeral*

141. The monarchic animals protecting the neck of the mummy. Incised gold sheets

held by a spirit surrounded by deities and amulets.

Over these five pectorals the priests laid another layer of bandages upon which they placed, not pendants this time, but gorgeous necklaces of gold cloisonné, inlaid with hundreds of pieces of the precious metal and multi-coloured glass-paste. It was necklaces such as these which funerary texts, dating from the time of the pyramids, decreed should be laid upon the neck and breast of the mummy. On the lower part of the chest lay a jewel consisting of the vulture and the serpent with two immense wings curved in a pattern of Oriental origin; upon this was a sheet of papyrus separating it from a great "necklace-pectoral" of the same shape but centred upon a single serpent of gold leaf. More bandages separated this layer of jewels from the next.

From the coffers they now took three bracelets, the first two of which were simple threads of gold, one with a lapis-lazuli bead and the other with a cornelian, but the third was of great ritual and historical interest since its ornament was a sacred eye in iron. This metal, foreign to Egypt and still almost unknown at that time, appears in three places upon the king's mummy. At this stage, the priests placed at the supposed level of the straps, the magical golden knots which only the gods wore, and on the breast, also separated from the rest by a sheet of papyrus, two more great necklaces of inlaid gold, one "the necklace of Nekhabet", the vulture, made of 256 gold pieces, and the other "the necklace of Horus". Over this went a vast collar, almost identical but worked in sheet gold. Four other similar ornaments, cut out of the same metal and incised with details of animals, were necessary to complete the protection of the chest: one was a copy of the bead collar with the two falcon's heads, another a winged *uraeus*, the third featured the two goddesses, the snake and the vulture, and the fourth the

230

142. *Bracelets on the king's mummy*

vulture alone (XXXVIIb). Beneath these four gold plates, and suspended upon a gold thread, was a black resin scarab encircled with gold and inlaid with coloured glass, representing the phoenix or *bennu* of rebirth.

The king's anthropoid coffins exactly reproduced the mummy's attitude; arms parallel with the body, and forearms folded across the upper abdomen, the left over the right. The fingers had been wrapped first, then the hands, the forearms and the upper arms, after which the limbs were folded against the body and bound in place. The thorax and abdomen had been previously bandaged, and at the level of the left and right wrists the priests had inserted between the wrappings two sets of objects, one set consisting of five and the other of eight rings of gold, lapis-lazuli, chalcedony, turquoise and black resin. They were in fact seals with the king's name, some with a scarab as the bezel. The mummy's bracelets were of two very different kinds; a simple gold band had been slipped over each elbow, the right one with a great green stone, intentionally uncut, and six amulets in the shape of the sacred eye threaded onto the bracelet. Over the left elbow, the bracelet upon which three beads were threaded, had a very fine cornelian amulet portraying a swallow supporting the solar disc with its wing —this is mentioned in *The Book of the Dead* in connection with the transformations of the solar god.

The forearms, however, were covered with many rich and heavy bracelets, seven on the right arm and six on the left (142). Gold, cornelian, gold-alloy, semi-precious stones and glass-paste formed geometric and granulated patterns consisting almost entirely of sacred *wedjet* eyes and scarabs.

Each finger was partially sheathed in gold, with the fingernail and first knuckle carefully outlined (143). A gold seal ring had been slipped on to the

231

ring and middle fingers of the left hand.

After the first bandages, gold sheaths were placed on the toes, and finally golden sandals put on the feet while the Reader priest intoned incantations which would permit the king to trample his enemies underfoot. Then, as they bandaged the places where the muscles had disappeared, the embalmers placed bundles of linen upon them to give shape to the natron-desiccated body, and between the legs they replaced the bandaged genital organ in a state of erection. Upon the thighs and between them were seven bracelets, separated by three successive layers of bandages, and on the knees and shins four collars of inlaid gold with their counterweights. In the hollow of the left groin a large bracelet lay just above the great *uraeus* of the diadem which rested against the left leg.

On the first bandages round the waist was a belt of gold and glazed terracotta beads; slightly above, a pectoral of bright blue varnished china, shaped like a *wedjet* eye, was supported by a necklace of brilliant beads of the same substance. To separate these archaic ritual objects from each other, the bandages had been wound several times round the pelvis and enveloped a belt made of a sheet of incised gold. Over the mummy's legs the priests fixed a sort of front-piece or narrow apron consisting of twenty rows of glazed terracotta and glass beads and small gold ornaments. Beneath the mummy, the ritual tail, worn by all the pharaohs since Narmer of the Ist Dynasty, was attached to the belt and wrapped in beaded material. Through the belt was thrust a dagger with its granular-gold, semi-precious stone and glass-paste hilt to the right of the abdomen, the blade

143. Gold finger-stalls and rings on the royal hand

XLIX*a. The coffer from the Treasury, divided inside into sixteen compartments. Wood and ivory with applied gold and silver*
b. A game of "senet" in ebony and ivory. This is the largest of three such objects found in the tomb

232

pointing to the left thigh. The blade and sheath were of gold; the sheath had feather-patterns worked on one side, and on the other an extraordinary hunting scene in which, along the full height of the sheath, animals friendly to man—two dogs, two tame lions and a cheetah—attacked savage and evil animals such as bulls and ibexes. With this ceremonial dagger, the blade of which was rendered invulnerable by the magic of the scabbard, the dead man might overcome all the demons in his path. Then these objects vanished beneath more bandages. On the left side of the abdomen, whilst reciting the formulas and pouring unguents, the priests laid a necklace of tiny dark blue glazed terracotta beads, probably corresponding to "the necklace of lapis-lazuli" already depicted upon the coffins of the Middle Empire. Beside it was a gold inlaid bracelet and several others of the same type were distributed along the legs. Around the waist yet another gold belt was placed, and along the right thigh lay one of the king's treasures: his dagger with the rock-crystal nob on top of its hilt and its blade of that miraculous metal: iron. (When the tomb was discovered, this blade still shone like steel.) Its sheath was of gold in an elegant palm-leaf design (XXI). An important object between new layers of bandages on the left side of the mummy was an oval gold plate intended symbolically to protect the incision made by the embalmers when they removed the viscera. Two signs cut out of gold sheets were also laid between the bandages; one T-shaped, on the left side of the abdomen and the top of the left thigh; the other, above, a Y-shaped symbol recalling the hieroglyph for woven materials and intended to render the bandages indestructible. Still more bandages concealed the last layer of objects.

Finally the mummy was wrapped in a large linen sheet held in place by four transverse bands and three tied lengthwise. On the mummy's head was placed a sort of cone of material, resembling the tall head-dress of Osiris, intended to fill the gap between the crown of the head and the top of the solid gold mask which was slowly and most carefully placed upon the young king's face while prayers were chanted (XXVI). Reciting the appropriate chapter from *The Book of the Dead*, one of the priests also placed a small headrest in the form of an amulet of rather crudely worked iron under the nape of the neck. This was the third object of the rare metal given to Tutankhamen. The symbolism of the object and the miraculous heat it generated would enable the king to raise his head as the sun rose on the horizon.

The artist who made the beaten gold mask had skilfully portrayed the delicate and rather melancholy features of Amenophis III's youngest son. The profile was so like that of Queen Tiye, that several of the officiating priests who had remained faithful to the Amarnan family remarked upon it while handling the mask, and alluded to the fine portrait of the queen which had earlier been carved in ebony and placed in one of her foundations in the Faiyum. The two small lines at the corners of the mouth enhanced the lifelike expression of the whole

L. *A cabinet with legs, ancestor of the modern commode. Cedarwood and gilded ebony decorated with hieroglyphic symbols ensuring divine life*

face with its eyes and eyebrows inlaid with blue glass-paste, and the ritual addition of Osiris' beard. The goldsmith had faithfully copied the king's typical little ears with their lobes pierced in childhood for earrings, but had not seen fit to reproduce the trace of an accident which had left a very deep scar on the mummy on the left cheek at jaw-level. The magnificent burial head-dress, or *nemset*, inlaid with blue glass-paste, bore the two Egyptian royal beasts on the brow. The mask ended in a very broad necklace made of several rows of lapis-lazuli, quartz and feldspar, with a falcon's head on each shoulder. Around the neck, under the beard, a priest had tied three rows of discoid yellow-gold, red-gold and blue-varnished clay beads. Another had fastened to a ribbon of inlaid-gold a great black resin scarab with the ritual text of the phoenix. Two golden hands, crossed on the breast and holding the crook and flail of Osiris had been sewn on to the linen. A pectoral of gold cloisonné portrayed the bird of the soul, with a human head and spread wings. Heavy bands of gold, tied together with strings of beads, bound the outer shroud; two long bands stretched to the feet. Four transversal ones, like those before, were covered with religious inscriptions all relative to the rebirth of the king and to the gods who would protect him: "O Osiris, King Nebkheprure, your soul lives and your veins are firm. You breathe the air and emerge (into the light of day) like a god . . .". The gold bands, which bore texts from the "Chapter of the Heart" of *The Book of the Dead*, showed traces of Smenkhkare's name but, although they must have been taken from his tomb, this does not seem to have worried the priests. The king's brother was forgotten and it was Tutankhamen's journey to the eternal world which had to be prepared—just in time—with all the appropriate funerary equipment.

There was only one day left before the funeral, and the mummy, now fully adorned and brought back to the royal palace, lay on the great gilt animal-shaped bed. The king's finely featured mask wore an expression of complete peace and glowed with the eternal youth which he had just lost and would recover, greatly enhanced, in the company of the gods. Upon the other coffins the court goldsmiths had given the features a weary and tragic air, but these different images, superimposed upon each other, were intended to convey the stages through which the king had to pass. The third coffin, of solid gold, the one closest to the mummy suggested triumph over death and human suffering. The gold mask represented the sovereign returning to life; it was the "renewed being", the phoenix, the *bennu*, as the inscriptions incised on the back of the breastplate proclaimed. According to Egyptian legend, the miraculous phoenix rose shining from the waters at break of day, radiant with light, and re-created itself, as does the sun. The gold mask showed the king resurrected and once more "divine flesh". "Hail to thee" was engraved on the back of the breast-plate, "alive is thy face . . . thy right eye is the boat of day (*mandjet*), thy left eye the boat of night (*mesketet*)". These symbolic boats carried the sun in all its peregrinations by day and by night, and this repeated succession of days and nights was thus assured for Tutankhamen, now partaking of the very essence of the sun and moon, and his immortality fully confirmed.

One April morning in 1343 the sun rose over a feverish Thebes. On the eastern bank, the northern part of the city, the priests of Amun held a final sacred council; should they or should they not attend the funeral of the young brother of the heretic, whose body, attired for its final journey, still bore, as some said, the mark of Aten, beloved god of the Amarnan traitor? Although the dead king had officially forsworn the worship of the Globe, his gold-encased throne bore the image of the sun, with the hands at the ends of its rays offering life to the young royal couple. However, he *had* officially changed his name and only Amun figured in his list of formal titles; his burial furniture had been made strictly according to the Osirian rites of his ancestors. But if there still remained a chance of avoiding the ratification of Ay's seizure of power, then they must not endorse the funeral rites which the old man would perform as heir to the throne. General Horemheb also remained undecided, but had not gone so far as to bar the road to Thebes to the Northern vizier who had been summoned to attend the obsequies beside the "Divine Father", vizier of the South. He was uncertain whether or not to cross the river and follow the procession, thus tacitly sympathizing with the last members of the Amarnan family. At any rate, he wished to underline his disapproval of the palace intrigues to which he had recently and firmly put a stop.

On the left bank, south of the great funerary temple of Amenophis III, the court of Malkata arose from the long period of silent mourning. The men of the family and their followers had shaved, and preparations for the funeral banquet were to end the long weeks of fasting and abstinence. The women of the harem had prepared the simple mourning-tunics of bluish white linen which they would tear and stain with the dust of the road during the procession. Long before dawn the servant girls were in the palace gardens at their task—which would continue throughout the burial period—of plucking flowers from which they would hurriedly make elaborate bouquets, wreaths and necklaces, not only for the corpse and the coffins, but also for the guests at the funeral banquet.

At the mummy's feet, Ankhesenamun, the young widow, recited the formulas evoking rebirth, and assumed the attitude of Isis by the body of Osiris. At the head of the bed, another princess of the family played the part of Nephthys, the sister-goddess of Osiris, who had helped Isis to lay out the martyred god. Then the priests entered. Despite the desperate supplications of the women trying, ritually, to hold back the dead king, they removed the mummy, bore it to the peristyle and placed it in a boat-shaped bier supporting an immense canopy and set upon a sled. Red oxen, of the colour of Lower Egypt, cradle of the ancestral religion, would draw the precious burden to the funerary temple. Behind them was assembled the most imposing procession seen since the death of Amenophis III-Nebmaetre.

The "Nine Friends of the King", a symbolic group similar to the privy council of the archaic kings of the north, were led by the official called "Mouth of God" or "Attached to the God", who was in charge of all the great oxen

144. Nobles of the realm drawing the royal catafalque : painting from Tutankhamen's tomb

for the king's sacrifices; he wore a ritual cape and held a pommelled cane. All the nobles taking part in this ceremony wore white sandals as befitted their canonical role (144). The men's procession naturally also included all the priests who had presided over or taken part in the embalming, and many other high officials. The women were grouped in serried ranks, and the queen, "the wife of the god", wore the same white mourning dress and headband as the others. Between the two groups of men and women the courtiers themselves carried the essential pieces of burial furniture which were to be placed in the "eternal dwelling". These included thrones, beds, coffers laden with jewels and ritual garments, vases and jars filled with unguents, wine-jars, boxes containing offerings, golden chariots, arms, games, ritual statues and funerary statuettes, lamps and boats. The four canopic urns, protected by their successive coffers, were drawn along in the centre of a procession similar to that accompanying the body whose organs they contained. The priests who walked in front of the two sleds regularly poured libations of the milk which would make rebirth possible and ensure the king's adoption into the world of the gods. The chanted dirges of the professional mourners rose above the laments of the people on both banks who had come to see their king buried.

Eventually the procession reached the canal leading from the Nile to the funerary temple. Boats awaited them and everyone embarked. The professional mourners crouched on the cabin roofs and resumed their keening, while the priests, led by the master of ceremonies directed the flotilla along the route prescribed by the rites of ancient royal liturgy. For the sovereign to be reborn it was necessary that a symbolic pilgrimage be made to the holy cities of the delta, where since the most ancient times Egyptian kings had always gone, among

238

which was Buto their necropolis. The principal halts of the journey corresponded almost exactly to the four cardinal points of the delta where these cities were situated (145). Sais, to the west, represented the necropolis where the body was buried; Buto to the north, with its famous canal, was an essential stage of the transformations within the aquatic world of the primordial abyss, evoking the water surrounding the unborn child; and Mendes to the east whose name could be written with the two pillars of Osiris, the *djed* pillars, evoking the concept of air. There, said the old texts, the gods Shu and Tefenet were reunited, or again, according to the 17th chapter of *The Book of the Dead*, that was where the souls of Osiris and Re had joined. Finally, the southern-most city which completed the cycle was Heliopolis, the city of the sun, symbolizing the fourth element, fire, where the heavenly body arose in youthful glory between the two hills on the horizon.

At each ritual halt the officiating priests disembarked and unveiled appropriate statuettes and objects. Offerings were left on the river-bank, exposed to the sun, which now shone high in the heavens. Then the water-borne procession reached the quay of the king's funerary temple, most of which was still unfinished. Priests awaited the body and its escort in the shade of a hall where the "Divine Father" Ay was to perform the first act of his brief reign as pharaoh.

At dawn the young widow, heir to the throne, had formally confirmed him as her co-regent, and this decision on the part of Ankhesenamun silenced, for a time at least, the claims of the pretender supported by the Memphite army and

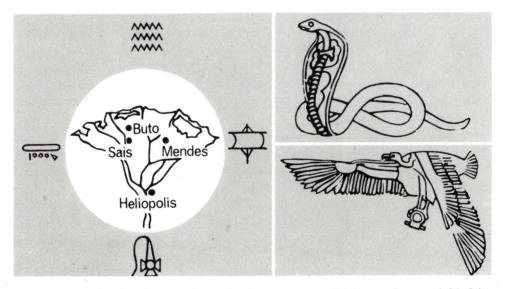

145. Diagram showing the sites of the principal holy towns which were the essential halting places during the royal funerary rites and evoke the most ancient pilgrimages. They correspond probably to the four cardinal points of the compass

the priests of Amun. Ay, succeeding to a child whose grandfather he may possibly have been, was to perform for him the duty which every son accomplished for his father, as Horus did for his father Osiris, the "opening of the mouth and eyes", or in other words the ceremony of restoring to the mummy the use of its senses (147). Numerous preparatory gestures were made over the statues of the dead king and all the priests of the sanctuary had their precise role to play in the accompanying purifications and fumigations. The whole ceremony lasted four long days, at the end of which the new king Ay appearing in the *Setem* priest's costume, wearing a leopard-skin, probably symbolizing his function as repairer of evil, and the blue leather *khepresh*, prepared to officiate. A bull had just been sacrificed and the forefoot and heart presented to the mummy. Ay then seized an adze and made the last magic gestures, ending by touching the mouth and eyes to open them to eternal life.

On the following day at dawn the procession again set forth, this time for the necropolis. The mourners again wept aloud and the men carried long stalks of papyrus, symbolic of the goddess Hathor's domain, for which Tutankhamen was bound. The red oxen had been left behind; now the "Nine Friends" and the two viziers—of the North and South—drew the ropes attached to the bier behind which followed a last high dignitary of the royal procession. At the necropolis, dancers called *muou*—dressed like the ancient spirits of Buto in short loincloths and tall reed head-dresses—emerged from a kiosk shaped like a primitive sanctuary of the Northern region, and performed a ritual dance as they moved forward to meet the immense procession; Tutankhamen was thus welcomed to the soil, where he would soon be laid, by ancient concepts which would help him in the recomposition of his body.

An atmosphere of feverish activity still filled the necropolis, where the sepulchre was barely complete, and the paintings were still drying on three walls of the burial chamber. The fourth could only be built up and painted after the contents of the bier, which were almost too large for the room, had been brought in and reassembled around the sarcophagus. This had been hastily finished, and its lid was not of the same beautiful compact sandstone, but of granite painted to match.

While the priests in the tomb supervised the setting of each piece of the burial furniture in its appointed place, those in charge of the "necklaces of the funeral procession" again removed from the coffers the magnificent long chains which they would pretend to place around the king's neck. For the mummy had now been removed from the bier and set standing, with infinite care, at the entrance to the tomb, upon a newly-strewn layer of fine sand. A libation of water recalling the purification of the great gods of the Osirian myth was poured over the mask and the shroud. Then the body was presented with the "crown of justification" made of olive-leaves, blue lotus-petals and cornflowers (146), and King Ay confirmed the opening of the mouth by a sacred gesture with the adze. At every move formulas from *The Book of the Dead* were recited. When the ceremonies were over, Tutankhamen's mummy, surrounded by huge elaborate bouquets,

240

146. The "crown of justification" on the forehead of the king's first mummiform coffin

was in possession of all the means of shaking off the bonds of death which are merely transient. It was reanimated since Ay, in the role of the *Setem* priest, had restored the escaped *anima* (or soul) to the body, which could now proceed upon the road to eternity.

At the moment when the mummy was to be placed in the tomb, the women of the royal family, moving away from the professional female mourners, rushed to the body and clung to its legs. Ankhesenamum clutched the body so tightly that the dust she had thrown over herself clung to the shroud. Tey, the wife of the new king and formerly "Nurse" to Nefertiti; Mutnedjmet, Nefertiti's sister and Ankhesenamun's aunt, and the surviving daughters of Akhenaten raised their voices in a pathetic complaint, a sudden human expression of pain shattering the atmosphere of sublime resignation. At the same time vessels of red earthenware were broken.

> I am thy wife, O great one—do not leave me!
> Is it thy good pleasure, O my brother, that I should go far from thee?
> How can it be that I go away alone?
> I say: "I accompany thee, O thou who didst like to converse with me,"
> But thou remainest silent and speakest not!

147. *Ay as king performs the ritual act of opening the mouth and eyes of the mummy*

To which the ladies of the court, in dramatic attitudes of mourning, replied:

> Alas, alas!
> Raise, raise ceaseless laments!
> O, what a downfall!
> Fair traveller departed for the land of eternity,
> Here he is captured!
> Thou who hadst many people,
> Thou art in the earth which loves solitude!
> Thou who didst move thy legs and didst walk,
> Thou art wrapped and firmly bound!
> Thou who hadst many linen garments and didst like to wear them,
> Thou liest in yesterday's worn linen!

When the mummy was taken away, Ankhesenamum did not leave it finally; she accompanied the few priests and the king's two most faithful friends, Nakhtmin and Maya, who escorted Ay into the tomb. The widow followed the king's mortal remains, surrounded by her sisters, Meritaten, who set an ivory palette at the feet of Anubis' statue and Neferneferure, who added to the treasure an inlaid box with coloured glass-paste with her own effigy on it (148). Most of the men had been made to leave the tomb after depositing all the requisite objects in the east chamber. In the antechamber (south), while the technicians hastily assembled the gilt shrines of the golden room (or western

242

chamber), with proper regard for their orientation as indicated by signs on their northern and western panels, the mummy had already been laid in its wonderful solid gold coffin. Before the lid was laid on it, unguents were again poured all over the body, and then the coffin was wrapped in its red shroud. At the neck lay a collar of fresh flowers and leaves in preparation for the banquet of eternity which the funeral escort concluding the burial ceremonies would also attend.

The heavy coffin was placed in the wooden and inlaid gold-plated one, and this, once closed, was in turn wrapped in a very fine linen shroud with a garland of olive and willow leaves, and blue lotus petals and cornflowers round the chest. The "crown of justification" was placed upon the linen on top of the sacred snake and vulture of the royal head-dress. Finally the third coffin of gilt wood received its great burden after which it was closed, and another crown of justification placed around the sacred animals of the coif. Lastly the whole was wrapped in several linen sheets. The final weight of the coffins containing the mummy when placed in the golden room, the adjacent burial chamber, was immense. The sarcophagus of compact red sandstone was decorated at each corner with the raised image of a winged goddess; Isis at the north-west; Nephthys at the south-west; Neith at the north-east and Serket at the south-east (XXXI). Against the southern end of the sarcophagus stood a tall *djed* pillar, the emblem which had become Osirian, painted in vivid colours.

The final burial rites were carried out comparatively swiftly, and only the specialists, a few priests and Maya, the chief of works, remained to supervise the closing of the granite lid. No doubt owing to lack of space this was awkwardly handled; first the feet of the last coffin had to be sawn for they prevented the lid of the sarcophagus from closing, and when the carpenters had rapidly planed the feet of the coffin, the lid was dropped and broke in two pieces. The crack was plastered over and repainted to match the sandstone.

During this time a chancellor had removed from the coffer, which bore a hieratic inscription saying that it contained the "seals of the funerary procession" (found in the antechamber), the seals with which he stamped the clay pellets prepared by his assistants. They also sealed all the blackened wood boxes and the chests which held the materials and jewels displayed during the mystic pilgrimage and procession. The big chest enclosing the canopic urns and the small sarcophagi containing the two foetuses were also closed. In the case of the latter the lustration rite had been repeated at the entrance of the tomb.

When the last panel of the outer gilt shrine was erected, it became possible to set all the objects in their appointed places. A priest closed the doors of the four shrines, one after the other, and sealed them, while the masons began to erect the mud-brick wall which would separate the golden room from the antechamber. The next day the wall would be dry and the great pictures of the gods which were to complete the decoration of this southern wall could be drawn upon it and then painted. Only a small doorway would be left, which would afterwards be walled up like all the others in the tomb, with the exception of the entrance to the north chamber.

Outside the tomb night had fallen, and the torches lit up the immense tent erected in the necropolis for the funeral banquet. The mourning period was now over, and the cries of the mourners were hushed. Each guest wore a floral collar similar to that on the king's solid gold coffin, consisting of nine rows of different elements upon a ground of papyrus; small blue discoid glazed terracotta beads mingled with tiny fruits, willow-leaves, date-palm leaves, cornflowers, blue lotus and other plants including slices of mandrake, the famous love-fruit.

The sound and rhythm of songs and dances performed during the banquet evoked the act of creation, and the ritual drunkenness of the goddess Hathor, who watched over the dead and presided over love, was intended to help the deceased who, however invisible, shared the *agape* or love-feast, to become a new being of his own making. The unguents which had been poured so liberally over the dead body to reconstitute its flesh were now placed, in scented cones, on top of the guests' wigs, and ran down their bodies during the meal.

Another offering would be made to the dead king at the next festival during that month, and in the funerary temple the priests were appointed to supervise the regular observation of the dead king's cult. But, before the living could leave the necropolis, it was important to place in a specially contrived store not only the dishes used for ritual episodes of the banquet and the linen which might have touched the burial objects (that is, the remains of embalming bandages or pieces of the statuettes' robes), together with the funeral mask of the longest of the two mummified foetuses which had, like the king's body, been given lustrations outside the tomb and which had been forgotten there, but also the beautiful necklaces—the last link between the living and the dead, which had served during the hours of mystical drunkenness to assist the young king, alone in the darkness of the tomb, to find his path towards immortality.

148. The lid of a box showing the effigy of princess Neferneferure

8 The dead god is reborn

THE KING WHO had officially returned to the traditional religion after the period of the Amarnan heresy was entitled to a strictly Osirian burial. Therefore Tutankhamen's mummified mortal remains had taken the form of those of Osiris. Osiris had been the victim of a death which removed him from human ken, but he had been transformed into an eternal body by the solicitude of the divine family.

The whole pantheon of gods and spirits was invoked, the innumerable resources of magic drawn upon to help him to reach the final stage: the dawn of resurrection. And it was this final stage which made possible the renewal of his supreme energy. At the end of his arduous search for survival, the dead Osiris would reappear in the aspect of the rising sun, Re. Those were the two basic tenets of Egyptian religious theory; simple but grandiose. There were not two entities; Osiris and Re were the two essential aspects, the dead and the living, of a single force whose constants and variants the Egyptians tried to describe and explain by every means including the use of countless symbols.

The royal tombs of the XVIIIth Dynasty from Tuthmosis I to Amenophis III, displayed on their inner walls material which might truthfully be called a "book", for there was a beginning and an end: the illustrations give an account of the twelve hours of the sun's travail during the night until its rebirth. This is known as *The Book of the Am-Duat* (or "What there is in the beyond"). None of these royal tombs have *The Book of the Dead* on their walls, nor any of the scenes of daily life which adorn the noblemen's chapels and give us such pleasure to observe. Until the Amarnan revolution, the graves of the masters of Thebes repeated the dramatic story of the sun's gestation and its rebirth at the fifth hour, when the god's boat slid over a pyramidal shape which protected the divine egg from which the sun emerged. The symbol of the god-to-come is the scarab which one finds as the image of "becoming" at the prow of the solar bark which rises from the horizon at the twelfth hour.

After the heretical period during which the traditional burial rites had fallen into disuse at Tell el Amarna by king and commoner alike, Tutankhamen's tomb, though architecturally rudimentary and barely decorated, marked a return to ancestral rites. Painted on the west wall of the "golden room", the twelve dog-headed baboons and the bark of the dead sun illustrated the first

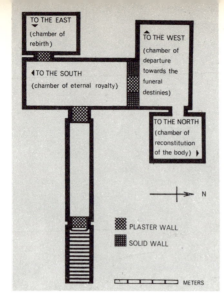

149. *Plan of the tomb showing the ritual purpose of each of its four chambers*

150. *The sarcophagus and the first mummiform coffin as they are now in the tomb in the Valley of the Kings*

hour of night. This was probably sufficient, symbolically, to allow the new Osiris to set out upon his journey towards solar rebirth. There had been no time to appoint the tomb with suitable—and complete—pomp and splendour, but everything it contained was arranged, according to the prescribed chapters, around the body which had been rendered as indestructible and everlasting as the gold, or divine flesh, with which it was covered.

In the shadows of the hypogeum, overlooked by the gigantic natural pyramid of the Theban peak, the dead king was to undergo the various phases of the cycle which had been evoked during his funeral to prepare him for the great journey. For the first time in a royal tomb, as guarantee that the rites had been properly observed these burial ceremonies were depicted on the east wall and part of the north wall of the burial chamber. The last magical gestures by the new king Ay over the mummy permitted the Osiris, Tutankhamen, to enter the other world where he was received by the "Lady of the Sky, Nut, mistress of the gods", who offered him a libation.

In fact, everything necessary for the tragic and sublime transformation was assembled in four rooms, and in spite of theft and the ensuing disorder, it is possible to discern that the burial furniture was arranged systematically.

The most important room of all royal tombs was the "golden room", containing the coffins and the mummy (67, 73-75). It communicated by a doorless opening with the little room which the excavators called the Treasury, in which had been placed one of the principal objects: the immense canopy over the canopic chest (151), where the viscera had been placed at the time of embalming. Only the heart was left in the body. The belly of each canopic urn was ascribed to a goddess, and the lids were carved heads of the four sons of Horus. Each of these spirits was in fact the sublimation of one of the dead man's organs: Imset stood for the liver which was protected by the goddess Isis, south-west (152b);

246

151. *The external canopic coffer on its sledge in the place where it was deposited on the day of the funeral*

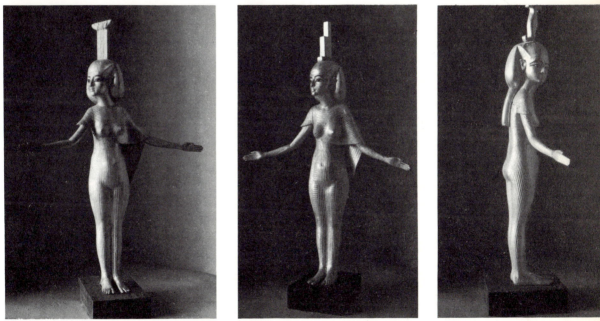

152. *(a) Nephthys, (b) Isis and, (c) Neith protecting the canopic urns*

Hapi was the lungs, guarded by the goddess Nephthys, north-west (152a); Duamutef, the stomach, was watched over by Neith, south-east (152c); and finally the goddess Serket protected the intestines (XXXI), evoked by the spirit Kebekhsenuf, north-east. The purpose of some of the rites performed at the funeral, which were to last for ever, was to re-unite the revived organs and the

247

153. *The god Ihy playing a sistrum*

154. *Menkheret carrying Tutankhamen in a shroud*

155, 156, 157. *Three statuettes used in the mystical pilgrimages during the funeral of Sethos II: from paintings in his tomb in the Valley of the Kings*

158, 159. Ritual statuettes preserved in their coffers

intact body to allow rebirth. No door, therefore, separated the small room containing the canopic urns from the burial chamber containing the mummy.

To help this fusion of the king's body, all the necessary equipment used in the archaic rites observed in the marshes at Buto was stacked against the walls and the canopic shrine, and some put in twenty-two black wooden shrines (158, 159). The origins of these mysterious rites were so remote that some of their episodes may have been forgotten by those participating in them, but all knew that they involved the parallel development of the germ which was the new-born deity.

Certain images are clear; for instance, Tutankhamen in his papyrus boat harpooning an invisible animal represented the triumph of right and innocence over the demon of the swamps, often personified by the hippopotamus (XLV). But

249

what was the significance of the deity called Menkheret, carrying on high the body of the king, wearing the red crown and wrapped in a sort of shroud (154)? Although the detailed interpretation of many objects still escapes us, it is possible to follow the mysterious phenomena of magically protected gestation.

The numerous barks and boats associated with the funerary pilgrimages would carry the dead man, once again a foetus, to the different stages in the aquatic region of the gravid mother-goddess's womb. Like the son of Osiris, in the swamps of Chemmis in the delta, he would encounter attacking demons, to oppose him as Seth had opposed his brother's son. Triumphing over evil by harpooning the demon, preserved from baleful influences by the benevolent cheetah which bore him on its back, he would cross various thresholds; with the aid of the spirit Menkheret, carrying him, almost inert, in the initial moments of his vegetative condition he would proceed, assisted by the gods of the cardinal cities, the holiest one, towards the final stages of his sojourn in the abyss.

All the wooden objects which had been gilded and painted in black—in ancient Egypt the colour of re-birth and not of mourning—are certainly connected with these primeval rites. The Osirian legend clearly alludes to them when it states that the goddess Isis, after being fecundated by the dead Osiris, whom she had invigorated by her magic, concealed her son in the marshes. It is certain that this episode concerns the pregnancy of the goddess and the fate of the child she bore within her, and not, as has been thought for so long, his first childhood. But many other symbols are still obscure and disconcerting to us; for example, Amun's goose, found between the golden shrines, is involved in the same rites, and it is known that this bird was connected with the birth of the sun. The two statuettes of the little child-king, in the image of the god Ihy, the sistrum-player, son of the goddess Hathor, also belong to the birth myths (153).

As for the head of the sacred cow, probably the goddess Hathor emerging from the papyrus thickets, this might well recall a very old legend of which there are three versions, originating in the myth of Horus. Hesa, the cow, a secondary manifestation of the goddess Isis, mother of Anubis—identified with Horus—had her throat cut by her son. The criminal was punished, his skin and flesh being separated from his bones, and order was re-established by the god Thoth. From the skin, the goddess made the famous *nebride*, known to have belonged to the god Anubis, and filled it with an unguent made of her milk, which would henceforth restore flesh to the dead and vitality to their skin. It was the mother-goddess Isis who gave it to the dead who thereby became her son Horus.

In the black boxes, the many black statuettes of the *ushabtis*, some entirely gold-plated save for their faces, others simply bearing accessories of the precious metal, were all portraits of the dead king (163). They were, in a manner of speaking, his servants, but not, as we should understand today, individuals attached to his service. Rather they were the projections of given aspects of the

LI. *Detail of the gilded shrine: the queen Ankhesenamun at the feet of the king*

dead man himself, enabling him to deal with any contingency in any place or at any time; in short, to be permanently ready to respond to his call. Probably at the dawn of time in Egypt, as in other civilizations, royal servants were systematically put to death when their master died.

To assist the deceased to reconstitute himself and be reborn, the great silhouette of Osiris, laid flat in a coffer at the bottom of the tomb, was covered with grain which was watered (160). The corn soon germinated, its tender young shoots giving promise of a harvest. This magical mechanism was intended to recreate the process leading to resurrection. At all costs the body had to remake itself, and must possess the silver bones of its father and the gold skin and flesh inherited from its mother; it was probably to underline the permanence of these two elements that within the chamber set aside for the mysteries of new life, in the coffins fitted within each other, were a statuette of Amenophis III, the king's father, and a curl of Queen Tiye's hair. Every effort was made to prepare for birth.

After the first two stages of the pilgrimages at Sais and Buto, the third halt was at Mendes, the eastern city of the delta where the *djed* pillar had been re-erected and the head replaced upon the dismembered spinal column of the sacrificed god; there the unborn creature received its two souls: that of its past body, Osiris, and that of its eternal one, Re.

These two entities attributed to the foetus on the eve of its birth can be associated with two aspects of the dead man's individuality, and to two principles of which one is masculine while the other may be feminine: the male genital organs and the vulva, or alternatively, the two royal crowns. This would correspond to the two placentas, mentioned in the texts, of which one, the invisible one, remains at birth "the non-manifested form of the king". If one is prepared to accept these basic notions of Egyptian funerary beliefs, which are common throughout Africa, one can understand why two small coffins, bearing Tutankhamen's name and laid head to foot and side by side in a plain chest, contained the mummies of two seven- or eight-month foetuses, one of them probably female (161, 162). It does not seem possible that in the midst of such a special collection of objects a place should have been set aside for two supposedly still-born children of Tutankhamen and Ankhesenamun. Why should such royal children, dying before their father, be buried in his tomb? There is nothing to confirm or to invalidate such an hypothesis, but the pattern of the archaic delta ritual invites one to consider the little mummies as the equivalents of the two placental (*khonsu*) images in Horemheb's tomb, which contained remnants of burial furnishings specifically connected with the delta ritual, as did the ravaged tombs of Amenophis II and Tuthmosis IV.

Like Horus in the marshes of Chemmis, the divine aspect of the king, prior to his rebirth, was vulnerable to all accidents lying in wait for a developing being. Isis must watch over him, and, "mistress of the two braziers", fan the flame of

LII. *Tutankhamen in the form of the dog Anubis during the course of his transformations.*

253

160. Osiris as a mummy sprouting in his wooden sarcophagus.   161. One of the two mummified foetuses probably necessary for the rites of rebirth.   162. The north-west corner of the north canopic chamber. Note the coffer containing the two foetuses

the lamps and torches to disperse the night and its miasmas. So that evil-doers lurking in the shadows might be permanently destroyed, light hunting chariots were heaped against the wall of the tomb, together with bows and arrows to allow the god Shed, like Horus the saviour, to massacre the infamous demons whose unbearably ugly and malefic shapes were poetically interpreted by images of desert animals pierced by arrows and bitten by dogs (represented on the quiver near the chariots). The protecting cheetah is seen everywhere, pursuing the enemy, and its familiar muzzle adorns both ends of the chest to confer even greater potency upon its contents.

Covered with the royal titles or magical hieroglyphs, the coffers held jewels to speed the sovereign's early "becoming"; the *wedjet*-eye promised a reconstitution of the being; divine boats bore the sun about to reappear in all its symbolic forms; and the scarab in particular, the central part of the royal given name, was the image of transmutation towards rebirth as well. Finally, Osiris himself, or the dead *djed* pillar, the image of the reconstituted body, occupied the central part of the elaborate pendentives, framed either by the goddesses Nephthys and Isis, the great guardians of the mummy, or by the two goddesses of Upper and Lower Egypt (also identified with the two placentas), Nekhabet the vulture of the South and Wadjet the cobra of the North.

In this context the little coffin of blackened wood dedicated by Maya, containing the image of the king on his deathbed, reveals its actual meaning. It was to remain in the room connected with these rites of revivification until both the mummy's souls (the two birds on either side of the corpse in Maya's sculpture) were restored to it. Three-quarters of the subterranean journey were therefore already assured, and before its solar rebirth the new being, still in the darkness but stirring with life, was ready to undergo the last stage of its transformations.

254

163. *Different ushabtis of Tutankhamen*

164. *The central part of the zodiac of Dendera: Graeco-Roman period (Louvre)*

For this reason the alert Anubis, wrapped in a linen garment from Akhenaten's looms, gazed at the golden shrines from his coffer at the entrance of the burial chamber (LII). Under the garment and around his neck was a floral necklace entwined in a sort of scarf tied upon a long ribbon, its ends falling to the forepaws. Anubis, with human eyes, was the young dog with whom the royal child was sometimes compared in his early years. According to some mythological texts Anubis was Horus himself, and is also identified with the child-god Harpocrates. Word-play explains his name as we find it in the Jumilhac papyrus in the Louvre: Anp(u). The hieroglyph *A* stands for the wind; *N* the water; *P* the *gebel* or rocky desert. By a strange coincidence those are the very attributes of three of the four primordial stations of the pilgrimage to the holy cities of the delta which the dead must visit to be reborn: Mendes, Buto, and Sais.

Anpu-Anubis, so often called *Imy-ut*, that is, he who is in the skin (or the placenta), therefore represents the unborn child, like Horus the infant in the papyrus thickets of the delta in the heart of the Chemmis marshes. Nothing remains but for him to appear once more after the final rites granting him possession of fire, to point at the horizon of the world like a rising sun.

On leaving this room which evokes the Northern marshes, one's eyes fall upon Anubis. According to an inscription on the temple at Abydos, it is he who inspires the fear of Osiris, and is called "god of the Northern gate", since he guards the entrance to the swamps of the North. Anubis destined for rebirth: that is the meaning of the figure of the black dog still held in the shadows and "master of mummification". In the centre of the sky within the zodiac of Dendera the deity whose life is written in the stars is also portrayed by the dog, standing upright, in the form of *Wepwawet*, "opener of the paths" (164).

Was it perhaps because of the connection of Anubis, "master of the chests", with scribes and scrolls of papyrus that the writing palette of the princess Meritaten was laid between his forepaws? *The Book of the Dead* devotes a chapter to the scribe's palette, instrument of the god Thoth, arbiter of all conflicts, restorer of harmony and of the proper rhythm of the world through his knowledge of the rites. The roll of plant fibres upon which he traces signs recording the divine word is made of papyrus from the primeval marshes.

One can therefore be certain that the room Carter called the Treasury corresponded to the first stage of the mummy's transformation into an immortal being and evoked the aquatic origin of the world. Let us return briefly to the tomb of Sethos II in the Valley of the Kings which—by sheer coincidence—was used as a laboratory for treating the objects of Tutankhamen's treasure. On the walls of one room at the end of the passage leading to the first hall of four pillars, were paintings identical with most of the statuettes of the king and of the spirits which were found undamaged in the northern room of Tutankhamen's tomb. Careful study of the paintings correlated with the Tutankhamen statues would certainly yield conclusive results (155, 156, 157). In the first place it strikes one

LIII. *One of the two life-size statues of the king:*
black wood with applied gilded plaster

256

that this chamber, preceding the first hall of pillars in the XVIIIth Dynasty tombs (excluding that of Amenophis I and Hatshepsut) corresponds to the well-hole, generally interpreted as a barrier against both thieves and infiltration by water. However one must now also admit that it represents symbolically the aquatic region in which the "becoming being" dwells as it were in his mother's uteral water. Of course there is no such "well" in Akhenaten's tomb, but one was scrupulously built into that of Horemheb, the merciless enemy of reform.

All the objects which are mentioned in later times as having to occupy four distinct and separate positions, although close to the burial chamber, were stored in this north room in Tutankhamen's tomb. A papyrus now in the Turin museum shows the ground-plan of Ramesses IV's tomb, in which, beyond the golden burial chamber, four other rooms contained the various items which had all been placed in Tutankhamen's single northern room. There was the corridor for the *ushabtis*, the resting-place of the gods (the statuettes figuring in the rites of Buto); the Treasury (for the jewels) and finally the chamber mainly devoted to the canopic urns. These areas surrounded a room called the "stopping room", which was the last trace of the earlier well.

We enter the burial chamber where the yellow background to the wall-decorations echoes the gold of divine life. On the back of the Turin papyrus it is also called the "hall of the chariot"—a forerunner, perhaps, of early Western chariot tombs. In the centre of the plan, surrounding the king's funeral sarcophagus, five yellow rectangles, one within the other, and the outer one separated from the rest by a thicker line at the corners, remained unexplained—until the discovery of Tutankhamen's tomb when it became clear that these represented the gilt shrines (165). At the end of the XVIIIth Dynasty there were normally only four of these.

Tutankhamen's burial chamber was intended to restore to the mummified monarch, treated as the god Osiris, all the royal prerogatives he had enjoyed on earth; that is why the gilded wooden shrines were of different shapes, for each symbolized a different facet of the king. The first, immediately next to the sarcophagus itself, an evocation of the archaic palaces of the northern kings, was the *Per-Nu* or "house of the flame" (166a), recalling the shrine where the king had been crowned with the divine *uraeus*. The doors of the large gilt shrine, both inside and out, showed Isis and Nephthys spreading their benevolent wings. On the outside, the rear panel displayed the two goddesses, facing each other, flapping their wings to restore the breath of life to the dead king. On the ceiling was a magnificent picture of the goddess Nut, the celestial vault, with her winged arms outstretched over the sovereign's body.

One of the greatest surprises, to the Egyptologists, was the absence of a richly illustrated papyrus: *The Book of the Dead* of Tutankhamen—or of anything similar. Moreover, the very unassuming decorations on the west wall of the

LIV. *Image of the king's mummy on its funeral bed flanked by the "two souls" of the dead man, dedicated by Maya*

259

165. Ancient plan of Ramesses IV's tomb. The coffin room (Museo Egizio, Turin)

"golden chamber" made only faint allusion to the many images of *The Book of the Am-Duat*. However, the panels of each of the golden shrines were wholly covered with the most important chapters of both *The Book of the Dead* and that of *Am-Duat*. Only the first, the Northern palace, had relief decoration; on its interior it bore the text of the 17th chapter of *The Book of the Dead*, in which the demiurge explains his own creation and the workings of his divine nature. The whole company of gods who protect the canopic urns are there.

The next two shrines had the outer shape of the Southern temple, or *Per-Wer* (166*b*). In the first of these two Southern chapels the incised reliefs again refer to burial ceremonies. Inside, near the right door-panel, two *wedjet* eyes symbolize the sun and the moon, and by sympathetic magic restore eternal life to the dead (167). Outside the doors infernal spirits grasping knives stand guard; they are evocations of the 147th chapter of *The Book of the Dead* describing the gates of the other world (168). The inside door-panels are again decorated with Isis and Nephthys.

166. a. Drawings of the gilded shrine evoking the sanctuary of the North; b. One of the two sanctuaries of the South; c. The shrine evoking the sanctuary of the feast of Sed

167. *Door of one of the gilded shrines similar to the first sanctuary of the South*

168. *The infernal spirits, on the door of a gilded shrine evoking the first sanctuary of the South*

The second of these two Southern shrines is decorated in a style strongly influenced by Amarnan art. Under the cornice and the lintel, on the two doors decorated with the solar disc, are portraits of Tutankhamen; on the left one, the sovereign, followed by the Isis, approaches Osiris; on the right, followed by the Maet, he faces Re Harakhti. He thus confronts the two entities which are to constitute his future being; Osiris, with whom he has already been identified, and Re, the sun god whose shape he has still to assume. Indeed upon the inside, he is shown stepping into the gods' bark with them (169). He will encounter the celestial powers, including the seven cows and the sacred bull which are to provide him with divine nourishment during his journey, flagged at the four cardinal points by the steering oars. This ceiling still shows the beautiful goddess Nut, whose arms are fringed with wings, and the inner panels of the doors are guarded by spirits of the other world. Various chapters of *The Book of the Dead*, concerning the dead man's transformations, cover the walls (170).

169. *The solar boat on which Tutankhamen is escorting the gods*

261

Inside the two golden shrines the mystery continues, and the sovereign, soon to be reborn, is swept along in a glorious flight towards the horizon of the eternal world, as pharaoh at the conclusion of a royal cycle. On the two long outer panels, the texts which accompany some of the illustrations are cryptographic in order to preserve the secrecy of the formulas. This composition describes for the first time the creation of the new solar disc. Anticipating Heraclitus, the Egyptians appear to have believed that the sun, having dispensed its heat during the day, had to recuperate its thermic power during the night, through the bodies of the gods who lived in the chthonian regions. Emulating the sun, the king was to draw from the world of the dead renewed strength for his morning rebirth. He is shown as a mummy and described as "he who hides the hours". Head and feet clasped by *Mehen*, the snake, he holds to the centre of his body the nocturnal disc which is inhabited by a bird with a ram's head. Further on, surrounded by fantastic spirits who are holding or even spitting out this disc, two immense dog- and ram-headed sceptres symbolize the head and neck of Re, evoking the creative power of the sun. Not far from these scenes, a chapter of *The Book of the Dead* relative to preservation of the heart alludes to the life and consciousness of the aspirant to eternity.

In the space between these first three gilt shrines the priests had placed various objects intended to increase the efficacy of the rites and facilitate the transformations. The weapons helped to frighten demons; the hunting of ostriches (demoniac creatures of the desert) suppressed evil spirits, and similarly, even upon the king's mummy the sheath of a dagger reduced to impotence the powers of evil by simply displaying the hunting of bulls and ibexes.

Of all the essential elements in the tomb, unguents were considered to be of prime importance; these had been poured over the mummy in unlimited quantities with the object of restoring to the corpse, by then almost skeletal, its former flesh. But a great deal was also deposited in pots and vases of alabaster, or more often calcite, of the most varied shapes. One depicted the joining of the two kingdoms of the South and North, assured by the vigilance of the spirits of the Nile; but the most original was the well-known pot surmounted by a peaceful lion with its protective tongue protruding—a symbolic image of the king himself (XLIII). The face of the god Bes on the top of two floral columns provided initial protection, and the belly of the vase, depicting an animal hunt, constituted still another safeguard. Oriental influence was very marked in this treatment of the pharaoh's lion attacking a bull (the Egyptian theme depicts the lion and the bull confronting one another). The contents of the vase, protected from putrefaction, were supposed to retain their efficacity as long as the body for which they were intended. To add to the power of the image, the container rested upon four heads with foreign features, representing Egypt's enemies, and set at the four cardinal points.

The walking-sticks, perhaps held by the "king's friends" during the funeral procession, may have been placed in the tomb to allow this escort to perpetuate itself in the other world. The most significant of these, however, from a symbolic

170. Shrine in the form of the second sanctuary of the South. The panels depict (on the left) the creation of the solar disc (and on the right) the king protected by winged goddesses

point of view, were those whose pommels, one of silver and one of gold, portrayed Tutankhamen in his early youth (*p.* 136). One is at once tempted to think of the orbs of night and day incarnated by the pharaoh to the very end of pharaonic times: "the living god, sun of Egypt and moon of all countries". Nevertheless, placed as they were between the catafalques where the ever-present, oft-repeated, basic idea was that of the reconstitution of the body, the two statuettes were probably intended to ensure by sympathetic magic the permanence of the bones, which according to ritual texts consisted of silver and were created by the father, and that of the flesh, of gold, issuing from the mother.

The last of the golden shrines was quite different from the others (166c). The two curves of its roof echoed the shape of the jubilee celebration pavilion under which, during the *sed* feast (*sed* means tail or end), after thirty years of rule the king had to restore his energy and vital powers by undergoing a simulacrum of death, reminiscent of the ritual murder of the primitive clan chieftains (171). He was shown wrapped in the robe of the dead, holding the crook and flail of Osiris, during this feast which was celebrated on the first day of *tybi*, the first month of the second season in the Egyptian year, *peret*, or the "emergence" of the fields from the floodwaters.

Clearly, under this golden edifice the sovereign was granted a new lease of life: Tutankhamen was promised immortality by his father Re, the sun. Like Atum, the setting sun, he entered his distant horizon, suggested by the concave roof of the chapel, within which the only decoration consisted of the *djed* pillar of Osiris and of Isis' knot, except for the two sacred eyes on a rectangular section of the left panel. The panels of the two doors were decorated, on the right with a mysterious image apparently of Anubis, standing with his head and paws cut off; from this corpse the reborn god must arise having triumphed over his enemies. Opposite was a crouching spirit representing Horus *Nedjitef*, (that is, a "replica of his father" rather than "his father's avenger").

This last shrine was the one which contained the essential images required to ensure the king's survival. On the back panel was the divine cow, its belly spangled with stars; between its fore and rear legs passed the solar barks, in one of which dwelt Re; the god of the atmosphere, Shou, supported the cow's abdomen and eight spirits supported its legs, symbolizing the pillars of heaven. This design appears here for the first time; the inscription alludes to a legend familiar to us from tombs of the XIXth and XXth Dynasties—Sethos I, Ramesses II and Ramesses III—concerning the last moments of the solar god's earthly reign. Aged and weary of ungrateful humanity, he proceeds to punish it before departing for celestial horizons, borne far away upon the back of the divine cow, and is replaced by Thoth, the divine scribe, god of the moon, who from the sky governs the world in his stead. It is the conclusion of the royal cycle, and the sovereign's entrance to eternity. In this shrine which also contained the *henu* bark and certain chapters of *The Book of the Dead*, not far from the sacred cow, are two spirits holding up the pillars of the sky; they are in the forms of a woman (*djet*) and a man (*neheh*) as symbols of the king's newly acquired immortality. Having reached the goal of his journey and knowing the password, he can say, as does the inscription beneath these two spirits, "I know the name of these two great gods; hers is Djet and his is Neheh".

This no doubt explains the light frame between the last chapel (in the form of a chapel of the South) and that reminiscent of the *sed* feast, which supported the light daisy-spangled veil, probably evocative of the sacred cow's star-spangled belly under which the solar bark had passed.

The oars by the north wall of the gilt shrine may have been for celestial navigation, and the flesh of the reconstituted god was to be perpetually nourished by unguents in the two copies of Anubis' *nebride* in the north-west and south-east corners of the room. Also, no doubt, the double coffers of black varnished wood in the north-west and north-east corners were reminiscent of the instruments which had served in the "ceremony of the opening of the mouth and of the eyes". Before the open door of the outer shrine were a silver trumpet, perhaps to announce the resurrection (?), and the solar goose to confirm the victory of the sun over the shadows. Thus the essential western chamber contained, under many layers, the body of the prince, to whom the royal prerogatives he had enjoyed on earth among men had been restored and strengthened for ever.

The antechamber, probably representing the South, must, before the robberies, have contained everything of importance connected with his pharaonic

171. Shrine in the form of the sanctuary of the feast of Sed

powers. First of all, guarding the entrance to the "golden room" came the two great black statues, the *Kas* of the king and indestructible emanations of his creative personality (LIII). The three large beds associated with embalming may also have served as vehicles for the sovereign in his sublime ascension: the goddess Tueris, with her hippopotamus-snout, protector of birth and child-bearing, bore the mummy towards a new destiny (XXX), and the protective cheetah, its eyes showing the characteristic tears in the corners, vigilantly guarded the pharaoh throughout his reconstructed reign (XXVIII). These two pieces of furniture correspond to the Northern and Southern shrines—those of birth and of the reign. And finally, for the ascension to the divine horizon, the cow-shaped couch was essential in its connection with the shrine of the feast of *sed* (XXIX).

Of the two thrones which were found, the one believed to be a sacerdotal seat, bearing the names of Aten and Amun, must have been used by the king during the great religious ceremonies, as was the stool, originally also placed in this room (XI, XII). The sceptre with which the king consecrated offerings and the coffers containing all the paraphernalia of official rule had been added to the assortment of pieces. But none of the numerous magnificent crowns worn by the king, depicted on all the sanctuary walls, was to be found in the tomb. They were the property of the throne rather than that of its occupant, and as such had to remain within the temple treasury. Only the *khepresh* helmet, which the king wore almost constantly, may have been put in a hatbox in the tomb (106).

Nevertheless, the excavators did find the great parade sticks in the image of the pharaoh's enemies which he could trail in the dust, as he strode majestically among his subjects, in a symbolic defence of his country (XVIII). These objects re-state the protective message of the hunting and battle scenes. The famous chest upon which the young pharaoh in his chariot is shown defeating the Asians and the African Negroes, the delicate painting in which he leads his horses in pursuit of ibexes, wild asses, ostriches and hyenas, or again his triumph over eight lions, is certainly the most splendid example of this symbolism (XVI). Of course, any of the details may be quite accurate: the horse's harness, Tutankhamen's own costume, the decoration of his chariot, the equipment of the cavalry and infantry escort, the Asians' garments and the armour of the Negroes, but the young and frail king cannot actually have lived through any of these scenes. These traditional images, so graphic in style, represented once again the triumph of good over evil and the pharaoh's determined ridding of the earth, and later of the other world, of everything contrary to harmonious patterns of life. The sandals found in the coffer had also their part to play, since they were made to crush underfoot the demons usually shown as bound enemies, as on his footstools (XI).

The gilt chariots, with vanquished and bound enemies as their principal decorative motif, were the official vehicles for his majesty, resplendent as the sun (XIX). Also stored in this antechamber was the dalmatic, possibly used by the kings for the jubilee feasts, its great frieze along the lower hem adding to the magical protection of the hunting-scenes (172). Gloves (173), travelling-cases (p. 58), jewel-boxes, the king's linen, the splendid chair on the back of which eternity protects the royal titles, the hunting corselet, the folding-stool with evil but enslaved ducks' heads for feet, the magnificent bow and the gold and silver-framed mirrors—may all have figured in the king's daily life, but nonetheless shows signs of having been made for strictly funerary purposes. It seems clear that this southern antechamber was intended to hold everything which could contribute, magically, to the recreation of the royal powers sublimated during the dead king's transformations.

There remained the last act of the drama: rebirth. The room the excavators called the annex was entirely dedicated to this, and its door, which faces east, suggests that it was deliberately orientated in this direction to favour the pharaoh's rising at the dawn of his new existence. Although the contents of the room when found were in disorder, the basic elements of the furnishings were sufficiently clear to give a mental picture of what was intended and what its significance was. There were food and drink, toys and childhood objects, an adolescent's furniture, delightful though hieratic poetry on a coffer and on a naos decorated with intimate scenes of the young king's life with his queen

LV. *Detail of the second mummiform coffin.*
Gold-plated wood inlaid with glass-paste

(VII–IX, LI). Sporting scenes rather than battles; a throne reminiscent of the Amarnan period upon which the queen is shown in an attitude more funereal than royal, cases containing headrests, games, the head and bust of a being re-born, a sort of homely shrine: the disparate assortment of objects had one common characteristic: that of magic awakening to life and to the joys of this world.

After his transformations Osiris the king was to spring from the horizon as Re, star of day. By the same token, the new pharaoh would appear upon the throne of "Horus-of-the-Living", succeeding his father and reflecting his image, as Horus, son of Osiris, had been reborn out of the labours of his father, whom Isis had invigorated after death in order to receive his seed. It is probable that the funeral banquet was primarily intended to induce scenes of procreation. Upon the back of the gold-covered throne Ankhesenamun, wearing the official headdress, seems to be anointing Tutankhamen seated in a casual attitude (VI). Although the names of the sovereigns are those of the Theban period (Amun having ousted Aten), the Amarnan globe extends the signs of life, as it did during the couple's childhood. This picture is important also because it shows the floral necklaces worn by the king and queen. Upon a small stand one was still recognizable; it was identical with that laid on the coffin and with those worn by the guests at the funeral banquet, found in such excellent condition in the cache in the Valley of the Kings.

In the depths of his tomb, Tutankhamen prepared for the *agapes* (love feast), but Ankhesenamun, though left among the living, did not desert him, and remained, wherever he was, his "favourite concubine". In commoners' tombs the wife's portrait accompanied the husband, and one often finds among funeral furnishings a small figure evocative of the "feminine principle", at the disposal of the dead man so that the latter may engender and be reborn of himself, becoming the *kamutef* (or bull of his mother). Not far away, the hippopotamus is shown as a paralysed and harmless demon, reduced to impotence in the marshes so that there may be no obstacle to the expected birth.

On a sublimated level, where the poetic elegance of the objects disguise the religious and magical aspect of the scenes depicted, the annex of Tutankhamen's tomb contained everything to favour this birth. Thus the gilt shrine on its sled, found in the antechamber but near the door of the annex from which it had clearly been removed at the time of the robberies, had an essential role to play. A ritualistic shelter for the royal couple, it should have contained statuettes of the king and queen but except for a stand with the king's footprints upon it, it was empty (174). The statuette itself and that of the queen, both probably of solid gold, must have been stolen. On the doors, as on the sides of the shrine, the decoration consists of scenes in which only the two characters, Tutankhamen and Ankhesenamun, appeared, in a variety of episodes centred upon their relationship as lovers and the pleasures of hunting in the marshes.

LVI. *Detail of the mummiform coffin. Gold with inlaid semi-precious stones and glass-paste*

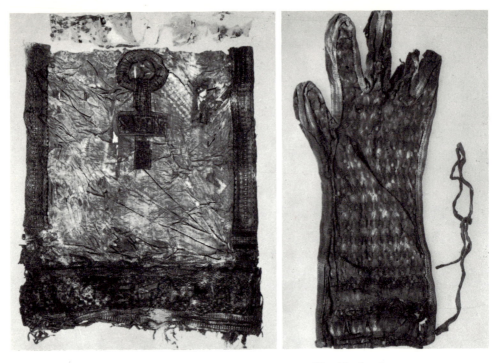

172. The king's dalmatic   *173. The king's glove*

Fondly the devoted wife heaps delicate attentions upon her husband. Dressed as a favourite she brings him the homage of the essential act, expressed by offering the symbols of the goddess Hathor; scent, flowers, and necklaces, presented by a woman who is at the same time presenting herself. And in order that no evil spirit should sap the king's renewed virility or abate the fecundity of his spouse, Tutankhamen is shown seated on a stool, escorted by his tame lion, showering arrows upon the evil wild duck in the papyrus thickets to put the evil birds to flight (176). Pious hands had also laid bundles of arrows in the "chamber of rebirth", that the queen might continue to hand to her husband the weapons he must have ready at every moment. The sovereign is also portrayed on a light papyrus boat, at the beginning of these rites, and Ankhesenamun is shown with him in a formal attitude. In his hand he holds a bunch of birds by the legs. This charming marsh hunting-scene, which is reproduced in almost all commoners' graves from the time of the pyramids, and even reappears in Ptolomaic temples, illustrates not only the obvious pastime of a nobleman, but once again the official ritual extermination of evil, achieved by the destruction of wild-fowl. This helps to explain the great number of boomerangs found in the "chamber of rebirth" for it was with this archaic huntsman's weapon the dead faced the demon (175). The queen is shown in most seductive apparel and is wearing the pendant ear-rings owned by the king as a child. But to ensure the efficacy of the rites, other furniture and coffers had been accumulated, each bearing on its sides representations of vital actions. Every variation on this single theme was present, and

270

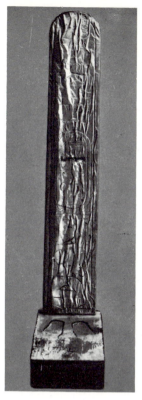

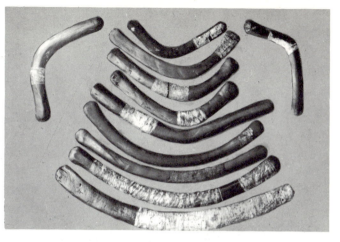

175. *Boomerangs from the eastern room of rebirth*

174. *The base and support of a gold statuette originally placed in the little gilded shrine*

176. *The panel from the desk-shaped coffer: the king hunting and fishing in the marshes*

repeated so often as to appear obsessive. Upon the ivory lid of the famous desk-shaped coffer, the queen offers the king two long bunches of papyrus and lotus entwined with mandrakes—the love-fruit. The couple is depicted upon a background of flowers and apparently beneath vines conducive of sacred drunkenness. The panels of the chest also show animals destroying each other; the propitious dog and cheetah attacking evil bulls and ibexes. Even the beasts were set to serve the dead.

The counterpart of the front panel with the love-scene shows the king seated before a pond in a flowered landscape, with the queen at his side, hunting wild duck in the surrounding thickets. Certain fish are evil. But in the centre of the pool *lates niloticus* and *tilapia nilotica* are symbolical evocations of the double aspect of the deceased in the "lake of life" at both poles of his watery voyage: Sais and Mendes. More than three thousand years later in parts of black Africa a similar concept of the souls of the dead still survives into the twentieth century.

The banquet, then, automatically led up to a Dionysiac conclusion, the ultimate scenes of which were to guarantee strength for survival. By the walls were stacked the king's requirements, preserves of fowl and beef and jars of the finest vintage wines. Scents and unguents were needed at these orgies and alabaster vases of the most elegant, original and sometimes startling shapes, were also an important part of the burial treasure. Here was a family souvenir, a vase in the name of Amenophis III containing precious ointment—there a bottle in the form of a rampant lion leaning against a sign of protection, imitating the attitude of the hippopotamus, goddess of births. But what could be the meaning of the elaborate centrepiece—a boat with an ibex head (184, XXIV)? The most delightful was a jar-lid consisting of a cup forming a nest for four eggs and a new-born bird (XLVII). No more evocative illustration could exist than part of the famous hymn to Aten, inspired if not actually written, by the heretic at Akhetaten:

> As yet unborn the bird already chirps in the egg,
> For thou hast given it the breath of life
> And set the time for it to break the shell,
> When it shall come forth and loudly raise up its voice.

Indeed, it was in this guise that artists sometimes represented a new prince. In fact the tomb awaited his advent. The low beds, some of which could be folded, grouped in this room, ensured that the king would not lack a marriage-bed, and that the new-born god would find all he needed. The little stools his majesty had used during his childhood on earth, his toy-box with the secret lock and case containing his tinder-box (177)—the ancestor of all lighters—and his sling—even castanets bearing Queen Tiye's name were set there.

The presence of some objects is less easily explained: why the sickles for cutting corn? Probably to perpetuate the sacrifice of the agrarian god. Why, in this place where the funeral banquet is depicted, are there no traces of musical instruments? Perhaps the grave-robberies provide the answer to this.

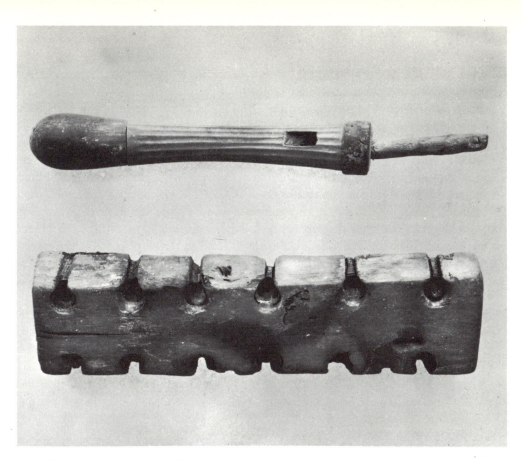

177. Tutankhamen's "lighter"

The votive shields were intended to ward off demons provoked by the king when he played the game of chance known as *senet* (from the word "passage") (XLIX*b*). The big thirty-squared board led the winner through pitfalls and the traps set by his adversaries to victory, when he was proclaimed *maa-kherou*, "right of voice", or rather, "animated of voice", implying that the rites had restored to him the use of his senses and the breath of life. It was a heated battle; the invisible enemy might be represented by pawns shown as prisoners with their hands bound behind them. Conversely, the dead man might choose the protective cheetah's head to adorn his own pawns. That is why the doors of Theban tombs were sometimes decorated with accounts of the magical passage, symbolized by the image of the dead man playing *senet*.

As in commoners' graves and in the fields, bust lararies throughout antiquity encouraged by the exercise of sympathetic magic the rebirth of the dead and the new shoots of the crops. Perhaps the so-called "dummy" of the king is linked with this concept (XLII).

There is no doubt, at any rate, about the function of the headrests, among the most original and beautiful objects of this room. The folding one declares its purpose by its decoration; the concave part shows two heads of Bes, god of births and protector against demons, and probably a reflex image of the benevolent cheetah aspiring to human form. The lotus-flower recalls the rebirth of the sun, and the legs consist of the heads and necks of wild duck, thus rendered impotent. But the most expressive of all the headrests in the tomb is the one of ivory with a column representing Shu, god of the atmosphere. On either side of it two lions of the horizon embody the concepts of today and tomorrow. Far too large, certainly, to be placed under the mummy's neck, these supports were stored in the room which the Egyptians called *mammisi* or "birth house". It will be remembered that under Tutankhamen's neck had been placed a tiny iron headrest. The 166th chapter of *The Book of the Dead*, devoted to this small piece of furniture, shows clearly that it was specifically designed to allow the dead man to rise again by gently lifting his head so that in due course his skull would leave the hollow of the headrest and move like the sun taking up its course at dawn.

At the end of the voyage, the battle won, all obstacles overcome and annihilated, solar birth could take place. The following address could then be made to the deceased:

> Awaken, O sick one, thou who hast slept,
> They have lifted thine head toward the horizon.
> Appear! Thou art justified against him who sought to harm thee;
> Ptah has overthrown thine enemies and has ordered
> Him who stood against thee to be pursued.
> Thou art Horus, son of Hathor,
> He whose head was restored to him
> After it had been cut off;
> Never again shall thine head be taken from thee;
> In the future never again for all eternity shall thine head be taken from thee.

The headrests thus served their purpose in the final transformations of rebirth. At one with the celestial god, the sovereign would share the existence of the rising sun and like Re at dawn could now spring from the primeval ocean above the blue lotus. In the corridor of the tomb, where daylight could at last penetrate, Tutankhamen's mourners had placed this flower, from which emerged the head of the solar child (11).

On the door between the annex and the antechamber, which opened to the east, the traces of seals again referred to the phenomenon of rebirth, on the level of divine incarnation, that is the coming of the pharaoh, god among men. His names might change, but it was always an element of the god on earth which quickened the reigning sovereign. He is not Re, but Horus, "Horus", as the inscription on the headrest says, "son of the goddess Hathor", represented here by Ankhesenamun, beloved of the king. That is why the texts on what is left of the brick door proclaim: "Nebkheprure-Anubis, triumphing over the Nine Bows (all the enemies of Egypt) . . . Anubis, triumphing over the four captive peoples (all the demons who during the voyage to the four cardinal points of the pilgrimage had failed to impede his progress towards rebirth)."

The transfiguration of the dead king, deified in the person of Osiris, took place on earth by a double phenomenon. Re rose on the horizon and, on the throne of the living, the young Horus, visible form of Anubis, the new pharaoh, renewed image of the god, would continue to exercise divine rule on earth.

9 The thrice-married queen and the vengeance of Horemheb

WHEN ONE THINKS of Tutankhamen's death one inevitably imagines the distress of his twenty-year-old widow, suddenly heiress to the throne of the pharaohs after two marriages. But there is no information to be gleaned on this subject from Egyptian annals, which are more silent than ever about this period.

The Hittite kings, however, were more methodical. Their records, no longer kept in Akkadian as their correspondence with Amarna had been, but in several other languages (the annals were written in Nesite or vernacular), give a most vivid picture of some of the events in which the Egyptian rulers of the XVIIIth Dynasty were involved. Among them is a letter from an Egyptian queen—a document so important and so unexpected that Mursil II, son of Suppiluliuma, who wrote the annals of his father's reign, devoted a whole section to it. The impossible had happened: a queen of Egypt had actually asked to marry a foreign prince and share her throne with him. Tutankhamen's widow had taken this unprecedented step, as one can see from this Hittite passage.

While my father was in the country of Karkemish, he sent Lupakkish and Teshub[?]-Zalmash to the country of Amqa [the region of Antioch]. They left; they ravaged the country of Amqa and brought back to my father prisoners and cattle large and small. When the people of Misra [Egypt] learned of the destruction of Amqa, they were afraid, for to make matters worse their master, Bibhuria [Nebkheprure, i.e. Tutankhamen] had just died and the widowed queen of Egypt sent an ambassador to my father and wrote to him in these terms: "My husband is dead and I have no son. People say that you have many sons [*or* that your sons are adult]. If you send me one of your sons he will become my husband for it is repugnant to me to take one of my servants [subjects] to husband." When my father learned this he call together the council of the great [and said to them]: "Since the most ancient times such a thing has never happened before." He decided to send Hattu-Zittish, the chamberlain, [saying] "Go, bring me information worthy of belief; they may try to deceive me; and as to the possibility that they may have a prince, bring me back information worthy of belief." While Hattu-Zittish was absent on the soil of Egypt, my father vanquished the city of Karkemish . . . The ambassador of Egypt, the lord Hanis, came to him. Because my father had instructed Hattu-Zittish when he went to the country of Egypt as follows: "Perhaps they have a prince, they may be trying to deceive me and do not really want one of my sons to reign over them"; the Egyptian queen answered my father in a letter in these words: "Why do you say 'they are trying to deceive me?' If I had a son, should I write to a foreign country in a manner humiliating to me and to my country? You do not believe me and you even say so to me! He who was my husband is

275

dead and I have no son. Should I then perhaps take one of my servants and make of him my husband ? I have written to no other country, I have written [only] to you. They say that you have many sons. Give me one of your sons and he will be my husband and lord of the land of Egypt." Because my father was generous, he granted the lady's request and decided to send his son.

Such an exchange of letters and ambassadors cannot have taken place without the knowledge of the "Divine Father" Ay who was vizier at Thebes; indeed it may even have been instigated by him. The young widow would certainly not have taken such a grave step without being encouraged, perhaps even forced, to do so. If one agrees that this is likely, one can appreciate the critical nature of Ankhesenamun's position. To safeguard the throne of her ancestors, she found herself obliged to marry a prince alien to the pharaonic crown who would thereby acquire a right to it. And she did not hesitate to say in her letter how distasteful she found the prospect of taking a "servant" as a husband. This servant can only have been the "scribe of the recruits", who had become the real dictator at the palace, Horemheb, and not, as is generally assumed, the "Divine Father" Ay who was a close relative of the queen's, indeed probably her grandfather. One can imagine the feverish court life of the time, the intrigues and interference of the priests of Amun over the succession to the throne. Between Karkemish and Thebes, during the minimum period of seventy days required for the preparation of Tutankhamen's mummy, the ambassadors and emissaries would have had the time to make several journeys, of which Horemheb's supporters kept him constantly informed. When the second Egyptian ambassador departed for the headquarters of Suppiluliuma, at the moment when he had just conquered Karkemish, to reiterate the queen's pressing desire for an alliance with the Hittite royal family, Horemheb must already have had his plans laid. Prince Zannanza of the Hittites duly set out with his escort but Horemheb's police, "the men and the horses of Egypt", murdered him on the way. This led to a state of war between Egypt and the Hittites, and Suppiluliuma decided to invade Egypt—or at least boasted that he would. One must, however, understand that Egypt in this context meant the pharaoh's Syrian protectorate; at any rate, Palestine was again invaded. The murderers were captured, judged, condemned and put to death. Horemheb probably went to the front to organize the defences against territorial invasion, but never it seems actually encountered the Hittites.

Henceforth the few who remained true to the heretical faith could no longer count upon the possibility of a marriage between the last legitimate heiress of the XVIIIth Dynasty and a foreign prince. Indeed, only immediate dangers, the threat of revolt at the very gates of Amun's temple and the despair of the royal family can possibly account for this inconceivable step; asking a Hittite to occupy the throne of Egypt was certainly one of the great mistakes of the Amarnan dynasty. But to the elderly vizier Ay, still perhaps loyal to Akhenaten's "international" ideals, it may have meant the acquisition by Egypt of a prince bringing with him the vigour of his race and the support of a powerful people. This policy might also have curbed Horemheb's ascendancy.

For want of a foreign prince, and repelled by the notion of a *mésalliance* in her

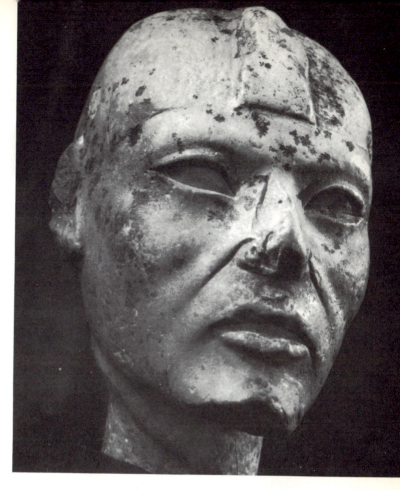

178. A head, thought to be of Ay when pharaoh (Cairo Museum)

own country, the young widow was now fated to share her sovereign's duties and privileges with a co-regent. Being a timid creature, utterly unlike her illustrious forbear Hatshepsut, Ankhesenamun chose her grandfather, the vizier Ay, to play this part. The decision was taken on the eve of the official funeral of Tut-ankhamen, and the "Divine Father" Ay, wearing the *khepresh* and animal skin, performed the ceremony of the "opening of the mouth and eyes" by the tomb as had been done throughout the ages by royal heirs succeeding their fathers (147). Reconstruction of these events, however, does not enable us to carry their interpretation any further. It has been alleged that Horemheb had Ankhesen-amun put to death at the same time as the Hittite prince, but if this were so how can one account for her presence by the side of Ay when king?

Another theory suggests that Ankhesenamun married Ay in order to confer upon him the right to the throne. There is no positive proof of this; only the discovery of a ring (a scarab in the Blanchard collection) bearing the joint cartouches of Ay and Ankhesenamun, confirms their simultaneous presence on the throne. The fact that they reigned together does not necessarily imply their marriage; for one thing, the queen's grandfather, who was also her great-uncle, may have recoiled from marrying his granddaughter, who had already been twice married to close relatives within the royal family. And there was also his wife Tey whom he made queen and who is portrayed as such in his tomb.

277

179. A lion dedicated by Tutankhamen in the temple of Soleb (British Museum)

Ay occupied the throne (178) for four years and displayed a tolerance towards
Aten which reflected his own convictions. By officiating at Tutankhamen's
funeral, he had made himself responsible for maintaining the funeral cult of the
king, and from the time of his ascension he seems to have carried out this duty.
Tutankhamen had gone on with a project of Nebmaetre to have two pink granite
lions carved and he intended to consecrate them to his father in his temple of
Soleb. Only one had been consecrated before his death and Ay undertook to
have the second taken to the same temple (179).

Less comprehensible is his behaviour over the funeral statues of the young
king, for, having built his own funerary temple, Ay proceeded to embellish it
with two statues—admittedly unfinished—of Tutankhamen, which he quite
simply usurped. This somewhat shocking conduct brought him no luck, for
after Ay's death the statues and reliefs (180) were usurped once more by Horemheb and marked with his cartouche.

What reason could there have been, not only for this usurpation by Ay of the
statues, but also for their removal? Was it the anxiety of an old man feeling the
approach of death and desperate to equip his burial chapel with every indispensable effigy—even if it meant stealing from the temple of his predecessor? The
funerary ritual required that the cult of a dead man was to be celebrated at
certain prescribed dates; how then could Ay, the reigning king, reconcile this
aspect of his duties with his covetousness?

And was Ankhesenamun still alive at that time? Did she live at Thebes or

180. *Tutankhamen offering incense to the god Amun. Relief appropriated by Horemheb (Temple of Luxor)*

181. *Fragment of a "marriage vase" found at Ras-Shamra (Ugarit). An Amarnan princess pays homage to her husband, King Niqmat (Damascus Museum)*

elsewhere? Nothing more is heard about the young queen and her delicate figure recedes into the shadows of time. What happened to the other daughters of the Amarnan pair? One of them may have married Niqmat, king of Ugarit (181).

In the royal necropolis, not far from the workmen's village to which, following their masters, they had returned from the heretical city where many had settled for a time, inspectors were negligent, sometimes even deliberately blind, in guarding the dead kings. Since Tutankhamen's funeral dazzling descriptions had circulated of heaped gold, silver and jewels, and the list of all the precious ointments and oils accumulated in the store had haunted the dreams of the greedy. The boldest among them decided to try and penetrate into the tomb. It is difficult to appreciate the effort involved in reaching the subterranean chambers by digging through rubble-filled stairways and passages and crawling through an almost airless tunnel to the bottom of the tomb. Yet this clearly happened twice, as two series of still visible traces in the tunnels and on the inner doors, which had been bricked up again, show. There is no need to assume, as the diggers did, that the pillage was systematic. It seems highly unlikely that a first raid was devoted to removing all the ointments and a subsequent one all the precious metals; the temptation to seize what was most accessible must have been irresistible. At any rate, the thieves knew what they were looking for and where to find it; they left the mummified provisions but stole the unguents and oils. Their raids were well planned; they brought wine-skins with them into which they decanted the greasy liquids—remnants of these skins were found in the tomb. Their knowledge of the tomb was so detailed that they were even familiar with its ground-plan, for they went straight to the little north room which held the handsome chests containing the gold jewellery of the funeral procession. There they burst open the locks and removed many of the jewels. Knowing the whereabouts of the loot they sought, they ignored the great black coffers, leaving their seals untouched. On both occasions they destroyed all semblance of order in the room, emptying some coffers on to the floor in their haste to pick out choice objects. It seems probable that the last of the intruders narrowly escaped being caught red-handed, for a rag bundle containing a number of gold rings was found abandoned in obvious haste. When the necropolis inspectors discovered the violation of the sepulchre, they had to inform Maya, who had probably personally supervised its construction. "Chief of works in the place of eternity, royal scribe, superintendent of the treasure", Maya, was devoted to the young king in whose tomb he had placed on the day of the funeral the little wooden cenotaph dedicating his lord to eternal life (182). Particularly agile inspectors were then sent into the tomb through the thieves' tunnels with instructions to restore order. But they worked too swiftly in the airless subterranean rooms and hastily replaced materials and jewels pell-mell in the gaping coffers. They closed the communicating door between the burial chamber and the antechamber, and in the annex, balanced on top of a pile of other objects, they heaped up pieces removed from the antechamber. They did not even take the trouble to fill in the hole pierced in the wall between the

182. The recumbent figure of the king, dedicated by Maya, in its wooden coffin

antechamber and the annex. Nor did they trouble to replace in this last room the little gilt shrine which had originally been there. But before leaving, the inspectors remembered to replace upon the threshold the fine lotus-shaped bowl which was to offer the reborn king eternal draughts of the elixir of youth.

By then Maya had realized the danger which threatened his dead king and had the entrance of the tomb concealed again under a thick layer of stone-rubble, which from then on formed the raised floor of the valley at this point. This was the second time Maya had sought to protect Tutankhamen from harm.

During his reign Ay had forbidden any manifestation of religious hatred or the profanation of any of Aten's sanctuaries. His death at last left the way open for General Horemheb—more concerned with preserving national institutions than waging war—to achieve his goal. History repeated itself in almost exactly the same way as at the time of Tuthmosis III; Amun's priests helped Horemheb to seize the crown. The celebration of the great feast of Opet was the ideal occasion for his already long-planned accession to power.

183. Horemheb and his god (Museo Egizio, Turin)

184. The alabaster boat decorated with a figure thought to be princess Mutnedjmet

Horemheb was now free to realize his dream. But he had somehow to legitimize his newly acquired rank as the lord of Egypt. There seems to have been no royal daughter whom he could have made his queen; but it seems likely that it was Mutnedjmet, the sister of Nefertiti, who became his wife. This girl was often to be seen nearly always escorted by two female dwarfs. The charming female figure crouching in the bow of the alabaster boat with the ibex figure-head may well be of the girl who was probably the daughter of Ay and Tey (184, XXIV).

This marriage did not encourage Horemheb for very long to honour the memory of his immediate predecessors, and he soon began his acts of destruction. He proceeded in two stages. First he attributed to himself all the more recent monuments, especially those of Tutankhamen and Ay, starting with their statues and temples. That is why the colonnade of Luxor, where the feast of Opet took place, was disfigured by scribe-sculptors instructed to hammer out

Tutankhamen's names and replace them with those of the new king (183).

At Karnak, however, there was one commemorative monument which he did not personally covet—that of Tutankhamen wearing the leopard-skin and standing before the god Amun in the attitude of a sovereign who had just buried his father according to the funerary ritual. Horemheb broke the head and limbs of the statue of the king and removed from the cartouches most of the hieroglyphs spelling his name, but he did not replace them with his own as elsewhere. The priests of Amun had set Horemheb on his throne, and in no circumstances would he wish to consider himself the successor of the Amarnan kings; it was a long time since, during the Atenist heresy, he had called himself Pa-aten-em-heb. If a royal ancestor was to be acquired, it would have to be Amenophis III, so he set to work energetically to proclaim this "truth" throughout the land, and succeeded so well with his propaganda that official lists even in the Ramesside period describe him as the legitimate successor of Amenophis III. In the court annals of the XIXth Dynasty, the years of his reign were counted from the date of Amenophis IV's accession, which explains why Egyptian inscriptions credited him with up to fifty years of rule.

Once established, the new pharaoh embarked upon extremely violent persecutions. In order to justify them, he published an edict, known as the "Edict of Horemheb", which was engraved upon a great stele at Karnak, found near the west wing of the tenth pylon. In this he described the deplorable state of the country at the time of his accession, and the abuses of officials and judges who were assisted by soldiers in their extortions from the poor. The king, whose main concern was to establish law and improve the lot of his people undertook to punish all injustice and to order immediate castigations: prevaricators were to have their noses cut off and exile was reinstated as a sentence.

Obviously he had to blame someone for the deplorable state of affairs he had inherited. The responsibility was ascribed to the four last sovereigns, and Horemheb was at last free to give vent to the hatred engendered by his wounded pride and to satisfy the priests of Amun who had acquiesced in his usurpation of the throne. Teams of workmen despatched to Tell el Amarna razed most of it.

At Thebes, too, he showed his destructiveness. It was at this time that he decided to add three new pylons to the great temple of Amun, so he had all the buildings dedicated by his predecessor to Aten taken to pieces and used more than ten thousand blocks of worked Amarnan stone for the foundations of his pylons. Nothing was fine enough for the dynastic god and Horemheb set himself up as champion of the rehabilitation of Amun's temples and of his clergy. He even surrendered a little of the pharaoh's supreme power by relying too heavily upon the priesthood. He offered his god a magnificent alley of sphinxes connecting Karnak with Luxor and also ordered the construction of the buildings which constituted a preface, so to speak, to the great pillared hall of Karnak. At the same time, with the most single-minded determination, he continued to pursue all those who had either directly or indirectly served the heresy. Ay's tomb was sacked. No doubt he also ordered the desecration of the hiding-place where Tutankhamen had brought together what was left of the Amarnan burial furnishings around the mummy of an anonymous king sheltering in a woman's coffin. Probably because of superstition the body was spared, but all the bricks of unbaked earth which were intended to ensure the protection of the tomb were destroyed. The portrait of Akhenaten on Tiye's shrine was effaced.

In the noblemen's necropolis Horemheb sought out the tombs of those courtiers who had remained faithful to the sovereigns and whom he had decided to annihilate. Huy, viceroy of Nubia was one of these: not only were Tutankhamen's portraits and names hammered out on the walls of Huy's burial chapel, but images of the viceroy himself were attacked.

It was the same in the provinces: from the delta to the Sudan, Horemheb struck everywhere, especially at Akhmim, the birthplace of some of the heretical family, and the steles dedicated by Nakhtmin, to whom we owe some of the most touching *ushabtis* of Tutankhamen, were stripped of King Ay's names. At the same time teams of workmen were despatched to rewrite the names and restore the monuments of the Theban god which Akhenaten had attacked with an equally passionate fury. Each new inscription recalled the harm done by the heretical king, who was now merely alluded to as "the scoundrel". With such evidence of Horemheb's ruthlessness it is not difficult to believe, as some do, that he was capable of assisting in the disposal of Ay and Ankhesenamun.

Everything seems to have been methodically planned and co-ordinated by Horemheb, the "virtuous" proselytizer, who to woo the leaders of the counter-reformation resorted to a type of fanaticism which has been responsible for so many crimes. There was only one flaw in his implacable logic: having done everything in his power to obliterate from human memory Tutankhamen, the young king "who loved Thebes itself better than its god", one wonders why he did not sack his tomb. Was it a belated flicker of respect for the dead, for the last son of Amenophis III, or was it fear of divine retribution? He had not hesitated to violate the tombs of Ay and Tey. Perhaps he thought it possible, without desecrating the divine body, to abandon it to oblivion in the Valley of the Kings.

One may of course prefer to regard this unexpected weakness of Horemheb's as due to yet another effort on the part of Maya, the "royal scribe, superintendent in the place of eternity" and Tutankhamen's faithful friend (185). But this very shrewd man won Horemheb's confidence and was in charge of the restoration of Tuthmosis IV's tomb, which had been damaged by pillage. Maya controlled the necropolis and managed to preserve his beloved king's tomb. But it cannot be denied that if the powerful Horemheb had ordered the destruction of Tutankhamen's tomb, he would certainly have seized for himself the treasure of whose value he was well aware.

One is therefore thrown back upon the first hypothesis: Horemheb, who set himself up as the champion of right and justice, owed it to himself to spare the one who was the first to bow once more to Amun. But this was the limit of his generosity; Tutankhamen was deserted and deprived of the rites and prayers which his now nameless statues in the sanctuaries could no longer claim.

185. Maya, the superintendent of finance, under Horemheb (Rijksmuseum, Leyden)

186. *The names of Tutankhamen which have survived on the "memorial statue" from Karnak (Louvre)*

Horemheb even succeeded in wiping Tutankhamen's name off the official list of Egypt's pharaohs.

At last the magical power of the funeral rites and the efficacy of the fantastic assortment of burial objects surrounding Tutankhamen were to be put to the test. Everything, or nearly everything, which had been done or assembled for the king had had the two essential objects of putting demons to flight and assisting rebirth to a new existence. Burdened with the moral weight of errors he had not committed, destined from birth to act upon orders from others, the young king had hardly learned to live before it was time for him to die. His departure for his ultimate transformations was attended by every possible curse. Even after his death, the deplorable situation into which his dynasty had sunk was made worse still by his widow's desperate and shocking attempt to deliver up the "beloved land" to a foreign sceptre.

However, the gods of whom Tutankhamen had "spent his life making images" were vigilant and the curse of Horemheb could be rendered powerless. On

187. *Ivory headrest showing the god of the atmosphere and the two lions of the horizon*

Tutankhamen's memorial at Karnak under the gold-plated plaster, the sculptor had carved the king's name into the stone in the right-hand corner of the statue's loin-cloth. It remained hidden and was spared. It can still be seen (186).

Thus in the night of the tomb the young king's journey through the nether-world was assured. As Osiris, whose "images he had also made and whose house he had built as at the beginning", he would be unjustly pursued by evil, but his innocence, after an infinitely long trial, would finally be proclaimed. Three thousand years later, the unbroken seals bearing the image of Anubis triumphing over all obstacles, were to be lifted, and the first golden sarcophagus in the tomb of the Valley of the Kings was to gladden the eyes of pilgrims for, like a new sun rising between the mountains of the horizon, Tutankhamen had reappeared (187).

Carter and Carnarvon had exorcized the curse of Horemheb and granted Tiye's youngest son the survival which every effort had been made to deny him.

*One of the statuettes of Tutankhamen used
during the ritual pilgrimages of the funeral*

AANEN
"Second prophet of Amun", "High priest of Re-Atum", brother of the queen Tiye and, therefore, son of Yuya and Thuya.

ABDIASHIRTA
King of Amor (or Amurru, present-day Syria), father of Aziru, his successor. Officially he was pharaoh's vassal, but he made an alliance with the Hittite king Suppiluliuma against the Mitanni, ally of Egypt and the loyal vassals of pharaoh in Asia. He was a contemporary of Amenophis III.

AMENOPHIS III
XVIIIth Dynasty king, son and successor of Tuthmosis IV and Mutemweya, husband of Tiye and father of Amenophis IV-Akhenaten, and probably of Dhutmose, who died before acceding to the throne, of Smenkhkare, Tutankhamen, the princess Sitamun, whom he married—and of several other princesses of whom the last was Baketaten.

AMENOPHIS IV-AKHENATEN
XVIIIth Dynasty king, the "heretic" who temporarily abolished the cult of Amun for political and religious reasons and gave pre-eminence to the cult of Aten. Amenophis IV-Akhenaten left the capital of Thebes and founded Akhetaten (present-day Tell el Amarna), his new city where he celebrated, with his queen Nefertiti and their daughters, the cult of Aten in enormous sanctuaries of a new type. Towards the end of his reign, this king who was too peace-loving to maintain the vast Egyptian empire, probably attempted a reconciliation with the powerful priests of Amun at Thebes, through the intermediary of his co-regent and son-in-law Smenkhkare. The last-named, after the king's separation from Nefertiti, had replaced the queen in official functions. We do not know what end this visionary king met, this exceptional personality in Egyptian history, but his doctrine, although it failed in practice, had a profound effect on Egyptian civilization.

AMENOPHIS, son of Hapu, called Huy
High official who played an eminent role under Amenophis III. He was invested with numerous offices: "chief of the secrets of the *Kap*", "master of ceremonies at the feast of Amun", "chief of the conscripts", and won renown as "chief of the king's works" (notably the transport of the colossi of Memnon for the funerary temple of Amenophis III). Towards the end of his life he became intendant to Sitamun, the daughter and second wife of Amenophis III. He lived to be 110, the age of wisdom.

ANKHESENAMUN: ANKHESENPAATEN
XVIIIth Dynasty princess, 3rd daughter of Amenophis IV-Akhenaten and Nefertiti; wife, niece and sister-in-law of Tutankhamen. By her first marriage to her own father she had a daughter Ankhesenpaaten Tashery.

Her name Ankhesenpaaten was changed to Ankhesenamun after Tutankhamen's coronation and the restoration of the Amunite cult.

ANKHESENPAATEN TASHERY
XVIIIth Dynasty princess, daughter of Ankhesenpaaten's marriage to her father, Amenophis IV-Akhenaten. She was, at one and the same time, niece, great niece and step-daughter of Tutankhamen.

AY
XVIIIth Dynasty king, husband of Tey, the "Nurse" of Nefertiti, and perhaps Nefertiti's father. Before his usurpation of the throne he was, under Amenophis IV-Akhenaten, "Divine Father", "commander of all His Majesty's horses" (= general of the chariotry), "the king's personal scribe". He ascended the throne as successor to Tutankhamen, to whom he was a shrewd adviser and vizier. It is possible that he married his widow Ankhesenamun in order to legitimize his accession to the throne, but no proof of this exists.

AZIRU
King of Amor (Syria), son of Abdiashirta, contemporary of Amenophis III and, in particular, of Amenophis IV-Akhenaten and Tutankhamen. He carried on his father's policies and, protected on one side by the Hatti alliance, and, on the other, by the intrigues of the Amarnan court (cf. Tutu), he succeeded in seizing the prosperous ports on the Phoenician coast. He was sufficiently cunning to convince Pharaoh—to whom he went to justify himself—that he was a loyal vassal, defending Egypt's interests at the frontiers of her empire. Suppiluliuma, who used Aziru as an instrument rather than as an ally, forced him to accept his suzerainty towards the middle of the XIVth century B.C. Although remaining Egypt's vassal officially, the Amurru thus became a tributary of the Hatti.

BAK
Son of the sculptor Men, and himself official sculptor to the young Amenophis IV-Akhenaten. The heretic king personally instructed him to create the new Amarnan style.

BAKETATEN
XVIIIth Dynasty princess, daughter of Amenophis III and Tiye, sister of Tutankhamen, Amenophis IV-Akhenaten, Smenkhkare and Sitamun; sister-in-law of Nefertiti.

BURNABURIASH (or Burraburriash)
King of Babylon at the time of Tutankhamen. He sought the support of the young king against the rising power of the Assyrians.

DHUTMOSE
XVIIIth Dynasty prince, of whom little is known but who is brought to mind by a whip found in Tutankhamen's tomb bearing the inscription "son of the king, captain of the troops, Dhutmose". He was probably the son of Amenophis III and Tiye, and therefore a brother of Tutankhamen.

GILUKHIPA
Daughter of Shuttarna, king of Mitanni (Naharina), secondary wife of Amenophis III. The king made a special issue of commemorative scarabs on the occasion of this marriage, where he recorded that the princess was escorted by 317 ladies-in-waiting.

HANIS
Envoy of Egypt at the time of Tutankhamen's death. He acted as intermediary between Suppiluliuma and Ankhesenamun in trying to arrange the marriage of the Hittite prince Zannanza to Tutankhamen's widow.

HIKNEFER
Son of a Nubian prince, brought up at the school of the "children of the *Kap*" at the pharaoh's court and a contemporary of Tutankhamen. He was prince of Aniba (Miam), in Nubia, when the viceroy Huy collected vast tribute from the Southern vassals of Egypt. He was buried on the eastern bank of the Nile in Nubia, on the site of the modern town of Toshka, where his tomb has just been discovered.

HOREMHEB
General and last king of the XVIIIth Dynasty. He played an important role under Amenophis IV-Akhenaten and Tutankhamen and acquired the most sought-after and important titles in the country's civil service and army. After Ay's death he seized the throne and proceeded to redress the political and military situation of the empire. With implacable hatred he pursued the Atenite heresy and the memory of its creator, Amenophis IV-Akhenaten, whom he did his utmost to obliterate from history. Probably, in order to give at least the semblance of legitimacy to his usurpation and to attach himself to the dynasty, he married Mutnedjmet, sister of Nefertiti and very probably the daughter of Ay—himself a usurping king—and of Tey.

HUY
Viceroy of Nubia under Tutankhamen, he was the son of a high official of Amenophis III. Under Amenophis IV-Akhenaten he had already accumulated the titles "sovereign's messenger in all foreign lands", "Divine Father", "fan-bearer on the king's right", "intendant of Amun's cattle in the Land of Kush", "intendant of the lands of gold of the lord of the Two Countries", "his majesty's brave in the cavalry". He was nominated to office by Tutankhamen, and amply justified, by his wise and efficient administration, the trust placed in him by his master.

HUYA
Majordomo of Queen Tiye's estates at Akhetaten. His tomb was prepared at Tell el Amarna, and its bas reliefs constitute evidence of the highest importance of the stay of Akhenaten's parents in the city of the Globe.

KIA
Unknown princess, mentioned in at least two documents as secondary wife of Amenophis IV-Akhenaten.

MAHU
Chief of the police at Tell el Amarna who maintained order in the heretic city at Akhetaten (Tell el Amarna) and one of the king's most devoted supporters.

MAYA
"Superintendent of construction work in the place of eternity", "superintendent of the treasure" under Tutankhamen, he dedicated a funerary figure to his king which is one of the few expressions of personal attachment found in the king's tomb. As intendant of the necropolis he seems to have looked after the security of his beloved master's tomb. This official was able to gain Horemheb's trust, to whom he was also minister of finance.

MEKETATEN
XVIIIth Dynasty princess, 2nd daughter of Amenophis IV-Akhenaten and Nefertiti: she died in year 12 at Tell el Amarna.

MEN
Amenophis III's sculptor and head of the traditional school of art. His son, Bak, was the moving spirit of the new artistic school under Amenophis IV-Akhenaten.

MERITATEN
XVIIIth Dynasty princess, eldest daughter of Amenophis IV-Akhenaten and Nefertiti, she became the sister-in-law of her own father and Tutankhamen, her uncle, by her marriage with Smenkhkare.

MERITRE
Egyptian princess who, according to some authors, might have been Tutankhamen's mother.

MURSIL II
Hittite king, son and successor of Suppiluliuma, responsible for the annals of his father's reign, brother of Zannanza who was chosen to marry Ankhesenamun, Tutankhamen's widow.

MUTEMWEYA
XVIIIth Dynasty queen, wife of Tuthmosis IV and mother of Amenophis III.

MUTNEDJMET

XVIIIth Dynasty queen (?), daughter (?) of Ay and Tey, sister of Nefertiti. Mutnedjmet probably married Horemheb who thus became Ay's son-in-law and legitimate successor to the throne.

NAKHTMIN

"Royal scribe", "fan-bearer on the king's right", "head of the army" under Tutankhamen, to whom he dedicated five ushabtis which were found in the young king's tomb and which are, with the little funerary figure of the loyal Maya, the only objects dedicated by a subject in the king's ritual furniture.

NEFERNEFERUATEN TASHERY

XVIIIth Dynasty princess, 4th daughter of Amenophis IV-Akhenaten and Nefertiti.

NEFERNEFERURE

XVIIIth Dynasty princess, 5th daughter of Amenophis IV-Akhenaten and Nefertiti.

NEFERTITI

XVIIIth Dynasty queen, probably the daughter of Ay and supposedly step-daughter to Tey but not, as some authors have thought, a Mittanian princess. She married Amenophis IV-Akhenaten by whom it is certain that she had at least six daughters.

She played an important role at her husband's side: she was the king's indispensable complement in the Atenite religious doctrine. It was by means of the royal couple—and a united couple solely—that life, dispensed by Aten, could be transmitted to all living beings on the earth. However, towards the end of Amenophis IV-Akhenaten's reign, she separated from her husband.

The beauty and charm of this queen can be seen from the famous bust in painted limestone now in Berlin.

NIQMAT

King of Ugarit (Ras-Shamra) and contemporary with the last pharaohs of the XVIIIth Dynasty. He married, very probably, an Egyptian who might have been one of the princesses of the Amarnan family.

PANEHESY

High priest of Aten at Tell el Amarna: remains of his house and tomb have been found in the city of the Globe.

RAMOSE

Vizier of the South under Amenophis III. His Theban tomb is famous for the beauty of its decor and the two styles, Theban and Amarnan, which can be observed there. He was a contemporary of the co-regency. He therefore took part in the festivities for Amenophis III's first jubilee in the temple of Soleb, in the heart of the Nubian province.

RIB-ADDI

King of Byblos, loyal to Amenophis IV-Akhenaten, his over-lord, who misinformed by his ministers, left him helpless against the Amorite attacks, led by Aziru with Habiru in his pay. The minister of foreign affairs at the Amarnan court, Tutu, was in league with Aziru, the faithless vassal, and knew how to present the situation to his master Amenophis IV-Akhenaten in a way which was advantageous to Aziru. The king demanded an enquiry without, however, any result. In the end, poor Rib-addi, forced into his city and abandoned by everyone, disappeared from the scene, probably assassinated.

SETEPENRE

XVIIIth Dynasty princess, 6th daughter of Amenophis IV-Akhenaten and Nefertiti.

SITAMUN

XVIIIth Dynasty princess, daughter and wife of Amenophis III, sister of three kings: Amenophis IV-Akhenaten, Smenkhkare and Tutankhamen.

SMENKHKARE

XVIIIth Dynasty king, co-regent, son-in-law and successor to Amenophis IV-Akhenaten, whose brother he probably was and, therefore, the son of Amenophis III and Tiye.

SUPPILULIUMA

Hittite king, contemporary with Amenophis III, Amenophis IV-Akhenaten and Tutankhamen. By his aggressive policy he created the new Hittite hegemony in Asia. In forcing the Mitanni under his power as well as the Amurru (and their vassals in Phoenicia and Palestine), he became a serious threat to the Egyptian empire. Conflict between the two great powers broke out at the time of the XIXth Dynasty pharaohs.

TADUKHIPA

Mittanian princess, daughter of Tushratta, king of Naharina (Mitani), sent to Amenophis III's harem in year 36 of his reign. On the pharaoh's death, she seems to have entered the harem of his son Amenophis IV-Akhenaten.

TAEMWADJSI

Sister or wife of Huy, viceroy of Nubia under Tutankhamen. She was this king's "Matron of the harem".

TEY

Ay's wife and Queen Nefertiti's "Nurse". She became queen on Ay's usurpation of the throne after Tutankhamen's death.

THUYA

Wife of Yuya, mother of the queen Tiye, of Aanen and, perhaps, also Ay. Thuya was "head of Amun's harem" at Thebes and, at Akhmim, "head of Min's harem".

TIYE

XVIIIth Dynasty queen, wife of Amenophis III,

mother of Amenophis IV-Akhenaten, Dhutmose (?), Smenkhkare (?), Tutankhamen (?), Sitamun and Baketaten as well as several other princesses.

Tiye was very probably of Nubian origin and not of royal blood. Her marriage to Amenophis III, which made her "Great Royal Spouse", must have constituted a revolution. A capable woman, she played an important political role and helped to safeguard the empire's interests, especially towards the end of Amenophis III's reign and during almost all the Amarnan experiment of Amenophis IV-Akhenaten.

TUSHRATTA

King of Mitanni, contemporary and ally of Amenophis III and IV, who had, both of them, married at least one Mittanian princess as a secondary wife. It was during Tushratta's reign that Suppiluliuma, king of Hatti—or Khatti—started to attack the Mitanni. After an abortive attempt, at the time of Amenophis III—who sent troops to his ally's aid—he took advantage of Amenophis IV-Akhenaten's apathy and the internal crisis which disturbed Egypt after the heretic's death, and took possession of Mitanni, in spite of the Assyrian "competition". Tushratta disappeared during the turmoil, probably murdered, and his son and successor Mattiwaza became a vassal of the Hittite.

TUTANKHAMEN

XVIIIth Dynasty king, probably the son of Amenophis III and Tiye, husband of Ankhesenamun the daughter of Amenophis IV-Akhenaten and Nefertiti. He came to the throne at the age of nine and died at eighteen and officially restored the cult of Amun after the failure of the Amarnan heresy. Tutankhamen owes his fame to the discovery in 1922 by Howard Carter of his funerary treasure, now in the Cairo museum.

TUTHMOSIS IV

XVIIIth Dynasty pharaoh, he married Mutemweya who gave birth to the future Amenophis III, his successor on the throne.

TUTU

Minister of foreign affairs under Amenophis IV-Akhenaten at Tell el Amarna. He betrayed his king's cause by becoming the accomplice of Aziru of Amor, Pharaoh's faithless vassal, and thus contributed to the decline of Egyptian influence in Asia during this reign. It is possible that he was party to the conspiracy which cost the unfortunate king of Byblos, Ribaddi, his life.

YUTI

Queen Tiye's chief sculptor, he executed effigies of the princess Baketaten, Tiye's youngest daughter. His tomb, which is famous for its reliefs, is preserved at Tell el Amarna.

YUYA

Father of the queen Tiye, husband of Thuya. He was "Divine Father", an important sacerdotal official of Amun at Thebes and, at Akhmim, "Min's prophet" and "superintendent of Min's cattle".

ZANNANZA

Hittite prince, son of Suppiluliuma, he was chosen to marry Ankhesenamun, Tutankhamen's widow. He was murdered on the orders of Horemheb, at that time still a general, whilst on his way to Egypt to join Ankhesenamun.

Notes on the colour plates by Dr Anwar Shoukry

I. **Royal diadem,** *page 5*

A skilfully worked example of the jeweller's art whose main characteristic is simplicity. The gold band is decorated with gold circles inlaid with round pieces of cornelian which are held in place by gold rivets in their centre. The lower and upper edges are picked out with turquoise and lapis-lazuli blue glass-paste. At the centre of the forehead are the double insignia of Upper and Lower Egypt. The head of the vulture-goddess Nekhabet has obsidian eyes. The cobra, or *uraeus*, of the goddess Wadjet, with its sinuous body, is inlaid with semi-precious stones and glass-paste.

At the back the knot of the band is inlaid with calcedony; the papyrus flowers on either side are of malachite. Two *uraeus* follow the lateral gold ribbons.

Found on the mummy's head.

Longitudinal diameter: 8 in; transversal diameter: 7 in; width of the band: ¾ in.

II. **Head of the child-king,** *page 6*

The head is the size of that of a new-born child and shows the elongation of the skull which is a feature of the Amarnan style. It portrays the young Tutankhamen emerging from a lotus flower as the sun god appears from the flower when it opens its petals.

Stuccoed and painted wood. Found at the entry of the tomb.

IIIa. **Pendant representing Amenophis III,** *page 23*

This tiny statuette of solid gold shows Amenophis III wearing the *khepresh* (wrongly known as a helmet). The king's necklace is made of little coloured beads. He is squatting and holds in his left hand a fold of his loincloth against his knee; in his right hand, he is grasping the crook and flail of the Osirian monarchy. The statue hung from a chain.

The whole was wrapped in linen and wrapped round a small mummiform coffin which contained a curl of Queen Tiye's hair. The two coffins were placed inside two other larger ones.

Height: 2 in.

IIIb. **Tasselled earrings,** *page 23*

Each of these ear ornaments was attached to a thick tube which called for a wide perforation of the ear lobe. In the centre of the ring a portrait of the king is flanked by two *uraeus*.

Gold, cornelian, coloured glass-paste, quartz, alabaster and glazed terracotta.

Length: 4 in; width: 2 in.

IVa. **The child-king's stool,** *page 24*

The feet in the form of a member of the cat family's paws are of wood painted white. Between them can be observed a gilded motif of the "Union of the Two Countries" in openwork wood, taking the form of lilies and papyruses entwined around the hieroglyphic sign signifying union. A cushion must have been placed on the curved seat.

Height: 17¾ in; width: 17¾ in; depth: 17 in.

IVb. **A scribe's palette and case for writing reeds,** *page 24*

The ivory palette bears the names and first name of Tutankhamen "beloved of the gods Atum, Amun-Re and Thoth". Two cakes of red and blue-black ink, still remain in their circular containers. In the hollowed central section seven reeds, or calamus, were found.

Length: 12 in; width: 1¾ in; depth: 1 in.

The case for writing reeds is in gilded wood inlaid with

cornelian, obsidian and coloured glass beads. It is shaped like a small column with a palmiform capital. The cap is made of a piece of ivory stained red and held in place by a catch acting as a pivot.

Length: 12 in; diameter: ¾ in.

V. Lid of a chest (detail), *page 29*

The desk-shaped lid of one of the precious chests is inlaid with carved ivory, and stained with very subtle colours: off-white, rose ochre and slate blue. Tutankhamen and Ankhesenamun are seen at the beginning of their reign, still adolescent in appearance. The king is leaning on a staff while the queen offers him two bunches of flowers: one of lotus and one of papyrus, decorated with mandrakes. Both are wearing pleated linen with long, flowing sashes. The modelling of the bodies and the expression of the faces are remarkably well executed. The scene takes place in an arbour of vines with little flower-shaped columns. In the lower part a servant girl (under the king) and a serving-man (under the queen) are picking mandrakes, the fruit of love.

Height of the scene shown: 12¼ in (approx.); width: 8 in (approx.).

VI. The centre of the back of the gold-plated throne, *page 30*

Sheets of gold and silver are used in conjunction with coloured glass-paste, glazed ceramic and inlaid calcite to form the scene which decorates this throne back.

The somewhat informal pose of the king is reflected by the affectionate attitude of the queen who appears to be anointing the king's collarette. This latter is very similar to the one she herself is wearing and to those worn by the guests at the funeral and decorating the mummiform coffins of Tutankhamen.

Although the sovereigns are marked with their names in the form "return to Thebes", the sun with rays in the form of arms ending in hands, shines down on the scene as in the days of Tell el Amarna.

21 in x 21 in (approx.)

VII. The little gold-plated shrine, *page 39*

The little shrine, in classical form (the roof is reminiscent of that of the archaic sanctuary of the South), is entirely plated with gold and rests upon a base in the form of a

silver-plated sledge. The outside and both sides of the double door (the bolts are of ebony) are decorated with scenes in relief depicting the young king and his graceful wife. The scenes on the double door are surrounded by friezes, royal cartouches and birds symbolizing vassals paying homage to the king. On the inside, only the pedestal bearing the king's name remained; the absence of the statue suggesting that the shrine had clearly been pillaged by robbers. It was found in the antechamber near the entrance to the annex.

Shrine without the sledge: height: 19¾ in; width: 10½ in; depth: 12⅝ in.

VIIIa. The little gold-plated shrine (detail), *page 40*

Tutankhamen wearing the *khepresh*, often called the blue crown, is seated informally on a chair with a thick cushion. The royal vulture behind his neck is proffering, in a protective way, the sign of life. The queen, wearing a sumptuous dress of pleated linen, appears to be anointing him with a scented unguent of which she is holding a cone standing in a bowl with lotus flowers.

VIIIb. The little gold-plated shrine (detail), *page 40*

Tutankhamen is seated in a pose as informal as on the scene above. This time he is wearing a short wig with little curls adorned with the diadem found on the king's mummy, but here only the *uraeus* (and not the vulture's head) is shown on the forehead. However the symbolic bird appears behind the king's head and neck.

The queen is placing on her husband's neck a double necklace composed of gold disks.

IXa. The little gold-plated shrine (detail), *page 41*

Seated on the cushion of a folding stool (similar to one found in the tomb) Tutankhamen is holding lotuses and mandrakes in his left hand. With his right he is pouring a scented liquid into the hand of his queen Ankhesenamun. Her hair is adorned with the two tall plumes of a royal consort and she is wearing the solar disk framed by horns. She is looking over her shoulder and is leaning her elbow informally on the king's knees.

IX*b*. **The little gold-plated shrine (detail),** *page 41*

Tutankhamen, armed like an archer, seated as above on a folding stool, assisted by his wife and accompanied by a tame lion, is drawing his bow and slaying wild duck with his arrows among the marsh papyrus where they live. The game appears unrealistically close to the human figures because of lack of space.

The sovereigns' head-dresses are different from those of the preceding scenes; Ankhesenamun's wig is adorned with the thick plait of hair only worn by royal offspring.

X. **The gold-plated throne,** *page 42*

This piece of furniture is a fine example of the great skill of the craftsmen of the New Empire. The carved wood is gold-plated and inlaid with multi-coloured glass-paste, glazed terracotta and semi-precious stones. Parts are covered in silver leaf. The arms of the throne are in the form of a winged serpent wearing the double crown and guarding the king's names. The cane seat is supported by animal feet. A pair of animal heads adorns the fore edge of the seat. The frame is strengthened by openwork motifs of which only the central elements have survived. They were initially flanked by intertwined lily and papyrus plants symbolizing the "Union of the Two Countries"

The back is decorated with a papyrus thicket in shallow relief in which water fowl are flying. A raised frieze in high relief of six *uraeus* can be observed, also worked in gold-plated wood. This throne was found in the antechamber.

Height: 45 in; width: 21 in; depth: 25 in.

XI. **King's ceremonial stool (details),** *page 51*

The king's foot-stool in the form of a small, low, rectangular box is decorated in incised relief on its exposed surfaces.

XI*a* and *b*. Four of eight human figures representing the Asian, Indo-European and African races, enemies of Egypt

are shown here. The men are portrayed as prisoners, lying prostrate with their arms bound behind their backs. The pharaoh trampled on them when he used his foot-stool. They are from top to bottom: a Syrian, a Libyan, a Nubian and a Sudanese. Each one has the clothing, equipment and features peculiar to these different peoples. The clothing of the two Africans is nearly identical, but the face of the Nubian is more refined than that of the Sudanese and his hair is adorned with a feather.

On the other hand the northern races are well distinguished from each other. The Syrian with his curled, spade-shaped beard is wearing a long skirt and tasselled loin-cloth. Round his neck hangs a characteristic pendant in the shape of a disk. The Libyan with his pointed beard and his hair plaited and drawn to one side, is wearing two ostrich feathers on the top of his head. His phallic sheath is hanging from his belt.

XI*c*. Below is the decorative panel of one of the longer sides of the stool. On one side of the sign symbolizing the "Union of the Two Countries", African prisoners are bound by the neck and arms to the plants of the South, lilies. On the other side various figures of the northern races are tied to papyrus plants.

Height: 3 in; length: 23⅛ in; width: 12⅝ in.

XII. **The "ecclesiastical throne",** *page 52*

It is generally agreed that this piece of furniture, very different from the gold-plated throne, must have been the king's ecclesiastical seat used during religious ceremonies. It is a prototype of the episcopal thrones of the Christian church.

The high, slightly curved back is fixed to a stool with crossed legs carved in the form of the necks and heads of wild ducks. The wood is partially gold-plated and inlaid with minute semi-precious stones, pieces of glass-paste and glazed terracotta, simulating lapis-lazuli and turquoise; ebony and ivory have also been used. The decoration consists of geometrical motifs which alternate with bands of hieroglyphic texts, amongst which appear the style of the king and the names of the two gods Aten and Amun. At the top a frieze of *uraeus* flanks the globe of Aten placed above the god's name inscribed in two cartouches. The curved seat (designed to hold a cushion) is decorated with ebony inlaid with ivory, simulating a spotted animal's skin which originally covered the seat of folding stools of which this throne is reminiscent.

The openwork motif of the "Union of the Two Countries" is partially intact.

Height: 40 in; width: 27⅝ in; depth: 17⅜ in.

296

XIII. Box in the form of a double royal cartouche, *page 69*

This double box is composed of twin cartouches. At the spot where the royal names appear, it is embellished with an image of the king. He is seated with the sun above him on a basket bearing an ornamental motif based on the hiero glyph meaning "feast".

He is wearing the side plait of a young prince, though in his hands are already the royal insignia. Above these boxes, each of which forms a separate container, are the solar globe and two tall ostrich feathers.

It is made of gold-plated wood inlaid with glass-paste. The base is plated with silver and decorated with a frieze composed of signs of divine life.

Height: 6 in.

XIV. Back of the cedarwood chair (detail), *page 70*

The finest chair of the treasure, in cedarwood, has a carved back whose openwork decoration depicts as the central element a spirit kneeling on the sign of the gold necklet. He symbolizes millions of years and is holding in his hands reed shoots (evoking years without number). The reed shoots are standing on tadpoles (signifying "hundred thousand") which in turn rest on rings of the eternal cycle.

The spirit's head has a disk above it, on either side of which are panels bearing the royal name and given name. Behind his forearms are two slightly larger panels consisting of the king's "banner" on which is inscribed the first name of the king's style; this latter is very rarely mentioned.

It is a masterpiece of harmony in design and plastic beauty in execution.

Height: 37¾ in; width: 18¾ in; depth: 20⅛ in.

XV. Votive shield, *page 79*

One of eight shields found in the tomb and made of incised and gilded wood, it depicts Tutankhamen brandishing a scimitar in one hand, while in the other he is holding aloft by their tails two lions symbolizing his enemies.

The scene is dominated by the winged globe. In front of the king a hieroglyphic inscription compares the strength of the king to that of the god Montu. Behind him the culture of Upper Egypt is, surprisingly, perched on a clump of papyrus instead of the usual lilies.

Below a decorative band suggests the mountains of the desert.

Height: 30 in; width of the base: 20 in; width at the top: 21½ in.

XVI. The painted chest, *page 80*

This famous chest made of stuccoed wood and painted with scenes of intense vitality is unique of its type.

It is worked in miniature in a style which, as was pointed out a few years ago, inspired the great mural compositions of the XIXth Dynasty, so well exemplified by the different versions of the battle of Kadech under Ramesses II.

The longer sides and the curved faces of the lid are decorated with scenes of war and hunting. The side facing the viewer illustrated the war which Tutankhamen may have waged against the Syrians. The corresponding panel of the lid shows ostriches, antelopes, hyenas and other desert animals in wild flight before the king and his attendants.

On the other side of the lid a lion hunt corresponds to the scene on the panel beneath in which the king is shown putting Africans to flight.

On the small sides of the chest the king appears four times in the guise of a sphinx treading his enemies underfoot.

Height: 17⅜ in; length: 24 in; breadth: 17 in.

XVIIa. The painted chest (detail). The destruction of the Africans, *page 81*

The young king standing in his chariot has the reins attached to his hips, leaving his hands free to shoot enormous arrows at the Africans which his soldiers and his dogs have only to finish off. He is attended by his chariot escort and by flail-bearers running behind him.

XVIIb. The painted chest (detail). The destruction of the Asians, *page 81*

In this scene, as in the above, the solar globe dominates the figure of the king who is also protected by the royal cultures. The Asian ranks are as serried as those of the Africans. The landscape is suggested by little clumps of flowers and bushes, some of which are flecked with blood. To the right in the foreground a soldier is busy cutting off the hand of a dead enemy, for this was how the number of enemies slain in battle was assessed.

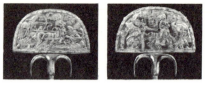

XVIII. **The lower end of a ceremonial cane,** *page 82*

a. Two figures typifying the two hereditary enemies of Egypt form the end of this baton (and not its handle as was previously sometimes thought). On this baton only the African appears. Ebony has therefore been used to portray his arms and head. The rest of the body and the clothes are of stuccoed and gilded wood.

Length of the baton: 45¼ in.

b. One sees here the Syrian whose hands and face look very lifelike owing to the colour of the ivory which has been only very slightly heightened by paint. The inlays are of glass-paste of various colours. The Asian and African turn their backs on one another and only their feet and legs touch (the foot of the African can be seen against the hand of the Syrian).

Length of the baton: 40⅛ in.

a. front. Alone on his chariot the king is hunting a pair of ostriches which he has brought down with his arrows. A dog is hunting with him amidst vegetation which suggests that the scene takes place in the desert.

b. back. The king returns in triumph to his place. Two men are carrying for him the savaged bodies of the ostriches whose long feathers are carried by the king himself. The handle ends in an elongated version of a papyrus umbel. An inscription incised into it states that the hunt took place "in the eastern desert of Heliopolis".

Length of handle: 37⅜ in; feather holder: height: 4 in; width: 7¼ in.

XIX. **Details of a panel of one of the ceremonial chariots,** *page 91*

a. Details of the right hand interior side of one of the chariots which were found dismantled (in the antechamber) and which are made of stuccoed wood with a sheet of gold applied. The decoration in relief is heightened by a border made of inlaid semi-precious stones and various coloured glass-paste. One sees the king here in the form of a human-headed sphinx guarded by the vulture. He is trampling an African underfoot and defying an Asian from whom he is separated by a decorative rosette which seems to have been added after the making of the panel as a reinforcement.

b. Another decorative detail in relief from this same panel shows the central portion of a frieze consisting of captive enemies. They can be recognized by their contrasted physical types which are depicted with elegant realism. Their clothes and their jewels add further to the picturesque effect and bonds ending in lily flowers and papyrus underline that these figures come from the South or from the North.

XXI*a.* **The king's two daggers,** *page 97*

The blade of one of the two daggers—or more likely poignards—is made of gold and its decorative elements are elegantly sober. A double line runs down the centre of the blade ending at the hilt in a stylized motif of lily plants. The sheath is made of gold. On one side it is decorated in relief with a succession of animals among which can be distinguished bulls and ibexes attacked by lions and dogs. This wild hunting scene takes place in a region which the vegetation suggests to be dry and mountainous. Below, on the tapering part of the sheath, there is a composite palm-shaped motif. On the reverse side the decoration consists of little feathers ending in a jackal's or dog's head, at the point.

Total length: 12¾ in; length of sheath: 8¼ in; width of sheath: 1¾ in.

The blade of the other dagger is made of iron which was, apart from a few specks of rust, still clean and shining at the times of its discovery. Except for one or two minor details, the handle is decorated in the same way for both daggers. The only major difference is that the one with the iron blade has a pummel of rock crystal. Its gold sheath is decorated in relief, on one side with lily flowers growing one out of the other; the other side is decorated like the reverse of the first sheath.

XX. **The king's fly-whisk,** *page 92*

This flail—or fly-whisk—is made of wood covered in gold. The curved edge is pierced with thirty holes into which white and dark brown ostrich feathers were fixed. The two surfaces depict scenes connected with the feathers which decorate the fly-whisk and which were necessary to the purpose which it was to serve.

XXI*b.* **Handle of the gold dagger (detail),** *page 97*

The different areas of the decoration consist of gold studs forming geometrical patterns. They are separated by bands in higher relief made of cloisonné of semi-precious stones and coloured glass-paste. Floral elements predominate at the top and there are falcons as well.

Length of the handle: 4½ in.

XXII*a*****. Object in red-gold openwork,** *page 98*

One of the gold objects found in the treasure and which still bears many traces of red "tinting". It depicts the triumphal return, probably more "official" than historic, of the young king driving his chariot and preceded by a group of captives from the South and the North. Behind the king the serpent goddess of the North protects him and moves in the direction of the vulture of the South who is proffering a sign of life.

In the lower register the scene of the "Union of the Two Countries" is framed by the two plants symbolizing royalty. They do not correspond with the enemies shown but with the deities protecting the king: lilies for the vulture goddess and papyrus for the serpent goddess.

Height: 2⅜ in; width: 3¼ in.

XXII*b*****. Drinking cup found at the entrance of the tomb,** *page 98*

This cup made of calcite is sculpted in the form of a half-open lotus flower, all of whose details are picked out in shallow relief. The inscription, engraved on the edge like the one on the bowl, is stained with blue pigment and contains parts of the royal style as well as a wish for the king's eternal happiness. The lateral handles each consist of a lotus flower and buds on which is perched a spirit of "millions of years".

Height: 7 in; width: 6¾ in.

XXIII*a*****. Alabaster lamp,** *page 107*

This is not a drinking cup but a triple lamp in the form of three lotus flowers which had been placed in the tomb. It consists of a central lotus wide open. On either side is one flower still in bud at the end of sinuous stems from each of which a leaf spreads out horizontally.

The overall effect is reminiscent of "modern style".

Height: 11 in; width: 11 in.

XXIII*b*****. Ivory jewel chest,** *page 107*

The most restrained and the most elegant of all the king's chests. Its sole decoration consists of knobs and the bases of the legs are sheathed in gold leaf. In shallow relief on the lid and the front panel can be seen the royal cartouches. A floral column adorns the centre of the back panel. An inscription, written in black ink in cursive or hieratic script, states that the chest contained the "rings of funerary procession".

Height: 5⅛ in; length: 6 in; width: 4¾ in.

XXIV. The alabaster boat (detail), *page 108*

Among the containers for scent (?) found in the annex the alabaster boat is the most elaborate and amounts to a real *pièce montée*. Standing on a base contained in a chest which suggests a square pool, the boat has a sort of cabin in the form of a shrine. This is sheltered by an awning borne by short columns which terminate in double capitals composed of lilies and papyrus motifs.

The figurehead takes the form of a Syrian ibex with real horns from a young animal. A young naked woman squats in the prow clutching a lotus flower against her breast.

At the stern a female dwarf is holding a pole to test the depth of the water.

Alabaster with inlays of coloured glass-paste and semi-precious stones, and gold leaf.

The boat: height: 14½ in; width: 10½ in; length: 11 in.

XXV*a*****. Model of the pharaoh's boat,** *page 113*

The room which Carter called the Treasury contained a considerable number of boats. Most of these were probably connected with the mystic pilgrimages of the king after death: those which inducted him into the suites of Osiris and Re; those which enabled him to claim his share of life and to take part in the hunt in the marshes.

This model, however, seems to be that of a boat which may have carried the sovereign during his trips up or down the Nile. One can still see the double mast to which, when the wind blew, a large rectangular sail was attached.

A central cabin sheltered the master. At the bow and the stern, two little cabins in the form of shrines are decorated in fretwork with the sphinx and the bull which symbolized the king.

Overall length: 46½ in; width: 8⅝ in; height of the hull: 3⅞ in.

XXV*b*. **Ring bezel,** *page 113*

Six tiny figures form the subject of this the most elaborate and the most ancient ring bezel which we know.

In the centre Tutankhamen can be seen between two dog-headed baboons. The baboons are carrying lunar disks and are worshipping the falcon-headed god Horus who is seated on a throne. The scene is, as it were, under the protection of two sacred birds, the falcon and the vulture, which are spreading out their wings.

Length: 1 in; width: ½ in.

XXVI. **The gold funerary mask,** *page 114*

This is the finest funerary mask ever found in the world and it shows in its finish workmanship of the highest order. It constitutes the best example of the goldsmith's art ever put to the service of portraiture. During the Ancient Empire a plaster mask was placed on the mummy. Then later, even before the Middle Empire, this was replaced by a mask made of *papier mâché*.

This mask, compared with the face of the mummy and with effigies of the king, appears to be an exact likeness of the young sovereign. It was placed immediately upon the bandaged face and is lifesize. It is made of beaten gold inlaid with semi-precious stones and coloured glass-paste. The king is wearing the head-dress known as "*nemset*" which falls on either side of his shoulders and which is tied by a cord in the form of a queue.

The two dynastic beasts protecting the king are shown on his forehead and the false beard of the gods decorates his chin. The eyes and the eyebrows are made up with lapis-lazuli.

The mask finishes in a large collar made of several rows of tubular beads of semi-precious stones and glass-paste.

Height: 21 in; width at the shoulders: 15½ in.

XXVII. **Door of one of the gilded shrines,** *page 131*

The third gilded shrine (third in the order in which the diggers discovered them one within the other) was made in the form of the primitive sanctuary of Southern Egypt.

Shown here is the inside of the left hand door, adorned with the goddess Isis whose arms were winged to reanimate the dead and who is standing on the sign of incorruptible gold. This piece of furniture is made of gilded and stuccoed wood and all the details of the goddess appear in shallow relief. The eyes are heightened with black colouring.

The hieroglyphs in incised relief recount the speeches of the goddess about the transformations of the king similar to those of the sun which lasts forever.

XXVIII. **Funerary bedhead in the form of an animal of the cat family,** *page 132*

Three tall and large beds found in the antechamber were reminiscent in their general form of the bodies of three animals.

Made of stuccoed and gilded wood, this bedhead evokes an animal of the cat family which for a long time was thought to be a lion. This is because even in the Ancient Empire the royal throne was sometimes depicted as borne by two lions which are usually associated with the person of the king. These large beds were funerary beds which could never have been used by a living person since they are too high. Three fine models of ordinary beds were discovered in the tomb.

The eyes of the animal's head are of crystal and their outline is picked out with blue glass-paste as is the end of the muzzle.

Length: 71¼ in; width: 36 in.

XXIX. **Funerary bedhead in the form of the sacred cow,** *page 149*

Like the other two funerary beds, the one having two sculpted sides in the form of the goddess of the sky is made of gilded and stuccoed wood. The head of the cow of heaven is wonderfully executed with its made-up eyes and its two tall horns in the form of a lyre framing the solar disk. The animal body, symbolizing the vault of the sky, is covered with regular pelt marks. The cow is a most classical evocation of the goddess Hathor and the goddess Nut, patroness of the sky.

XXX. Funerary bedhead in the form of the goddess Tueris, *page 150*

The most monstrous of the animals, being a hypostasis of a god, is certainly the hippopotamus which evokes the goddess Tueris, often shown bearing on its back a crocodile and having the paws of a lion.

The third funerary bed had sides in the form of this very popular goddess, patroness of birth, who protected the living as well as the dead.

The three beds, probably used during the funeral ceremonies, were perhaps connected with rebirth.

The teeth and tongue made in ivory, in this case stained with red for the tongue, are to be noted.

Length: 93 in.

XXXI. Detail of the canopic chest, *page 159*

One sees here Serket, one of the four delightful goddesses who protected the dead and were supposed to guard the viscera of Tutankhamen. His viscera, placed in four gold mummiform sarcophagi, were placed in alabaster compartments with covers in the form of the king's head. These were then enclosed in a chest, which in its turn was contained in a veritable little shrine of gilded wood, itself protected by a canopy of gilded wood. Against each of its panels was placed a goddess keeping guard over what was entrusted to her.

Gilded all over, Serket gives an intensely lifelike impression thanks to her eyes painted in black and white and to her blackened eyebrows.

Canopic chest: height: 78¾ in; width: 59 in; depth: 60¾ in.

XXXII. The alabaster canopic chest, *page 160*

This chest of singular beauty shows workmanship of a remarkably high standard and is made of alabaster of the first quality. The massive sloping lid is surrounded by the "Egyptian gorge" of architectural effect and ends in a band of inscriptions referring to the goddesses which appear at each side of the chest. In point of fact the goddesses adorning the angles are Isis, Nephthys, Serket and Neith.

The cover was fixed to the base by little cords attached to gold rings and sealed with the seal of the necropolis.

The four sides of the chest are incised with hieroglyphs stained with black pigment evoking the words pronounced by each of the goddesses to protect that part of the royal body which was placed in the care of one of the four spirits: Imset, Hapi, Duamutef and Kebehsenuf.

The base is made of a frieze of *djed* pillars and "knots of Isis" and was placed on a gilded sledge.

Apart from the sledge: height: 34 in; length at base: 17¼ in.

XXXIII. Cover of one of the canopic urns, *page 161*

One of the four covers of the compartments hollowed out of alabaster, each of which formed an urn. The four covers bear the effigy of the dead king wearing the *nemset* headdress which is adorned on the forehead with the vulture and with the complete body of the cobra.

The eyes and the eyebrows are painted black, the lips are red.

Height: 9½ in.

XXXIV. One of the sarcophagi containing the viscera, *page 162*

The alabaster chest contained, in each of its four compartments, under a lid in the form of the royal head, a miniature gold sarcophagus inlaid with cornelian and glasspaste. The viscera of the king had been placed inside, bandaged like a mummy. The sovereign is wearing the *nemset* head-dress adorned with two divine animals, the vulture and the cobra. His chin is adorned with the beard of the gods. He is holding in his hands the flail and the crook.

The wings of tutelary goddesses envelop his arms and the body is wrapped by a decorated motif reminiscent of feathers.

This sarcophagus corresponded to the canopic urns placed under the protection of Isis and Imset.

Height: 15⅜ in.

XXXV. One of the king's ushabtis, *page 171*

This little statue represents Tutankhamen—the body is mummified but the face is visible—he is wearing the crown of Lower Egypt. A large number of similar statuettes were found in the tomb: they were, in one way or another, substitutes or emanations of the king, supposed to represent him in the accomplishment of certain acts in the beyond.

The text of the 6th chapter of *The Book of the Dead* refers to this type of statuette and is engraved in vertical columns on the body.

Gilded and stuccoed wood.

Height: 25¼ in.

XXXVI. **Pectoral with a bird-scarab,** *page 172*

This is one of the richest jewels of the treasure. The central motif consists of a bird with upward curving wings whose body and head have been replaced by a fine scarab in translucent calcedony. It represents the sun about to be reborn. The bird's claws are holding a lily and a lotus flower flanked by buds.

Instead of a ball, the scarab is pushing a boat containing the sacred *wedjet*-eye which is dominated by a darkened moon, holding the image of Tutankhamen become a god, guided and protected by Thoth and Horus.

Heavy tassels of lotus and composite bud forms are the base of the pendant.

Length: 20 in.

XXXVIIa. **Pectoral of the vulture Nekhabet,** *page 177*

The finest of the pendants in the treasure found on the mummy represents a vulture in gold cloisonné, lapis-lazuli, cornelian and green glass. The bird is holding in its claws the ring of the infinite cycle.

On the back the bird is made of solid gold and from its neck is hanging the king's name in a cartouche.

The necklace to which it is attached is made of alternating rectangles of gold and lapis-lazuli bordered by little gold and glass beads.

Height of the vulture: 2¾ in; width: 4½ in.

XXXVIIb. **The pylon pectoral containing the vulture,** *page 177*

This is the pectoral whose form is the most classic. It evokes a rectangular shrine, or a pylon.

The vulture is similar to that of the preceding pendant but it is executed with less suppleness of line in the technique and less success in the choice of colours. In addition it is not made with precious stones but with multi-coloured glass-paste. On either side of the vulture's head is the first name and the name of the king.

Height: 4¾ in; width: 6¾ in.

XXXVIII. **Necklace and pendant of scarabs,** *page 178*

The pendant is formed by a boat in the centre of which is a large scarab surrounded by two *uraeus*. The latter have disks and are separated from the insect by three hieroglyphs: the *djed* pillar, the sign of life (*ankh*) and the sign of eternal youth (*ouas*). The same elements (the boat is re-

placed by the sign of feasts in the form of a basket) are used to adorn the necklace.

Gold, lapis-lazuli, cornelian, turquoise and green feldspar.

Overall length: 19⅝ in.

XXXIXa. **Wedjet-eye pectoral,** *page 187*

A very fine pendant, also found on the mummy, consists of the eye of Horus, symbol of the entity of the body.

On the right the *uraeus*, wearing the royal crown of the North, on the left the vulture of the South seem to defend and protect the *wedjet*-eye which is to help rebirth.

Gold, precious stones and glass-paste.

Height: 2½ in; length: 4 in.

XXXIXb. **Scarab pectoral under the protection of Isis and Nephthys,** *page 187*

Another pectoral whose exterior shape is massively architectural. The interior decoration is very, even too, elaborate and has as its principle motif a stone scarab with wings in gold cloisonné and coloured glass-paste. Its protection is assured by Isis and Nephthys. The words of the goddesses and names of the king are inlaid in gold bands above the scarab. The scene is dominated by the solar disk, winged with rich feathers and accompanied by two protective *uraeus* whose long bodies fill out the empty spaces with sinuous curves.

Length: 9½ in.

XLa. **Alabaster vase,** *page 188*

This elegant vase is discreetly decorated with three bands of inlaid glass-paste in the form of a ribbon made of blue lotus petals.

Length: 24 in.

XLb. **Mirror case,** *page 188*

This mirror case is in the form of an *ankh*, sign of life. Carved in wood it is gold-plated and inlaid with the king's name flanked by lotus flowers. The names and titles of the king appear in shallow relief on the handle and on the upper surround.

Length: 10⅝ in; width: 5⅛ in; depth: 1⅛ in.

XLIa. **Headrest of blue glass-paste,** *page 193*

This headrest whose proportions are very satisfying is a remarkable example of the craftsmanship of Egyptian artists. It is made of turquoise-blue glass-paste and it consists of two parts whose jointing is concealed by a gold band showing the symbols of divine life.

A vertical inscription gives the names and titles of the king.

Height: 7¼ in; length: 11 in; depth: 3⅝ in.

XLIb. **Ivory headrest,** *page 193*

This headrest is similar in shape to a folding stool. It is made of ivory stained dark green, red-brown and black. Three bands made of alternating pieces of black and white form the part where the nape of the neck was placed and end in two heads of the god Bes. These are adorned at the base of the skull by the image of a calice-shaped lotus flower turned towards the ground.

The feet of this folding headrest are sculpted in the form of wild ducks' heads.

Height: 8 in; length: 7¾ in; depth: 4 in.

XLII. **The king's "dummy",** *page 194*

This effigy in painted and stuccoed wood gives a very strikingly lifelike impression. The flesh is red, the pupils, the eye make-up and the eyebrows are black. The shoulders are covered with a sort of white tunic. The body is shown as far as the waist and the forearms were never attached. The ears are pierced to hold earrings. This lifelike portrait of the king is wearing the mortar head-dress with the flat top, yellow in colour and complete with frontal *uraeus*.

For a long time it was thought that this object was a dummy of the king to wear his robes and necklaces.

Height: 30 in; width at the shoulders: approximately 16½ in.

XLIII. **Unguent jar,** *page 211*

This cyclindrical jar in alabaster is of an unusual shape. The lid is adorned with an animal of the cat family—possibly a lion—sticking out its tongue of reddened ivory. Its fore-feet are crossed. The scenes are incised and stained with red, green and dark blue paint. They represent lions and dogs hunting bulls and gazelles.

On either side two columns with capitals in the form of

lotuses support each one a head of Bes. The base rests on bars crossed at right angles and which end in four heads of prisoners sculpted in red and black stone, two Africans and two Asians. This jar was found in front of the door of the second gilt chapel and still contained a cosmetic made of 50% animal fat mixed with a sort of resin.

Height: 10¾ in; diameter: 5 in.

XLIV. **Detail from the unguent jar,** *page 212*

The front part of the unguent jar is very finely sculpted in the form of an ibex, which is shown crouching and bleating, its forefeet folded under it. It has often been said that this is an example of the imaginative gifts of the artist in his choice of new forms to give various containers. The neck of the vase is broken at the back of the ibex and one can still see the beginning of the opening. The horns are real, one is still in position. The eyes were inlaid with bronze and glass-paste, the tongue is made of ivory stained red. The other marks borne by the animal, such as the royal cartouche, are dark blue.

Height of the whole lid: 11 in; width: 7¼ in; length: 15 in.

XLV. **Tutankhamen on a light papyrus boat,** *page 217*

Gilt wood statuette depicting the king wearing the red crown of Lower Egypt. His loincloth is typical of the period. It is pleated and goes down in front as well as coming up fairly high at the back. Tutankhamen is standing on a raft and with his hands he is holding a harpoon whose cord in bronze wire is coiled and which he is ready to throw. The light bark of papyrus is here made of wood painted green and gilded in the places where the details of the papyrus should appear.

The statuette, which is one of the most harmonious and elegant of the whole collection, shows the king like Horus harpooning Seth, the enemy of his father and transformed into a hippopotamus. Like all the statues of this group, this was found in a varnish-blackened chest and was wrapped in a piece of linen. Only the face was left uncovered.

Height, including the base: 29½ in; width: 7¼ in; length: 27½ in.

XLVI. **Statuette of the king,** *page 218*

Like the previous statuette, this one was found in the room which the diggers called the "Treasury". The king is depicted here wearing the red crown of the North and in a walking position. He is holding in one hand the flail (?) and in the other a long crook which he is using as a walking stick. These objects, in spite of having rather different proportions from usual, are reminiscent of the emblems of Osirian kingship which are held in the hands of the royal mummy.

Height: 29½ in.

XLVII. **Jar cover,** *page 227*

This is a delightful cover imaginatively and surprisingly conceived. On the flat, circular part which closed the container a fine bowl, also in alabaster, contains a fledgling which has just been born from the egg. It is surrounded by four eggs.

The young bird is carved in painted and stuccoed wood, its tongue is made of ivory stained red.

Diameter: 5⅓ in.

XLVIII. **Head of the sacred cow,** *page 228*

The head of the sacred cow usually is one of the forms of the goddess Hathor, patroness of the west who dwells at the entrance of the Theban necropolis. It is fixed to a wooden plinth, stained with black varnish. This same varnish, painted somewhat hastily, has stained the elegant horns which are made of wood plated with bronze leaf. The eyes are of crystalline limestone and obsidian. Black glass outlines the eyes and forms the eyebrows. The rest of the head is made of gilded and stuccoed wood.

Height, including the plinth: 36 in.

XLIX*a*. **Coffer with fretted decoration,** *page 233*

This delicate wooden chest is decorated with fretwork motifs of a series of ivory sticks inlaid with hieroglyphs picked out with black paint and giving the names and titles of Tutankhamen and his wife, Ankhesenamun. The rest of the decoration is openwork and is formed of groups of the *ankh* sign of life surrounded each one by two *ouas* signs. Each small group is placed on a basket together symbolizing

"all divine life".

The two knobs are made of ivory stained with red and feet are fixed into silver ends. Inside sixteen regular compartments are formed by ivory partitions.

Height: 16¾ in; length: 19 in; width: 17¾ in.

XLIX*b*. **Ebony and ivory gaming set,** *page 233*

The funerary equipment included three games of *senet*. It has not yet been possible to work out the rules according to which the pawns were disposed on the marks of the box. However it is known that certain details of the game are similar to those of the "goose game", rather like our snakes and ladders. This applies to the "big" game which is shown on one of the long surfaces of the box as well as to the "little" game on the other. It is clear that the moves of the pawns were directed by a die of small sticks whose two surfaces were usually painted in different colours.

The stand for the gaming set is supported by legs of an animal of the cat family.

Ebony, gold, ivory and silver.

Height: 2¼ in; width: 3½ in; length: 10¾ in.

L. **The chest on legs,** *page 234*

This is the only chest of the funerary equipment which had legs as high as the chest itself.

It is made of dark red wood and ebony. The decoration consists of hieroglyphic inscriptions (the names and titles of the king) which stand out against the sombre ebony background and also by a large band in openwork consisting of a group of the signs of divine life standing on the basket. The latter are in ebony and gilded wood. The two knobs are gilded and enable the chest to be shut by a cord tied between them which bore a clay seal. The hinges of the cover are made of bronze.

LI. **Detail of the gilded shrine,** *page 251*

The queen Ankhesenamun, seated on a cushion, is wearing a bandeau on which is a *modius* consisting of a frieze of *uraeus* bearing disks. On her forehead there is not one snake as the king usually wears, but two. The curled plait usually

worn by the young princes adorns one side of her head-dress and from the nape of her neck hang two ribbons which are often seen on members of the Amarnan royal family. On her cheek the tasselled earring can be seen. A large necklace covers the collarette of her dress which is of pleated linen. The queen is handing an arrow to the king and with her other hand she is pointing towards papyrus shrubs as though to indicate the target, in this case probably wild duck.

(cf. plate VII.)

LII. **The dog Anubis,** *page 252*

The animal of the god Anubis was for a long time thought to be a jackal particularly as it was always depicted black and therefore evoked the jackals that roam the necropolis at night.

It is made of wood varnished black and the details are gilded except for the claws which are made of silver. The eyes are made of alabaster and obsidian. Standing on a gilt wood chest in the form of a shrine which in turn had been placed on a sledge by means of which it had been brought into the tomb, it stood at the opening between the room containing the gilded shrines and the room which the diggers called the "Treasury".

Anubis alone: height: $23\frac{1}{2}$ in; the shrine: height: $21\frac{1}{4}$ in; width: $14\frac{5}{8}$ in; length: $37\frac{1}{2}$ in.

LIII. **A lifesize statue of Tutankhamen,** *page 257*

One of the two lifesize statues which faced each other on either side of the walled-up entrance to the funerary chamber. They are both made of wood covered with brilliant black resin and gilded.

The king is in a walking position, wearing a *uraeus* on his forehead and a gorgette on which is placed a necklace with a pendant. In one hand he is carrying a club and with the other he is leaning on a long cane. His eyes and eyebrows are made of gold; the *uraeus* and the sandals are gilded.

Height (without the plinth): 68 in; width at the shoulders: $18\frac{1}{8}$ in.

LIV. **Image of the king on his funerary bed,** *page 258*

Here in miniature is the mummiform image of King Tut-ankhamen lying in the position of the god Osiris on a bed which suggests the elongated body of an animal of the cat

family and which is reminiscent of the gilded bed on which the mummiform coffins were placed in the stone sarco-phagus.

On either side of the dead king two birds, one of which has a human face, are stretching a protective wing over the torso of the mummiform figure. The wood out of which the whole has been carved has been left in its natural state; only one or two details have been picked out in paint.

The inscription which decorates the bandages, which in fact kept in place the winding sheet, carry the names and titles of the king, and protective formulas.

Between the paws of the animal the dedication by the "royal scribe, chief of works in the place of eternity, super-intendent of the treasure" Maya is noted.

Height: $1\frac{1}{4}$ in; width: $4\frac{3}{4}$ in; length: 16 in.

LV. **The second mummiform sarcophagus (detail),** *page 267*

The upper part of the second mummiform sarcophagus containing the solid gold sarcophagus. This one is made of compact wood covered with sheets of gold and inlaid with multi-coloured glass-paste and semi-precious stones. Once again it depicts the mummified figure of Osiris with his arms crossed on his chest holding his insignia. He is wearing the *nemset* head-dress, the "wide collar" and the long beard of the gods. On his arms can be seen the two animals of the monarchy, the vulture and the winged cobra. The cover was fixed in place by little silver-headed nails.

The face is impressive by its expression of suffering view of death. This is emphasized by the yellowish colour in the cornea of the eyes.

Height of the sarcophagus: 31 in; width: 27 in; length: 80 in.

LVI. **The gold sarcophagus (detail),** *page 268*

The upper part of the third mummiform sarcophagus, the one which contained the mummy wearing its mask and covered with a whole network of jewels and amulets. It is made of beaten 22 carat gold.

It depicts with a precision and delicacy greater than in the previous sarcophagi the image of the god Osiris, the first mummy. The inlay is again of semi-precious stones and glass-paste. The face gives an impression of great serenity and its majestic air is heightened by the frame of gold formed by the side parts of the *nemset* head-dress which is no longer striped blue and gold but offers to the eye a unified zone of calm grandeur.

Height of the sarcophagus: 20 in; width: 20 in; length: 74 in.

I must limit myself here to a summary bibliography as I mean in due course to prepare another work—at the suggestion of the Director of the Institut Français d'Archéologie Orientale at Cairo, to appear in a scientific series published by the Institute, *Bibliothèque d'Études*—which will deal with the present state of knowledge of the events mentioned in this book. These problems concerning the Amarnan period (the co-regency, the coronation and the reconstruction of the funerary rites, etc.) are discussed in more articles and studies than can be mentioned in so limited a space.

CARTER, HOWARD, *The Tomb of Tut·Ankh· Amen*, 3 vols, Cassell, London, 1923-33. This is the basic work on Tutankhamen.
Vol. 1, in collaboration with A. C. Mace, with photographs by Harry Burton, 1923.
Vol. 2, with appendices by Douglas E. Derry, A. Lucas, P. E. Newberry, Alexander Scott and H. J. Plenderleith, and photographs by Harry Burton, 1927.
Vol. 3, with appendices by Douglas E. Derry and A. Lucas, and photographs by Harry Burton, 1933.

CAPART, JEAN, in collaboration with M. Werbrouck, E. Bille de Mot, J. Taupin and P. Gilbert, *Tout-Ankh-Amon*, Vromant, Brussels, 1943.

FOX, PENELOPE, *Tutankhamun's Treasure*, Oxford University Press, London, 1951. The German translation (*Der Schatz des Tut-ench-Amun*, Wiesbaden, 1960) is one of the best-illustrated editions of this book.

Tutankhamun's Treasure, with an introduction by Rudolf Anthes, American Association of Museums and Smithsonian Institution, 1961-1962. This is the catalogue of the first Tutankhamen exhibition to be held outside Egypt.

The following sources have also been consulted in the preparation of the present work.

The papers and notes of field research of Howard Carter, at the Griffith Institute, Oxford.

The treasure itself, in the Cairo Museum.

A very important series of specialist articles on the excavations in the region of Thebes and Tell el Amarna and on the monuments and artefacts of the "Amarnan" period and of that which followed; that is to say, from the middle of the reign of Amenophis III to that of Horemheb. These articles are by Maspero, Borchardt, Roeder, Newberry, Glanville, Gunn, Frankfort, Peet, Winlock, Engelbach, Černý, Brunner, Gardiner, Fairman, Hayes, Wolf, Aldred, Helck, Seele, Doresse, Bonnet, Barguet and others.

Studies in Egyptological journals, including: *Recueil de travaux relatifs à la philologie et à l'archéologie égyptiennes et assyriennes*, Paris; *Ancient Egypt*, London; *Zeitschrift für ägyptische Sprache und Altertumskunde*, Leipzig; *Annales du Service des Antiquités de l'Égypte*, Cairo; *Journal of Egyptian Archeology*, London; *Chronique d'Égypte*, Brussels; *Bulletin de l'Institut Français d'Archéologie Orientale*, Cairo; *Revue d'Égyptologie*, Paris; *Journal of Near Eastern Studies*, Chicago; *Bulletin of the Metropolitan Museum of Art*, New York (supplement: "The Egyptian Expedition"); *Mitteilungen des deutschen Instituts für ägyptische Altertumskunde in Kairo*, Berlin; *Orientalia*, Rome; *Journal Asiatique*, Paris; and the *Rapports sur les fouilles de l'Institut Français d'Archéologie Orientale à Deir el-Medineh* by BERNARD BRUYÈRE, Vols 1-26, Cairo, 1921-51.

DRIOTON, E., and VANDIER, J., *L'Égypte* (Clio series, *Les Peuples de l'Orient Mediterranéen*), new edition, Paris, 1962. This book can usefully be consulted for its brief summary of the period and more particularly for its bibliography.

HAYES, WILLIAM, *The Scepter of Egypt*, Vol. 2: *The New Kingdom*, Cambridge, Mass., 1959. This is a useful general survey of all aspects of the period; equally useful are the same author's contribution to *The Cambridge Ancient History*, Vol. 2, chapter 9, parts 1 and 2, Cambridge, 1963, and the studies mentioned above, by Engelbach

(*Annales du Service des Antiquités de l'Égypte*), Fairman and Aldred (*Journal of Egyptian Archeology*), and Hayes and Seele (*Journal of Near Eastern Studies*).

DAVIES, N. DE G., *The Rock Tombs of El Amarna*, edited by Griffith, 6 vols, The Archeological Survey of Egypt, London, 1903–8. This work includes all the basic information on the Amarnan period. An initial volume was published earlier as *Monuments pour servir à l'étude du culte d'Atonou en Égypte*, by U. BOURIANT, G. LEGRAIN, and J. JÉQUIER (Mémoires publiés par les membres de l'Institut Français d'Archéologie Orientale du Caire, Vol. 8), Cairo, 1903.

The City of Akhenaten, 3 vols, Egypt Exploration Society, 1923–51. This work presents the most recent reports on excavations at Tell el Amarna and their important results.
Vol. 1 by E. PEET, L. WOOLEY, B. GUNN, P. GUY and F. NEWTON, London, 1923.
Vol. 2 by H. FRANKFORT and J. PENDLEBURY, one chapter by Fairman, London, 1933.
Vol. 3 by J. PENDLEBURY in collaboration with J. Černý, Fairman, Frankfort, Murray-Thriepland and Samson (Part 1: text; Part 2: plates), London, 1951.

DAVIES, N. DE G., and GARDINER, A. H., *The Tomb of Huy, Viceroy of Nubia in the Reign of Tutankhamûn* (Theban Tombs Series), Egypt Exploration Fund, London, 1926.
DAVIES, N. DE G., *The Tomb of Nefer-Hotep at Thebes*, 2 vols, The Metropolitan Museum of Art, Egyptian Expedition, New York, 1933.
These two books are the most noteworthy publications on the Theban tombs.

PIANKOFF, ALEXANDER, *The Shrines of Tut-Ankh-Amon*, Bollingen series 49, Vol. 1 of Egyptian Religious Texts and Representations, New York, 1955. This is a fundamental work concerning the dead king's solar voyage.

DAVIS, THEODORE M., in collaboration with Sir Gaston Maspero, *The Tomb of Iouiya and Touiyou*, London, 1907.
DAVIS, THEODORE M., in collaboration with Sir Gaston Maspero, *The Tomb of Queen Tiyi*, London, 1910.
DAVIS, THEODORE M., in collaboration with Sir Gaston Maspero, *The Tombs of Harmhabi and Toutankhamonou*, London, 1912.
These are very useful accounts of the excavations of Theodore Davis in the Valley of the Kings.

MACADAM, L., in collaboration with F. Ll. Griffith and L. P. Kirwan, *The Temples of Kawa*; Vol. 1: The Inscriptions, London, 1949; Vol. 2: History and Archaeology of the Site (Part 1: text; Part 2: plates), London, 1955. This book contains reports of excavations in the Sudan concerning this period.

KNUDTZON, J., *Die el-Amarna Tafeln*. Vol. 1: *Die Texte*; Vol. 2 (by O. Weber and E. Ebeling): *Anmerkungen und Register*; "Vorderasiatische Bibliothek" II, Leipzig, 1915. This superb edition of the correspondence of the pharaohs with their Asiatic vassals during this period, which was found in the archives at Tell el Amarna, has been reprinted as *The Tell el-Amarna Tablets*, by S. MERCER, 2 vols, Toronto, 1939.

VERGOTE, J., *Tutankhamon dans les archives hittites*, Nederlands Historisch-Archaeologisch Instituut in het Nabije Oosten, Istanbul, 1961. This study, after Sayce, Sturm and Edel, has resolved the problem of the references to Tutankhamen's family in the Hittite archives discovered at Boghaz-Keui, and of the identification of his name in the Hittite language.

List of monochrome illustrations

Index

This index includes the names of gods and goddesses; the names of kings and queens, high Egyptian court officials, foreign royalty, and people mentioned in the book; the names of sites and places; Eygptian terms used—in italics; and the principal rites, feasts and ceremonies discussed.